MOTORCYCLE JOURNEYS THROUGH

THE ALPS

AND CORSICA

THIRD EDITION

JOHN HERMANN

A Whirlaway Book
Whitehorse Press
North Conway, New Hampshire

A Whirlaway Book. Published by
    Whitehorse Press
    P.O. Box 60
    North Conway, New Hampshire 03860 U.S.A.
    Phone: 603-356-6556 or 800-531-1133
    Fax: 603-356-6590

Whirlaway and Whitehorse Press are trademarks of
Kennedy Associates.

ISBN 1-884313-32-9

5   4   3   2

Printed in the Hong Kong

WARNING!
**Alpine roads and scenery and culture are known
to cause Alpinitis, a disease that creates an almost
uncontrollable urge to return. There is no cure.
The only relief is more Alpine riding, which
results in reinfection.**

Dedication

All these roads have been discovered and enjoyed and played on and replayed on with such a wondrous company of friends as any person could hope for.

To ride the roads again, or to write of riding them, or to read of riding them, is to recall those good friends with whom they've been shared. Indelibly etched on my mind with each hairpin, each view, each culinary delight, is the memory of good friends who were there with me. To them, with the hope that they too remember, I would like to dedicate this book.

Until we ride again in the Alps.

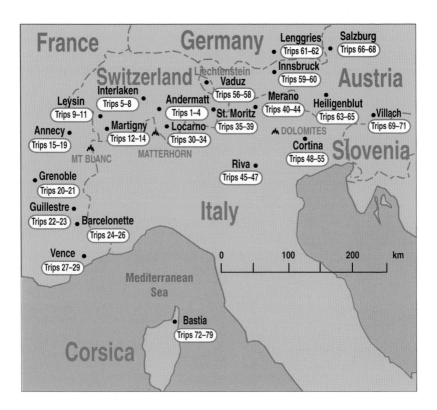

France

Germany

Lenggries
Trips 61–62

Salzburg
Trips 66–68

Switzerland Liechtenstein
Vaduz

Innsbruck
Trips 59–60

Austria

Interlaken
Trips 5–8

Andermatt
Trips 1–4

Trips 56–58

Merano
Trips 40–44

Heiligenblut
Trips 63–65

Leysin
Trips 9–11

St. Moritz
Trips 35–39

Villach
Trips 69–71

Annecy
Trips 15–19

Martigny
Trips 12–14

Locarno
Trips 30–34

DOLOMITES

Cortina
Trips 48–55

Slovenia

MT BLANC

MATTERHORN

Riva
Trips 45–47

Grenoble
Trips 20–21

Italy

Guillestre
Trips 22–23

Barcelonette
Trips 24–26

Vence
Trips 27–29

0   100   200   km

Mediterranean
Sea

Bastia
Trips 72–79

Corsica

Contents

Foreword

My intention is to make this third edition the best and most complete guide to the roads of the Alps available in any language.

Since the second edition came out, I've been back in the Alps a couple of months each year, checking roads, looking for new ones, checking hotels and fun spots. Terrible work. So this edition is really full of new stuff. New roads, new details, new trips. And new color.

Check the Pass Bagging List in the Appendix. Each of the 271 mountain passes in this book is listed there from the highest to the lowest. Beside each listing is a country and trip reference so you can find the pass and the good roads near it in the text.

I hound book stores and shops all over Europe and in America, buying lots of Alpine guide books in Italian, German, French, and even some in English. Some of them have beautiful pictures. Some are good in specialized or select parts of the Alps, or perhaps on the most famous pass roads. But some are little more than road maps.

In the Alps, they've been building roads for centuries, and they still are. I believe that this book is the most thorough and up to date guide to all those roads.

And Corsica. You've heard about it. You should go there. I've been there ten times, and it's in this book.

You should know that the maps don't always agree on the spelling of place names. Italian maps have their opinion. German maps insist on theirs, etc. Are Swiss maps a good compromise? I lean toward Swiss map maker Kummerly and Frey. They use readable color contrast and produce accurate maps of Switzerland and one of the whole Alps called Alpen Strassen (Alpine Routes). Recently, Kummerly and Frey has marketed maps produced elsewhere, but packaged in their familiar blue folder. Some aren't quite so good. Fretag and Berndt has wonderful maps of Austria, and Touring Club Italiano has the best of Italy. Because none of the countries is square, most of the maps include detail of adjoining areas. I also use maps by Kompass, RV, Studio, F.M.B., Hallwag, and Michelin. Occasionally maps may show roads that don't seem to be there, and more often, they fail to show roads that are there.

All the roads in the book I have ridden. Most of them many times, in both directions.

In the high Alps, the road is THE road. There is no other. In lower elevations, roads proliferate, many going nowhere of particular interest. Consequently, some of the trips here in lower, more populated elevations have a bit more detail to help locate THE road that goes through and is worth exploring.

Here are some assumptions I've made while writing:

German nouns are almost always capitalized. Italian and French nouns are capitalized, as in English, when they are the name of something. For example, Pass is always capitalized if it's German, but the French equivalent, col, and the Italian, passo, only when they're part of a name.

I lean toward Anglicizing plurals of a few German and Italian words. The plural of the German word, Autobahn is Autobahnen. I say Autobahns. The plural of Italian autostrada is autostrade. I say autostradas. Gelato, gelati, gelaterias. You get the idea. What I have written may not be completely correct linguistically, but I have tried to capture the international flavor while keeping the words familiar to other Americans.

In the text, there will be no German umlauts or French accent marks. Their chief function is to guide pronunciation. There are some phonetic aids in the text.

The French don't use the d' or l' in alphabetizing place names, so Val d'Isere is under I, not v or d.

St. is the abbreviation for Saint in French and Sankt in German (it's Sankt Moritz). Rather than make that distinction, I put both French and German saints alphabetically under "St." in the index.

I start the book at Andermatt, Switzerland, in the very middle of the Alps, a very good place to start a book or a trip. Then, in what I hope is an orderly and reasonable fashion, I describe every road and some facilities to the west, all the way to the Mediterranean, then to the south, and, finally, to the east of Andermatt.

You'll find most paved Alpine roads, and even a few unpaved ones, described here. Most have been tested many times in both directions, and all have been rated by stars—two stars (★★) shouldn't be missed! All are discussed as part of a trip that includes a home base, hotels, and attractions. The trips and bases can be combined to fit almost any time frame and interest.

The following conventions were used on the maps:

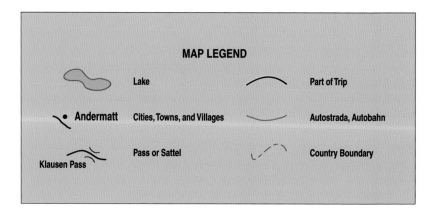

MAP LEGEND

Lake

Part of Trip

Andermatt   Cities, Towns, and Villages

Autostrada, Autobahn

Klausen Pass   Pass or Sattel

Country Boundary

Worth a Special Trip

Imagine the most exciting, the most beautiful, the best possible motorcycle trip.

There'd be roads, endless roads, climbing and sweeping through forests, past waterfalls and glaciers, bursting out into meadows, twisting past snow-capped mountains.

There'd be green pastures with flowers and cowbells and farmhouses with flower boxes.

There'd be good food and shiny clean rest rooms, and maybe even motorcycle parking by the door.

And there'd be other motorcyclists, riding every kind of bike available on this planet.

Imagine this, and you've imagined the Alps. Motorcycle heaven with scenic overload.

There are other mountain ranges, but only in the Alps of Europe have people spent centuries building roads into each high valley and in between each peak. Only in the Alps can you expect good food and drink at the top of the mountain.

In the Alps, good roads, good food, good hotels, good health standards, and a standard of living to equal or exceed any other all come together with exotic scenery and a general appreciation of motorcycling and driving.

Starting on the Mediterranean coast, the Alps arc across Europe, cutting Italy's boot from the rest of the continent. Deep valleys cut into the mountains from all directions. Since ancient times, people have been trying to get from one valley to the next. They hacked through gorges and hung roads on mountainsides, finally reaching a pass, into the next valley. The ancients must have agonized over which pass to risk, how to carry supplies for a long journey, how to trade with the natives. Now, those roads make a motorcycle paradise.

Just bring a credit card.

The south slopes of the Alps speak Italian, drink cappuccino, eat pasta at ristorantes and gelaterias, and drive Fiats and Moto Guzzis with skill on an amazing maze of mountain roads. They call a road over the mountain a *passo*.

The westerly slopes speak French, drink wine, eat French fries and glace and French bread at restaurants with French doors, and drive Citroens and Renaults (say wren oh) over some of the highest roads in the Alps. They call a road over the mountain a *col*.

The north and east slopes of the Alps speak German, be they Austrian, Swiss, or Bavarian. They drink beer, eat Wiener Schnitzel (cutlet Viennese style) and Eis (say ice) at Gasthofs. They drive BMWs and Mercedes very seriously on spectacular roads. They call a road over the mountain a Pass.

There's something satisfying about a through road, one that goes up one side of the mountain and down the other side. In the Alps, such roads are known by the pass they traverse: Passo Sempione, or Grimsel Pass, or Col de l'Iseran. Each pass seems to have a unique personality.

At the Alps' core is Switzerland. We call it that. Germans living there call it *Die Schweiz,* the French call it *Suisse,* Italians who live there call it *Svizzera,* and Swiss stamps call it *Helvetia.* By any name, it's motorcycle heaven.

When the snow melts, Swiss put away their skis and get out their motorcycles. Motorcycling is so popular that German-speaking Swiss have a special slang for it: Toff (say tough). A Toffler, of course, is a biker. A Gasthaus may have a sign, TOFFTREFFPUNKT, meaning a motorcycle meeting place. Tiny Switzerland even has its own motorcycle press, including a weekly magazine, *Moto Sport Schweiz,* published in both German and French, and a glossy monthly called *Toff.*

Most Americans will enter the Alps from international airports at Zurich, Munchen, Frankfurt, or Milano. Andermatt is almost as close to Milano's airport as Milano is.

Half a day and a ferry trip away is Corsica, the only close second to the Alps for riding. It's chock full of fun roads.

Imagine you and your bike in the high Alps at Andermatt, in *der Schweiz.* Every road in every direction is a great road. Select roads are marked here with a star. The *creme de la creme,* the absolute best roads, rate two. Some rate none, by Alpine standards, but those roads still must be among the best in the world. There isn't a bad one.

Switzerland, like many Alpine countries, has signs addressed to motorcyclists. This one is on Grimsel Pass.

Good Stuff to Know

Of Shower Curtains, Window Screens, Sealing Wax, and Hair Dryers

Okay, if the Alps are so great, how come:
1. There aren't any window screens?
2. Or wash cloths?
3. The shower curtains are too small or non-existent?
4. My hair dryer fries?
5. Double beds aren't?
6. The feather bed is too hot and too small?
7. The steak is tough?
8. Water's rationed?
9. There aren't any laundromats?
10. There's that extra appliance in the bathroom?
11. They can't count?

    1.   It's true. The Alps are full of cows and all. They tinkle their bells and so forth everywhere. And there are no window screens in the Alps. Mechanically, there isn't a double-hung window in the Alps. All windows are on hinges, so screens aren't handy, and so the finest establishment may have flies. Almost all hotel rooms have a sheer curtain that can serve as a screen at night.

    2.   In the Alps, only branches of American hotel chains have wash cloths. Others may have a tray of toiletries, needle and thread, a razor, and an assortment of towels of all sizes, but no wash cloths. If a wash cloth is important to your life-style, bring one from the New World.

    3.   For some reason, you're expected to sit down in the tub to shower with a hand-held shower on a flexible hose. So, why would you need a shower curtain? Some suggest that you are expected to wash before you shower. Maybe because Americans have flooded too many bathrooms, shower curtains are gaining a foothold in the Alps.

    4.   American appliances will not fit European plugs, voltage, or cycles. European plugs are round, and the prongs are too. Adapters are available, but their use usually burns up the appliance and trips the circuit breaker, leaving everybody unshaven, undried, and in the dark. Some electric razors will switch to 220, and will work with an adapter. Some hotels have outlets in the bath good for 110 SHAVERS ONLY. They will not work with hair dryers. Hair dryers of modest price are available in Europe. Better to buy one there if it's absolutely needed.

But they take up so much room! To save them and us the hassle, many hotels now have built-in hair dryers.

5. Almost all double beds are two singles pushed together. Sometimes, expressing a desire for a *grand lit* (a big bed, say grahn lee), or a "matrimonial bed," will help.

6. Everywhere that the Alps speak German—in Germany, Austria, north and west Switzerland, and the Sud Tirol part of Italy—beds have feather beds. A feather bed is like a giant pillow, or maybe a fat comforter. It rests in a big hump on the bed, which otherwise is more or less similar to a bed anywhere. That means there's a sheet on the mattress, but no blankets, no cover sheet, and no bedspread. Just a luxurious feather bed stuffed inside a washable cover. Feather beds vary in size and quilting. Without quilting, all the feathers may end up in one spot. Hardly ever will the thing cover the shoulders and feet at the same time. Some, in frustration, have been known to take the cover off the feather bed and crawl inside the cover. Better to curl up with the feather bed. It can be wonderful. If hot, leave a leg out, or more.

7. Steak is not an Alpine specialty. The hills are alive with music . . . it's cow bells. *Cow bells.* Not bull bells or steer bells. Boy cows become veal. The Alps have wonderful veal in all kinds of creative ways. But steak is very likely a mature cow. Schnitzel is a cutlet, usually veal, but sometimes pork. Wiener Schnitzel can be either. Pork is usually cheaper.

8. Drinking tap water is very American. It's not customary in Europe. There's absolutely nothing wrong with drinking tap water in the Alps. It is always safe. But Europeans don't think it's a nice thing to do in public. Most hotel operators know that Americans have the uncouth habit of drinking water, even with meals, and they probably will make a modest carafe available upon request, but don't be surprised if the cook objects. It's reassuring to note that in the interest of safe driving, even the French have cut wine consumption dramatically in recent years, and Oktoberfest tents in Munchen are required to have alcohol-free drinks available. If it becomes an issue, get mineral water, with or without "gas." Some presumptuous hotels with stocked refrigerators in the room may have a little sign in the bathroom advising against drinking the tap water. It's a ruse.

9. There are hardly any self-laundries in Europe. For whatever reason, entrepreneurs don't deem them worthy. Be prepared to hand-wash whatever needs washing. Detergent works better than soap. Finer hotels will have pricey laundry service.

10. Hotel baths in Italy and France very often have bidets. They're for washing what's hard to wash in a basin. And for rinsing socks. (Don't be confused by the European use of the word "dusche." It means shower.)

11. In Europe, the ground floor of a building is just that, the ground, the earth, terra firma. So the next floor up must be the first floor. And what Americans would call the third floor is clearly labeled "2," etc.

Here, several riders carve their way down the northeast side of Passo dello Stelvio in Italy. On Alpine roads there are no double yellows. You get no more road than you need or can claim. This photo is of late summer, after the snow has melted (Trip 38).

Rest Stops

A roadside Gasthaus, hotel, or restaurant is a logical rest stop in the Alps. It's diplomatic to order something from the bar before using the facilities. Coffee, tea, and hot chocolate come from the bar in Europe, and each is made one cup at a time. No refills. In the home of Swiss chocolate, hot chocolate is a cup of hot milk and a package of powder (the real thing is in Italy). A hot fudge sundae is always good in Switzerland and is called a Coupe Danemark. In Switzerland, Sinalco is a carbonated grapefruit drink, and Rivella tastes something like ginger ale. If you like the fizz, stop the waiter before the drink is dumped in a glass. There's always beer and wine, though most Euro restaurants feature only one local brew and few bars have hard liquor. Since the waiter will be charged for your order, pay and tip the waiter directly. In the Swiss countryside, the only currency is the Swiss Franc (a credit card slip signed in Swiss Francs will come home in dollars). If the bill is hand-written, remember that a European numeral "1" looks like an American "7," while Euro sevens have a horizontal line through them, and Europeans use a comma where Americans use a decimal point.

Spezi (say SPAIT zee) is a cola drink available in Bavaria and Austria. Soft drinks are a little less varied in France and Italy, so mineral water should be a safe bet.

Cold drinks hardly ever have ice. Ice cubes (*Eiswurfel* in German) are a rarity. Some warmer climes have started serving ice water.

When

When is the best time to ride the Alps? Spring? Summer? Fall? The best time is as soon as possible, of course.

Late spring, May, and June, are spectacular. Eighteen hours of daylight illuminate meadows carpeted with new yellow and blue flowers. Flower boxes have new geraniums. High mountains, still snow capped, are awesome backdrops to larch trees, just showing new green needles. Gorges are gorged with white water. Temperatures are moderate, yet the high passes cut through deep canyons of snow. Even the southernmost reaches of the Alps should be temperate. The only

It's a puzzlement. The station sign says *aperto*, open. But nobody's there. Only this machine which will take money—clean crisp bank notes—and swallow them. Once swallowed, pushing the right combination of buttons should start one of the pumps nearby. Good luck.

problem is that some passes may still be snowed in. Any pass needed for access or commerce will be open, but those just for playing on, the more remote ones, may be awaiting sun and snow plows.

Come summer, all the passes open, and the south warms up. Seldom are the Alps really hot by American standards, but Italy and the south of France can be. August is vacation time in Europe, so major areas can be peopled, and prices may reflect "high season." Flower boxes are masses of pink, red, purple, and yellow. Whole families rake and mow steep mountain meadows. Cow bells tinkle until dark.

Fall can turn the meadows pink. Mountain ash trees are loaded with orange berries. Near the tree line, larch needles are turning yellow. Last winter's deep snows are long gone and the mountains show rocky faces. Streams are drier. Days are shorter. Most of the tourists go home. Sometimes a passing weather front can dust the mountains with new snow, perfectly etching each formation and crevice. Fields of brilliant yellow-gold are "rape," a plant whose seed produces vegetable oil and biodegradable plastic.

Each Alpine country has special holidays. Sometimes, only one part of a country has a holiday. On one side of a pass, everything is closed. Across the pass, everything is open. Like in the U.S., holidays are arranged to make a three day weekend. Then everything closes and everybody goes someplace. In order to avoid arriving for a big trip only to find everything locked up, it's wise to check ahead. Many family run hotels and restaurants close for one day a week. In Germanic areas you may be greeted by locked doors and a little sign, RUHETAG, quiet day.

Some claim that there is less rain in the fall but any season in the Alps is a good season.

What to Wear

Europeans *expect* motorcyclists to be fully dressed in motorcycle gear, probably full leathers. A motorcyclist in full gear will be welcome anywhere in the Alps.

Ideally, wear full leathers as the primary article of attire all the time. They're lightweight, versatile, protective, not too bulky, and good in most Alpine weather conditions. All that you need under them is easily washed and dried underwear, and possibly a turtle neck.

A rain suit should go on easily over the leathers. The simplest is a hip-length jacket over elastic-waisted pants. (The jacket goes on first, so you don't get soaked pulling on the pants and so either top or bottom can be entered easily for keys or passport or whatever, without removing the other part.) One-piece rain suits work fine at keeping water out, but they sometimes are hard to get into and out of, especially dancing on the edge of the traveled lane, or in a small WC (water closet; toilet—the term "rest room" is meaningless in Europe). Soleless, snap-on rain booties are effective and easy to use. Some Gortex boots really are waterproof. Most rain boots are very hard to get on, and won't last if walked in. Remember, the boots go under the pants. Stores selling safety equipment have cheap and effective rain gloves to wear *over* leather gloves.

For cold, there should be a jacket to wear *over,* not under, the leathers. American softies have been known to enjoy an electric vest.

Leathers can be wiped off and debugged at the end of the day, and underwear washed in the basin if necessary, but jeans draped over the flower boxes on the balcony probably won't dry overnight.

Sport clothing, maybe just a colorful warmup suit, will last a long time between washings if it's worn only a couple of hours in the evening.

Two-Night Stands: A Home Base

When you're reading a tour brochure at home, it does seem exciting to actually contemplate 12 exotic hotels in two weeks. But that takes a lot of packing and unpacking and hotel adjustment to move lineally along the road. Instead, how about establishing a base camp in an interesting smaller town like Andermatt? That means at least a couple of days of baggage-free riding; convenient, almost familiar, stores and shops; and a familiar home base at the end of each great riding day.

Gas and Oil and Service and Tires

Some Alpine roads seem otherworldly, like a wild moonscape. But the Alps are not Siberia, or even Alaska. Even the most remote mountain pass is just a few kilometers from civilization. Europe has a well-motorcycled population. There are services and probably motorcyclists in every town and village, down at the bottom of the pass. And if you're at the top of the pass, everything is downhill.

Gas stations are plentiful, but not on mountain tops. Since they weren't in any medieval town plan, most are located outside the historical old parts of cities and towns and near the edge of smaller communities. Everything about a gas station looks familiar, with pumps and islands—everything, that is, but the price, which will be three or four times the U.S. price. Both gas and oil are sold by the liter. Leaded gas is being phased out, but both leaded and unleaded have higher octane than is available in the U.S.

In many smaller localities, stations close for a two-hour lunch at noon. Some stations announce that they are open (little signs, APERTO, or OUVERT), but only for drivers paying via automated credit card or cash machines.

Air is most likely available from a portable canister with a dial on the top. The canister hangs from a filler valve. Usually, the dial has pressure readings in both metric and pounds. Take the canister over to your tire. It should have a plus and a minus button for pressure regulation. The metric unit of pressure is kilograms per square centimeter (usually called "bar"). One pound per square inch equals

This gas station in the Dolomites is *Geoffenet, aperto,* with an attendant who will take credit cards.

0.07 bar; 33 pounds per square inch is about 2.33 bar. Finicky tire adjusters might want to carry a pocket gauge.

Most communities of any size have at least one motorcycle shop. At many the staff may appear busy even if they are not, so scheduling service in advance is wise. Store hours and days vary. Most depend on overnight delivery of parts from some central warehouse. Best way to find a shop is in the phone book, the yellow pages, or in motorcycle magazines, or by asking another biker. Smiles and pointing always help in an emergency. Pointing at a worn tire or a brake pad or a headlamp, etc., will register with most riders, dealers, and mechanics. They've probably been on the wrong side of a language barrier themselves.

An American on the Italian island of Sardinia once cracked a wheel hub on a BMW ST, not a very common bike. Calling around and using all possible translators, he learned about an overnight ferry from Sardinia to Genova on the mainland. The broken BMW was to take the ferry to Genova. Meantime, the BMW dealer in Genova would order a new hub from the BMW importer in Verona, Italy, and the hub would get to Genova overnight, too. The bike made it on the ferry. Other bikers on the ferry helped find the dealer in Genova. The hub arrived from Verona as scheduled, delivered by a 3-wheeled Lambretta truck. The wheel was laced and the American was off and running for the Alps that day (Italian headquarters for BMW bikes are now in Milano).

Accelerating and braking and leaning on twisty roads all day long may wear tires faster than normal. Nothing spoils the enjoyment of a good road like worrying about a tire. Many motorcycle shops do not sell motorcycle tires. Tire stores do and usually they will mount them for you. A motorcycle dealer may send out to the tire store for the needed tire and then mount it for you. Dealers will want to follow the law, which requires them to mount only matching, factory approved tires.

Calling America

Most U.S. telephone companies have a "USA Direct" service. In each foreign country there's a toll-free number to call and the U.S. operator answers. It's cheaper and it's easier than dialing direct. The charge goes on your credit card or phone bill. A call from a hotel room using the USA Direct number should not record on a hotel's billing machines. Before you leave, get the toll free numbers for each country you plan to visit from your company (AT&T, MCI, Sprint).

Calling Europe

It's really cheap during low-rate hours. Mid-day in Europe is early morning in the U.S.—the cheapest time to call.

In the U.S. dial 011 to get the international circuit. Then dial the country code (43 for Austria, 33 for France, 49 for Germany, 39 for Italy, or 41 for Liechten-

At European gas stations, air comes from a canister which hangs from a filer valve. It can be removed to a convenient spot by the tire being checked. Atop the canister, a dial reads both metric and pounds per square inch, and there are buttons marked plus and minus.

stein and Switzerland), then the area code (for example, the area code for Andermatt is 41) and the desired number.

Most Europeans list their phone with the area code first, and a zero in front of the area code. The zero is like a "1" in America. Use it the same way. Dial it first to call out of the local area from within the same country. It isn't necessary if the call is originating inside that area, or if calling from another country. When calling to a European country from America or any other country, just use the country code and the area code. No zero. Except Italy. Italy has changed to require the zero on international calls.

Of course, the answering party may speak very fast in German or Italian or some other language. If uncertain, ask for "English, please."

Except for big city hotels, hotel staffs in Europe go to bed, so there may not be any answer in the middle of the night.

Almost every European business has a fax.

Cell Phones

Cell phones are big in the Alps. The street sweeper has one. Everybody has one. They're usually called "Handys."

Most North American cell phones use CDMA technology. Europe uses GSM. And European GSM uses a different frequency than GSM phones in North America.

Most cellular phone companies offer a program to make your North American phone compatible. With some you can keep the North American number. Check before you go.

Demi-Pension

All the hotels listed in this book have been enjoyed. All will serve well. All rooms have private baths. Some are exceptionally attractive, worth a special journey just to stay in them. Please note, none are in cities, none are expensive by American standards. Most will seem reasonably priced, especially if meals are considered in the total. The few that are a bit more expensive will have clues here, like "exceptionally attractive," and "pampering service." Keep in mind that French hotels are likely to expend more resources on dining than on accommodations. Prices will vary by season and the exchange rate. Policies in Washington, or New York, or Zurich will affect what you pay more than what the hotel actually charges, so it doesn't seem practical here to quote prices.

Almost every hotel in Europe will make a special price for "demi-pension," half pension, which is room, dinner, and breakfast. Full pension includes lunch. Quite often demi-pension is a good deal, and may be a necessity in remote locations. Sometimes there will be a choice available at dinner, sometimes not. Most of the time, breakfast is a buffet with a variety of wonderful fresh breads (no breakfast until the bakery has delivered), cold cuts, cheese, and possibly nowadays, juice and fruit, but hardly ever eggs.

Demi-pension prices are per-person. Often a hotel is listed as a "garni," or "pension," usually meaning it has no public restaurant, although it should serve breakfast.

Bread and rolls are delicious in Europe and are served at all meals. Most Europeans visiting the U.S. say what they miss most is good bread. Good beer is a distant second. In Europe, butter comes only at breakfast.

Campgrounds abound in the Alps and usually have fine facilities.

Addresses, phone, fax, and e-mail addresses for hotels listed in the text are in the Appendices.

Cash Money

It's best to have cash money for small purchases like coffee or cappuccino. One side of a border may have cappuccino and the other side not, but it can be bought with the same currency, the Euro. No more lire (one lira, two lire) with columns of zeros. No more Deutsche Marks, no more French francs, no more Austrian schillings. Money is the Euro. Except in Switzerland. Swiss Francs still rule in Switzerland.

So, away with little baggies to keep currencies and coins separate. No more of those little purses, no more billfolds with multiple pockets. No more long division or multiplication problems trying to figure out just how much 43,000 lire is going to cost in dollars.

It's never advantageous to change twice, for example, to get Euros for dollars in Switzerland. There'll be a fee for changing to Swiss francs, then another for changing to Euros. (In some languages "Eu" is pronounced "oy" like in boy or toy, so the money is called "oy row" not "you row").

The Euro has paper bills varying in size and color in accordance with the denomination, each decorated with pictures of different epochs in European history. Each epoch has a bridge on one side (the Pont du Gard in France, for the Roman period), and a window on the other side. Coins are all the same on the front, with the back side varying with the country of origin. Presumably, they're good everywhere. Except, of course, in Switzerland and Slovenia. Neither belongs to the European Union.

There are banks in all international arrival airports. That's the recommended place to acquire Euros or Swiss francs. You don't need them before you get there.

Credit card transactions are always in the local currency, and ATMs usually accept American cards and spit out Euros or Swiss francs. Your account will be charged in your currency at a bank exchange rate that is probably better than any other. Banks and train stations usually have exchanges. In rural train stations, the ticket seller may do the changing. Sometimes it's necessary to go to one teller to

With the coming of the European Union, most national border crossings are no longer manned. About the only manned crossings left in the Alps are at Switzerland, which is not in the EU. Swiss guards will be pleased to sell you a "Vignette," the sticker which is good for one calendar year and must be affixed to any vehicle using a Swiss freeway, Autobahn, autostrada, or autoroute. The finger points to a picture of the vignette.

make the exchange, and then to a cashier to get the money. Banks often have a double door system that admits people one at a time. Sometimes you have to push a button.

Most American credit cards have toll-free numbers to call in each European country in case the card is lost. It's probably good to keep these numbers separate from the card.

Passports and Stuff

Border guards between countries in the European Union are fast disappearing. (Switzerland isn't in the Union.)

When there are guards (also at airports) there are two checks: a passport check, to identify the person; and a customs check to identify the "stuff." At most small border crossings in the Alps, the same official checks both. But there will still be two checks. The country you're leaving will check you out. Then, after you've crossed the border, the country you're entering will check you in. The two checks may be some kilometers apart. Usually, the customs folk are more interested in what natives may be bringing back than what visitors are carrying. With the coming of the European Union, there is less hassle, even about insurance, since it's assumed that everyone must be legal. Should a border guard note a non-European license plate, he'll very likely decide to check insurance papers.

On some remote unstaffed crossings, a little sign may say something to the effect of, "If you have something to declare, stop in the next town."

Remember that you and your bike are passing through, not staying, so Americans don't need visas, but you must have a valid driver's license, and preferably an international one (available from auto clubs in the U.S.) as well as a passport.

A thin wallet on a string around your neck is handy for passports and official papers. Hiking, camping, and bicycle shops in America, and motorcycle shops in Europe sell inexpensive ones. A passport in your luggage is almost useless.

Photocopies of passport, driver's license, traveler's check numbers, vehicle registration, and airplane ticket (the big long ticket number is important should the ticket be lost) can be stashed in various bags.

So What Are We Going to Call It?

We call it Germany. Italians call it Germania or Tedesco! French call it Allemagne. But the Germans call it Deutschland.

We call it Lake Geneva. Germans call it Genfer See. The folks who live there call it Lac Leman.

We call it Venice. So do the French. The Germans call it Venedig. Italians call it Venezia. When you're there, Vienna is Wien (say vean).

Most of us call it the Matterhorn. But half of it is in Italy where it's Monte Cervino.

Most signs will be local. So will most maps. So, it's the intent here to use local names. The exception: herein it's Germany and Austria and Italy, not Deutschland and Osterreich and Italia, even though that's what local signs will say (except in Italy, where signs pointing to Austria will say Austria). The international code is used everywhere in the Alps, and here: (D) is Deutschland, Germany. (A) is Osterreich, Austria. (CH) is Die Schweiz, Switzerland. (I) is Italia, Italy. (F) is France. (FL) is Liechtenstein, (SLO) is Slovenia. Accordingly, Swiss bikes and cars are identified by a "CH" sticker, presumably for *Confederation Helvetia.*

Germans put two dots over some vowels. They are called "umlauts" and are supposed to help in pronunciation. For example, there are supposed to be two dots over the "u" in Zürich and also over the "u" in München. Some texts leave out the dots but add an "e", so it's Zuerich and Muenchen. That all seems confusing. Here, there will be no dots and no "e"s.

Sometimes Germans use a letter that looks something like a capital "B" (β) instead of a double "s" at the end of a word like "pass." Here, it will always be double "s".

And, Germans have the habit of tacking modifiers onto a word without spacing, so that a menu item might read "Grandmothersrecipeforsteakontoast," or a highway sign, OBERALPPASS. Here it will be "grandmothers recipe for steak on toast," and "Oberalp Pass."

Besonder Uberwachung und Versicherung und Umleitung, or, "Special watching and insurance and detour"

Some German words don't slide easily from the English tongue. The French and Italian equivalents almost make good sense. But a couple of German words like those above are not in most handy "where is a good restaurant?" guides.

BESONDER UBERWACHUNG is on signs around Austria under a picture of a motorcycle. Motorcyclists will be especially watched! Other signs at Austrian borders advise that Austrian police use radar "in the whole land." Radar traps exist, especially in Austria. Typically, there is an unmarked radar in some area with a speed limit, like a village of a couple of houses, and the police wait farther along the road at the edge of the village and pull hapless drivers or riders over, waving them in with a red "ping pong" paddle. Friendly as Austrians are, their police will extract fines on the spot in cash for speeding. Most police in Europe do the same.

Police waved a bunch of motorcyclists into a big parking lot on the edge of Interlaken, in Switzerland. Seems there'd been a radar back in the town where the speed limit is automatically 50 kilometers per hour (about 30 mph.) Each biker was fined on the spot, one modestly for a mere four kilometers over the speed limit, others several hundred Swiss francs. The police accepted Visa and Mastercard!

Recently, Austria has put signs along the road that show a motorcyclist with an angel above, and words to the effect of "give your guardian angel a chance." Switzerland has had signs picturing a rider with the words "look out." Most auto drivers assume it is the rider who is supposed to look out! Both countries keep the motorcycles pictured up to date.

Helmets are mandatory in the Alps. Some countries require headlights at all times.

The international sign showing a motorcycle (usually ancient) in profile in a red circle means "motorcycles forbidden." The key is the little white sign underneath it, reading something like "between 2230 and 0600." There's often a second white sign that reads something like "except for bikes with business in the area."

Germany has a lot of low speed limit signs, even on Autobahns. The key is the little white sign underneath that says BEI NASSE, "when wet."

Versicherung, insurance, is mandatory. Proof of liability insurance is required before a vehicle license plate is issued in Europe. And it's expensive, like thousands of dollars a year. Many motorcyclists turn in their license plate for the winter to save money. Rental bikes should already be insured. Insurance should be included with any bike purchased in Europe. Bikes brought from America must have proof of European insurance before they're allowed out of customs.

Americans living or stationed in Europe can get motorcycle insurance like car insurance. But few U.S. carriers will or can sell it to American motorcyclists

Motorcyclists in Switzerland wait for a green light so they can proceed through a one-way-at-a-time construction area. "LU" is canton Luzern, Switzerland. "VA" is Italian.

traveling for pleasure. European insurance companies complain of bad luck with American bikers. Proof of insurance is a green piece of paper called a green card. That's what police and border agents will want to see. It should be in hand (or pocket) before operating on any European road.

European liability (and optional collision/comprehensive) insurance can be purchased for U.S.-registered vehicles from several sources. Most companies that specialize in shipping bikes to Europe will arrange for the insurance needed (see Appendix E, "So, How About a Bike?").

European automobile clubs are inclined to be more motorcycle friendly than those in America. Some think its worth joining a European club, like ADAC in Germany. Check with your American club about reciprocal services abroad.

Fun mountain roads are labor-intensive, and the labor usually can only be done in summer, when the roads are open and the ice is gone. Detours are a possibility, labeled *deviazione* in Italian and *Umleitung* in German. Sometimes a portable traffic signal allows traffic past the repair area one way at a time. It's common, though not legal, for bikes to go to the front of any line waiting for the green, with the obligation, of course, to take off fast when the light turns green so as not to delay others. A tardy response to the green will elicit some angry responses from other drivers with whom the road may have to be shared. On popular bike roads, the light may collect quite an array of motorcycles, and the green light is almost like the start of a race. It does make sense to get ahead of any trucks or buses.

Where Are They From?

Everybody plays the game of guessing where their fellow travelers are from. License plates help. Cognoscenti can tell which town a long French license plate comes from. Some insist that shoes and socks (or lack thereof) are telltale. Chances are that any American will be identified as such without saying a word, especially while eating. Only right-handed Americans hold a fork in the right hand. Only Americans ever put the other hand below the table. Right-handed Europeans hold the knife in the right hand and the fork in the left. So, it's hard for an American to hide. In Europe, there have been plenty of wars, with bombings and occupations and refugees and invasions, unpleasant invasions of tourists as well as soldiers. Everybody has had plenty of opportunity to develop prejudices as well as preferences. In the long run, you might as well be identified as American as anything else.

Europeans all know of U.S. speed limits, and presume no American can go over 55. Keeping up with local traffic can be helpful as well as entertaining. British and Dutch drivers usually stand out because they have orange license plates. Both are usually very cautious in the mountains—the Dutch because they have no mountains to practice on, and the poor British because the driver is seated on the wrong side of the car and can't see the road ahead. At least both speak good English. (How far can you go speaking Dutch?) Locals are almost always more aggressive drivers than visitors.

A couple of American customs need modification in the Alps. The forefinger raised when ordering means two, like "two beers" (it is the second finger). The thumb raised means one beer. And the thumb and forefinger touching, the okay sign in America, is not okay in the Alps. The middle finger? Let's hope it's three beers.

News

In America, many newsstands carry *The European,* a British paper of continental news. It is a good way to find out what's happening in the Alps, including weather, road conditions, and status of Alpine passes. In Europe, most newsstands have three American newspapers, the *Herald Tribune, USA Today,* and the *Wall St. Journal,* all printed at multiple sites in Europe.

Road Signs and Drivers

Alpine signs almost always point toward towns and passes. Route numbers are obscure. It's best to know which town you're going to.

City limit signs are automatic speed limit signs, and villages and towns are where speed laws are usually enforced. Conversely, the end of a city, the city sign with a slash through it, means "resume highway speed."

Signs in Andermatt point at three pass roads, the Gotthard, the Furka, and the Oberalp. The white "Furka Oberalp" points to the train which can carry cars and bikes through a tunnel under the pass. "Kaserne" is a military base (Trip 1).

Direction arrows often point *at* the road, which may not necessarily be the direction of travel. For instance, an arrow on the left side of the road pointing right most likely does not mean turn right. It means that "this is the road."

Schematic signs of anticipated intersections don't necessarily mean "now." There are often signs diagramming how roads will intersect in the next town.

You usually can't go around the block. If you miss a corner in a city, there probably will be another sign to the destination. If all else fails in a city or town, head back for the middle and start again. All towns have signs to the middle: STADTMITTE, in German, CENTRO, in Italian. French have a wonderful sign: TOUTES DIRECTIONS, meaning "you can get anywhere going this way." The yellow diamond sign used in Europe means "this road has the right of way over all entering or cross traffic." A slash mark through any sign means the end of it, whatever it was. A slash across a white circle means the end of whatever was being regulated, like the speed.

European drivers are usually very good and alert. Drivers' licenses are expensive and hard to get, and motorcycle licenses almost always require expensive schools and long periods of probation. European drivers will expect you to be competent and alert, too. If you are, they will usually accommodate you. Just remember, they consider the road to be a commodity in short supply. Anybody on it should be using it. Don't block the road. Some rules of the road and right of way are different than in America, and it sure helps to know them (for example, no turn on red in Europe, and no passing on the right on a freeway).

National attitudes about driving vary. Italians especially are inclined to think, "if it works, why not?" French riders are very aggressive about passing against oncoming traffic, sure that the other vehicles will make room. Observe. Then do what suits you. Just don't dawdle in the traveled way.

In all European towns and cities it's quite customary for motorcycles to park on the sidewalk, making sure to leave room for pedestrians.

French highways are numbered and well marked. "N" numbers are national roads and "D" numbers are department roads. These numbers are reliable (except in cities) and are used in the text here.

In a Hurry

You can get from one part of the Alps to another in a hurry by taking a freeway (an autostrada) across Italy. The Alps arc around northern Italy from the French Riviera to Austria. So Italy is in the middle. Its autostradas are like a chord that connects ends of an arc. They may not be as romantic as riding the roads of the Alps, but you can get from one end of the Alps to the other in a few hours on the autostradas of the Po Valley. (They're toll. Push a button and take a ticket when you enter. The toll is computed from the ticket when you leave).

The train is another way to make time, maybe while you sleep. You and your bike go on the train: the bike, well-strapped down on a double deck vehicle carrier, you in a chair car or sleeper. For instance, a train loads in Munich in the afternoon and the next morning you and the bike are in the south of France. Going to or from Germany, it's the DeutscheBahn Autozug. Check the web pages.

Skid marks on mountain roads are evidence that not all drivers have been perfect. Sometimes the marks head in unsatisfactory directions.

Tourist Info

Each Alpine country has a tourist office in the U.S. Be warned, they are more into hiking than motorcycling.

Austrian National Tourist Office; Box 1142; New York, NY 10108-1142; T 212 944-6880; F 212 730-4568.

German National Tourist Office; 122 East 42nd Street, 52nd floor; New York, NY 10168-0072; T 212 661-7200; F 212 661-7174.

Italian Government Tourist Office; 630 Fifth Avenue, Suite 1565; New York, NY 10111; T 212 245-4961; F 212 586-9249.

Slovenian Tourist Office; 122 East 42nd Street, Suite 3006; T 212 682-5896; F 212 661-2469.

Switzerland Tourism; 608 Fifth Avenue; New York, NY 10020; T 212 757-5944; F 212 262-6116; www.myswitzerland.com.

Time to ride.

Around Andermatt

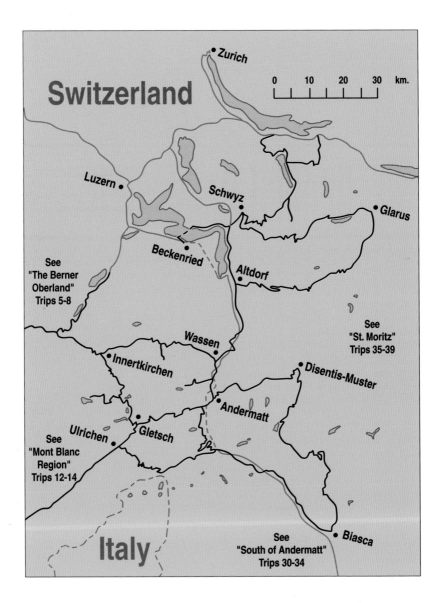

Switzerland

Zurich

0 10 20 30 km.

Luzern

Schwyz

Glarus

See
"The Berner
Oberland"
Trips 5-8

Beckenried

Altdorf

See
"St. Moritz"
Trips 35-39

Wassen

Innertkirchen

Disentis-Muster

Andermatt

Ulrichen

Gletsch

See
"Mont Blanc
Region"
Trips 12-14

See
"South of Andermatt"
Trips 30-34

Biasca

Italy

Andermatt

Draw a straight line across the Alps from Milano, Italy, to Zurich, Switzerland. Right in the middle of that line, in the very middle of the Alps, is **Andermatt, Switzerland.**

Imagine you and your bike in Andermatt, in the mountain canton called Uri. There are four major Alpine trips over some of the highest passes through some of the most spectacular country in the Alps starting right in Andermatt. Uncluttered by cities, these trips are good in any order, in any direction.

The village of Andermatt, at 1,450 meters, is almost as high as **Zermatt.** Zermatt has the Matterhorn and hoards of tourists. But Zermatt doesn't have any roads. Andermatt does.

For centuries, Andermatt was the crossroads of the Alps: Italy to the south, France to the west, Germany to the north, Austria to the east. Now, thanks to one of the longest highway tunnels in the world, tour buses and trucks, everybody

From the Oberalp Pass the whole village of Andermatt can be seen, the whole thing, nestled in the corner of its high mountain valley. The Reuss River is at left, along with the last, lower sweepers of the Oberalp. To the right is the Glacier Express train station, and the hypotenuse road that takes through traffic toward the St. Gotthard Pass. In the distance, the Furka Pass road.

with fear of heights, and anyone with urgent business, all go through the mountain instead of through Andermatt. Andermatt is for Alpinists and motorcyclists. That's what this book is about—where the crowds don't go but motorcycles do.

Park by the cafe of the **Hotel Monopol-Metropol** in Andermatt. You're on the inside corner of one of the best sweeper roads in the world, the **Oberalp Pass.** It starts right there at the hotel. The first sweep goes around the hotel. The road continues, arc after arc of smooth asphalt, never straightening out, up the face of the mountain.

In mid-summer, it's light until after 10 p.m., and bikes come from the great cities in the valleys to drive the Oberalp in the evening. The pass is worth several passes. (Mind the decreasing radius in the tunnel, coming down.)

Looking down from the sweepers of the Oberalp, you can see Andermatt huddled in a corner of its mountain-ringed valley, some modern buildings, some shingled chalets, some log buildings, with a Baroque church tower above all. The cobblestone main street has smooth granite slabs for wagon wheels. The street looks ancient, but was brand new in the 1980s.

A hypotenuse bypass leads across the valley from the granite **Kaserne** (military base) toward the **St. Gotthard Pass.** A cable car goes from the west side of the village up on **Gemsstock Mountain,** 1,500 meters above the town. The cog railway weaving around the Oberalp road leads down to a train station in

The westerly approach of Susten Pass has several tunnels, including this one, under a waterfall.

Andermatt, where it meets two other cog lines. This is the land of the **Glacier Express** train between Zermatt and St. Moritz.

Andermatt has restaurants, gas stations, banks, shops, and the Post, Switzerland's post office, telephone exchange, and bus station. You can dial anywhere in the world from the Post and pay when the call is completed. Just remember that the east coast is six hours behind the Alps, and the west coast nine hours. So 6 p.m. in Andermatt is noon in New York and 9 a.m. in California. All the Alps have daylight saving time. They just start and end on different dates than ours in the U.S. and even than other countries in Europe.

The Post is where all those yellow buses park, the public buses that deliberately motor into every cranny of Switzerland, sometimes towing a baggage trailer and tootling their three-note horn. The horn is supposed to send all other traffic scrambling to get out of the way. Most importantly, the Post sells freeway stickers, called "vignettes," that all vehicles must have to drive on a Swiss freeway, including many tunnels and many two-lane roads that have limited access. Swiss vignettes are annual. The vignette does not substitute for tolls, and there are a couple of toll roads in Switzerland. (Austria also requires a vignette to use the Autobahn, although Austria has short term ones, good for a week or a month).

Andermatt's travel bureau is: **Verkehrsburo;** CH-6490 Andermatt, Switzerland. (In Euro addresses the ZIP comes before the town. In this instance, 6490 is the ZIP, CH is the code for Switzerland.) T 41 887-1454; F 41 887-1185; www.andermatt.ch; e-mail: info@andermatt.ch. (Note: The telephone country code for Switzerland is 41 and the area code for Andermatt is also 41. So, calling Andermatt from another country dial two "41s".)

A sampling of the many hotels in Andermatt includes:

The **Hotel Monopol-Metropol,** on the corner where the Oberalp begins, is a building with an international flavor and a kitchen that blends Swiss and French cooking.

The **Drei Konige Hotel** (three kings, as in "We Three Kings of Orient Are") is located in the crook of the cobblestone street through Andermatt, right beside a rushing mountain torrent. It's traditional Swiss. The German author, Goethe, stayed at the Drei Konige in the 18th century. It's been updated since.

The **Sporthotel Sonne** (sun) is a multi-story log building in the village center, with a door that opens directly onto the cobblestone street. It's much more modern than it looks, with a cozy dining room and a garage for motorcycles.

In Switzerland, those proposing to build a new building must erect a scaffolding to show the actual size and shape proposed. Then those concerned can see what view might be affected, and what shadow cast. Such was the case for the **Alpenhotel Schlussel** in Andermatt. The scaffolding was up for years. But now, there's a brand new hotel.

Find postal and e-mail addresses along with telephone and fax numbers for these hotels in the Appendices.

After you ride the roads around Andermatt, you'll understand why many motorcyclists come back to the Alps again and again (Trip 1).

The main road through Andermatt was recently repaved in authentic cobblestones with smooth slippery granite slabs for carriage wheels and motorcycles.

In any language, Swiss money is called a Franc. Traveler's checks and money can be changed at a bank or at any Swiss train station.

German is the working language of Andermatt, but most locals can speak some English. The waitress may be a Norwegian who spent her last holiday in San Francisco, while the clerk in the sport shop very likely can discuss slopes at Aspen.

One evening, visitors in Andermatt heard band music. Rushing to the balcony, they observed a military band coming down the cobblestone street with a very deliberate drum major. European bands march much slower than American bands at football games. Tum . . . tum . . . tum . . . tum. But this band was in strange uniforms...greenish: It was a Russian Army band, in Andermatt, Switzerland, commemorating the 200th anniversary of a battle between the Russian army and Napoleon in the **Schollenen Gorge** just north of town. Come back in 2099 for another concert.

Besides the Oberalp Pass heading east, three roads lead out of Andermatt. West across the valley beyond Andermatt, the **Furka Pass** snakes up the mountain. Compared to the Oberalp, it's narrow and tight and irregular. Working up the mountain south is the **St. Gotthard Pass.** To the north an unbelievable road squeezes down through a gorge called the Schollenen, made by the Reuss River.

Information on road conditions in English can be obtained from Swiss auto clubs: **ACS (Automobilclub Schweiz);** Bern, 31 312-1515; **TCS (Touring Club Swisse);** Geneve; 22 735-8000; www.tcs.ch.

Trip 1 Furka, Grimsel, Susten ★★

Distance *About 120 kilometers from Andermatt*

Terrain *Steep twisting climbs into glacier worlds, three steep twisting descents, plus the narrow Schollenen gorge, mostly modern highway. Some tunnels*

Highlights *Rhone Glacier, Aareschlucht water storm, favorite motorcycle cafes, Sherlock Holmes site, Devil's Bridge and stone, Autobahn tunnel entrance, ★Furka Pass (2,431 meters), ★Grimsel Pass (2,165 meters), and ★Susten Pass (2,224 meters), the Schollenen Gorge, Oberaare road, Goscheneralp road*

At 2,431 meters, the **Furka Pass** is one of the higher roads in the Alps. Just a few kilometers from **Andermatt,** up among glacial peaks and rushing water, it's easy to feel civilization is very far away.

Starting up the Furka Pass toward the tiny village of Gletsch, the mighty retaining walls holding the traverses of Grimsel Pass tower overhead. Although this picture is of the Grimsel, the road in the foreground is below Gletsch (Trip 2).

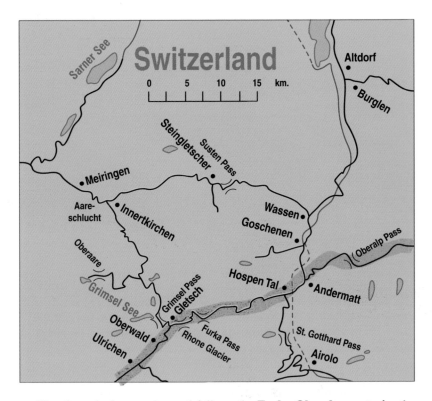

West from Andermatt the road follows the **Furka-Oberalp cog train,** the route of the **Glacier Express,** through **Hospen Tal,** a village with a stone watch tower, and where the **St. Gotthard Pass** road turns up and south. The cog train and the Furka road continue on west across the valley to **Realp** where the train enters a tunnel under the pass. (So the Glacier Express folk never see the pass or its glaciers. They ride the train through the tunnel in the dark. When the pass is closed, cars and bikes have to take the train, too.)

Across the top, on the west side there's a parking lot on the south side of the road. From it there's a magnificent view of the Rhone Valley, called the **Goms,** and the mass of the **Rhone Glacier,** and the cantilevered hairpins of the Furka road down below, and the zig zags of the **Grimsel Pass** road climbing the far mountain, and the lake at the top of the Grimsel, and the peaks beyond, and . . .

Climb down below the edge of the parking lot. Look closely. The lot is atop a gun emplacement that commands the whole scene. It's so well camouflaged that it defies detection just a few feet away.

The westerly side of the Furka is mostly new alignment. Then at one hairpin, you're face to face with the Rhone Glacier. Drive right up to the base of the ice, source of the **Rhone River.** Water melting from this glacier runs to the Mediterranean at Marseille, France. (Back at Andermatt, all the water was running to the Rhine and the North Sea.) At the glacier there's a parking lot terraced on the edge

Coming down the west side of the Furka Pass, all of a sudden you're face to face with the Rhone Glacier. It's possible to park and walk into the glacier. It is the source of the Rhone River which flows through Switzerland and France to the Mediterranean.

of the mountain, with an outdoor cafe that's popular with bikers. Restrooms are down under the parking lot. A tunnel carved into the glacier permits a walk into the blue world inside.

It's only 31 kilometers from Andermatt, across the Furka Pass and past the Rhone Glacier, down to **Gletsch,** where the Grimsel Pass road intersects and heads up and north. Gletsch is just a couple of stone buildings at the tree line.

Once some American bikers got trapped at Gletsch by avalanches and mud slides on the pass roads. The Grimsel was closed. The Furka was closed. The Goms road west was closed. The stone hotel building had no electricity. But the cog train was running back and forth through the Furka train tunnel. So, the bikers went down below Gletsch to **Oberwald** and put their bikes on a flat car. They sat on the bikes through 25 minutes of dark tunnel and debarked at Realp over by Andermatt.

The traversing road up the Grimsel from Gletsch leads to hairpins supported by walls of massive stones and offering great views of the Rhone Glacier.

Several restaurants around the lake at the top of the Grimsel (don't ask the lake's name) are popular with motorcyclists. The one farthest north, **Hotel Alpenrosli,** has a large parking area marked for motorcycles only. It's often full of bikes, while the riders enjoy the sunny restaurant terrace.

Just west of the Hotel Alpenrosli (to the left, facing the hotel) is a tiny short road you have to try if it's open—the **Oberaare.** It looks like a driveway with a traffic light. About ten kilometers long, it snakes up high above the top of the Grimsel Pass and then down to a lake, the **Oberaare See.** Views are awesome ... glaciers, snow-capped peaks, icy white lakes, and the ribbon of the Grimsel Pass road winding down north. Traffic is one way at a time, controlled by the traffic light at each end of the road.

It's only 37 kilometers north from Gletsch, across the Grimsel, past the Hotel Alpenrosli, down past dams and lakes and hydroelectric plants and through several tunnels, one of which has a decreasing radius curve, into forests and through meadows to **Innertkirchen,** where the **Susten Pass** road heads east. This is countryside known in song and story as the **Berner (Bernese) Oberland,** canton Bern, the valley of the **Aare River.** Just a few kilometers below Innertkirchen, the Aare goes through a very narrow gorge called a *Schlucht,* as in *Aareschlucht.* It's a spectacular display of enormous volumes of frothing water. There's a parking lot on a hairpin where a wooden catwalk leads into the water storm.

The Devil's Bridge

By the freeway entrance to the long tunnel is a giant rock with the flag of canton Uri on it: gold, with a black bull's head with a ring in its nose and a red tongue hanging out. The big rock was moved aside at great expense during freeway construction because:

Long ago, the villagers failed to get a bridge across the gorge. The devil offered to build it in exchange for the soul of the first to cross the bridge. But the villagers fooled the devil by sending a goat across the bridge first. Enraged, the devil hoisted the huge rock to smash the bridge, only to drop the rock when a villager made the sign of the cross.

The rock's still there to prove it. Pictures of the **Teufelbrucke (Devil's Bridge)** abound around Andermatt. ∎

A newer Devil's Bridge decorated with a red devil and the goat crosses over the old Devil's Bridge in the Schollenen Gorge.

Just below the Schlucht is the base of the **Reichenbach Waterfall,** the great cascade where **Arthur Conan Doyle** had Sherlock Holmes fall to his death in a fight with the villain Moriarty. A marker at the base of the falls says it happened on May 4, 1891. It must be so, because the monument was erected by "The Norwegian Explorers of Minnesota!" The marker is in the parking lot of a "Klinik." There's a statue of the great detective in the nearby village of **Meiringen.** (Meiringen and the roads of the Berner Oberland are in the next chapter, Trips 5, 6, 7, and 8.)

On the west side of the Susten Pass, a couple of hairpins before the summit, is **Hotel-Restaurant Steingletscher** named after the glacier on the peaks to the south. Explore the dead-end military road that starts beside the hotel and works its way up to the base of the glacier. Narrow, but mostly good asphalt. Usually there are troops around, sometimes firing artillery. If there's a gate down across the entrance to the road, it may be necessary to buy a ticket at the hotel.

Hotel Steingletscher can arrange accommodations at a Gasthaus way up above the top of the pass. Access to it from the top of the pass is a steep road that passes in front of the restaurant there.

The climb up the Susten Pass from Innertkirchen goes from meadows back up to the land of glaciers. The parking lot at the top of the Susten Pass, sur-

From the Grimsel Pass, look for the Furka Pass snaking up the far mountainside with the village of Gletsch down below.

rounded by glaciers, is another favorite motorcycle gathering place. The restaurant has a view terrace from which there's free access to the restrooms below (Euro restrooms are usually marked "WC").

The road on the east is a tunnel. Sit on the terrace and try to identify the bikes coming from the east by their exhaust note magnified in the tunnel.

It's 53 kilometers across the Susten Pass from Innertkirchen on the west to **Wassen** on the east. The east side, east of the tunnel, after a couple of hairpins, is delightful, open sweepers until the final tight curves and tunnels down into Wassen. From the curves, if you can take your eyes off the road, there are views of one of the major engineering feats of the Alps, the four-lane freeway in the gorge of the **Reuss River.** It connects Zurich with Italy through the **St. Gotthard tunnel.** The gorge is so narrow and steep that the road is either on a bridge or in a tunnel. Here it's called an Autobahn, and it leads to the tunnel under Andermatt, once the longest vehicle tunnel in the world. The tunnel daylights as an autostrada in **Airolo** (see Trip 2).

It's only a couple of kilometers south, up the **Schollenen gorge** from Wassen to **Goschenen,** where the freeway enters the long tunnel, and where the really steep part of the gorge begins. The main line of the railroad goes in a tunnel, too, leaving only a cog line to grind on up to Andermatt alongside the hairpins of the gorge road. (There's a fun dead-end road westerly from Goschenen to a high Alpine dam and lake called **Goscheneralp.** There's a restaurant at the dam.)

The climb up the gorge toward Andermatt goes right by the Devil's Bridge and another bridge of Roman origin. And there's a spot in the gorge that will be forever Russian. A turn-off near the Devil's Bridge leads down to an enormous carving in the mountainside with script in Cyrillic. Seems it commemorates the Russian army. Defeated by **Napoleon** on the plains, it retreated south and was trapped in the gorge.

The monument's named after the Russian general, **Suworow.** Turn into the monument parking lot and continue on down the old gravel road over the old Teufelbrucke. (The road is closed to cars.) The best view of the monument is from this road. (For other Russian monuments in the Alps, see Trip 56, Filzmoos and Tauern Passes, and Trip 60, Three Country Loop.)

A final short tunnel opens out onto the high Andermatt valley. The main road is the hypotenuse bearing right toward the St. Gotthard and Furka Passes. A mini interchange leads into the village, past the vast stone **Kaserne,** home to much of Switzerland's citizen army. In the village, soldiers patrol around and occasionally roar by in rubber-treaded tanks, or astride an army Condor motorcycle, assembled in Switzerland with a Ducati engine.

Remember the DB-1 Bimota that was on the cover of every bike magazine once? There it was, parked in Andermatt. Tiny, beautiful. Tracked down, the owner allowed as how it had indeed cost a bundle of Swiss Francs. "You could have bought a Harley for that!" The owner reached into a pocket and pulled out a card. He was a Harley dealer.

43

Trip 2 St. Gotthard, Nufenen, Furka ★★

Distance *About 110 kilometers from Andermatt*

Terrain *Three steep twisting climbs and descents, mostly modern highways*

Highlights *St. Gotthard Museum, a favorite motorcycle cafe, concrete-roofed sweepers, in and out of Italian-speaking, cappuccino land, St. Gotthard Pass (2,108 meters), ★Nufenen Pass (2,478 meters), ★Furka Pass (2,431 meters)*

It's a good sweeping ride up the **St. Gotthard** to the top, where all of a sudden, it's no longer the St. Gotthard, but the **San Gottardo.** The south slopes of the Alps speak Italian, eat pasta, and drink cappuccino, even in Switzerland. The old-time hospice at the pass summit has been turned into a museum of the historic attempts to conquer the pass, including the history of the **Devil's Bridge.** Water here runs to the **Po River** in Italy, and thence to the Adriatic. A monument out front commemorates aviators' attempts to conquer the pass. Crossing the Alps in early planes was a major undertaking.

Near the top of the Furka Pass in Switzerland, the Finsteraarhorn dominates the western horizon. Under it, some of the best motorcycle riding in the world, the Grimsel Pass and the Furka Pass, meet down in the valley called Goms (Trip 1).

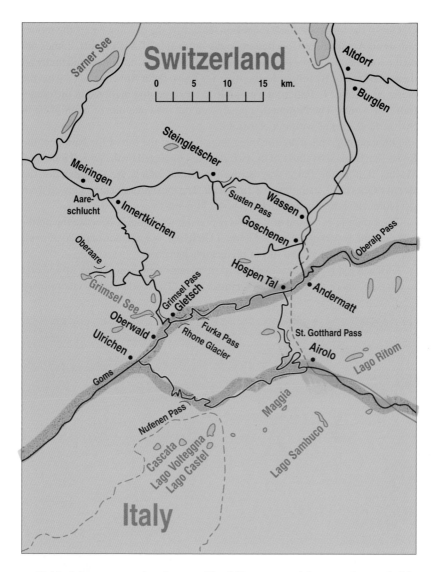

Behind the museum there's a an old cobblestone road down to the south. It's known in Alpine lore as the **Tremola,** and many feel the urge to try its many rough and convoluted hairpins. Sometimes it's closed to through traffic. The best views of it are from the newer, main road.

The main road down the southern slope of the San Gottardo starts in kilometer-long, covered concrete sheds designed to protect motorists from avalanches. The sheds are open on one side and the road surface is good at highway speed. About halfway down there's a view spot cafe, and lower, some military fortifications. A couple of hairpins are built out in space on stilts.

One of the longest vehicle tunnels in the world, the one that enters the mountain as an Autobahn at **Goschenen** on the north side of **Andermatt,** comes out on the south slopes of the pass at **Airolo** as an autostrada, having passed under all these good roads. By following the signs for **Passo della Novena** (that's what the Nufenen is called in Italian) it's possible to avoid getting involved in the tunnel traffic at Airolo. The **Nufenen,** a newly laid out road and one of the highest in Switzerland, climbs west out of Airolo.

Often photographed are the three flags flying at the top of the Nufenen, the Swiss flag flanked by those of the two cantons connected by the pass, **Ticino** and **Wallis.** Behind the flags, way across the **Goms** valley, are the peaks of the **Berner Oberland,** including the **Jungfrau.** The most prominent as viewed from the Nufenen is the **Finsteraarhorn** at 4,274 meters.

The cafeteria at the top of the pass is popular with bikers, because the northerly descent, way down into the Goms at **Ulrichen,** is a wonderful piece of road: good pavement, steep, and full of predictable hairpins.

Ulrichen is down in meadowlands, so it's a real climb from it back up and east to **Gletsch** where the **Furka** and **Grimsel** meet. The road passes some military

Often called the *Tremola,* the old cobblestone road snakes up the south slope of the St. Gotthard *(San Gottardo)* toward Andermatt. It's been replaced by a sweeping modern road from which this picture was taken, which, in turn, has been replaced with one of the (ugh!) longest vehicle tunnels in the world.

Often photographed are the three flags flying at the top of the Nufenen Pass, the flags of the two cantons united by the pass, Ticino and Wallis, with the flag of Switzerland in the center. The restaurant is just a cafeteria, but its parking lot is a favorite bike stop.

airstrips and the railroad loading ramps at **Oberwald,** where cars and motorcycles can be driven right onto the train for a tunnel ride under the Furka Pass back to Andermatt. Should you choose this method, just ride onto a flat car and take a seat in a passenger compartment, or maybe sit on your bike. Switzerland claims to be planning a steam cog train using the old abandoned tracks over the pass.

Climbing up to Gletsch from Oberwald the awesome switchbacks of the Grimsel Pass are straight overhead. They've been rebuilt in recent years. There's lots of concrete behind those huge stones.

The parking lot of the **Rhone Glacier** revealed a bunch of bikes, including a YB-1 Bimota. The rider turned out to be a dentist from Disentis, over the Oberalp beyond Andermatt. "Your English sure is good." "Oh, I teach part time at the University of Illinois!"

CHAPTER

1

Trip 3 Oberalp, Lukmanier, St. Gotthard ★

Distance *About 154 kilometers*

Terrain *Three climbs and descents, plus a valley run*

Highlights *Oberalp Pass (2,044 meters) and the world's best sweepers, less-traveled Lukmanier Pass (1,914 meters), St. Gotthard Pass (2,108 meters), a taste of Romansch culture, deeper into Italian-speaking Switzerland*

Sweep up the **Oberalp** from **Andermatt** into canton **Graubunden** (sometimes called Grisons in English), where buildings are usually stucco with arches and deep set windows and stenciled decoration. The official language is Romansch. Nobody speaks it, but they print signs in it. The working language remains German. (Elementary school children in many parts of Graubunden are taught in Romansch.)

Across the Oberalp, at a pretty good-sized town called **Disentis-Muster,** the **Lukmanier Pass** road heads south. Disentis is famous for a big monastery church visible just above the town. To visit it, you have to park below on the main road and hike up. The interior is sort of Spanish baroque. To head for the Lukmanier, take a sharp right in the middle of the town down across the **Vorderrhein River.** The sign for the pass in Romansch will be CUOLM

On long summer evenings, bikers come from the great cities of Europe, not to mention the rest of the world, just to ride the sweepers of the Oberalp Pass above Andermatt.

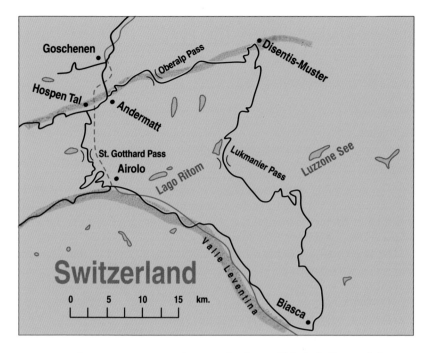

LUCMAGN. As soon as you cross the pass, the signs will be in Italian, and the pass will be called **Passo del Lucomagno.** The pass road is modern all the way to Biasca. There's a functional restaurant at the top of the pass.

A pleasant stop might be the **Hotel Olivone and Post,** about 18 kilometers down the **Ticino** (south) side.

The Passo del Lucomagno meets the **San Gottardo** autostrada at a town called Biasca.

Biasca is in one of those major valleys that cut deep into the Alps, the **Valle Leventina.** It's the best route from the great cities of Italy to Zurich, via the long St. Gotthard tunnel. So a lot of traffic is heading for the St. Gotthard (called *San Gottardo* here), and since it's about 35 kilometers north, the autostrada may be the viable route to get there. Just be sure to exit the autostrada at Airolo, or you'll be treated to at least 20 minutes of tunnel behind a diesel-belching bus or truck, all the way to **Goschenen.**

On the climb up the St. Gotthard from **Airolo** there are a couple of tight sweepers on stilts out over the valley, with big metal expansion joints that are slippery when wet. A turnout has a little restaurant with a fine view of the can-of-worms interchange squeezed into the valley down in Airolo where the autostrada, the tunnel, the Nufenen Pass and the St. Gotthard Pass roads all meet.

A Kawasaki pulled into the restaurant at the top of the Lukmanier once. The rider was all in white—white leathers, white boots, white gloves. He allowed he worked for Swiss-air. "How do you keep it white?" "Oh, that's my wife's job!"

Trip 4 Klausen, Pragel, the 'eggs' ★★

Distance *About 200 kilometers from Andermatt*

Terrain *Tight climbs and descents on narrow, less-traveled roads*

Highlights *William Tell country, a historic highway on lakeshore, Klausen Pass (1,948 meters), Switzerland's little-known ★Pragel Pass (1,550 meters), Ibergeregg (1,406 meters), Sattelegg (1,190 meters)*

Dash north down the **Schollenen Gorge** from **Andermatt** and hop on that Alpine masterpiece, the Autobahn, down toward **Luzern.** In a couple of minutes, you'll be in **Altdorf.** almost at sea level, at least the level of **Lake Luzern. Klausen Pass** climbs east from Altdorf.

The lake that we call Lake Luzern the Swiss call by the tongue twister **Vierwaldstatter See** (four forest state sea) after the four cantons of William Tell's day. And we call the country "Switzerland" after **Schwyz,** one of the four forest cantons.

There's a helpful and well-stocked Kawasaki-Yamaha shop called **Gisler Motos** at **Shattdorf,** on the main road just south of Altdorf.

Climbing out of Altdorf on the Klausen, the next village is **Burglen,** Tell's home, where there's a small statue of Tell.

About halfway up the Klausen from Altdorf on the inside of a 180, there's an attractive hotel and restaurant called **Hotel Posthaus Urigen.** It's handsomely decorated inside and out and advertises itself as a motorcycle meeting place.

East of the Klausen summit, still in canton **Uri,** the road crosses a high, mountain-ringed valley called **Urnerboden.** It's open range populated by cows. Thousands of cows. Signs beg vehicles to stay off the pastures. It's also desirable to dodge cows and cow pies.

The bottom, on the northeast side of the Klausen, is in canton **Glarus,** with a capital city of the

William Tell

Altdorf is famous as the home of **William Tell** and there's a monument and statue of him and his son in the center of the town. Tell was not just a good marksman, but a symbol of Swiss independence. The guy who had him shoot the apple off his son's head back in the middle ages was the evil count, an outsider. It seems that four of the Swiss forest cantons around **Lake Luzern** decided they'd like to be independent. The count was against it. Tell was for it. The evil count dreamed up the ultimate punishment for a father—the life of his son. He was sure that the son would flinch or Tell would miss, or both. We all know that the son didn't and Tell didn't. ■

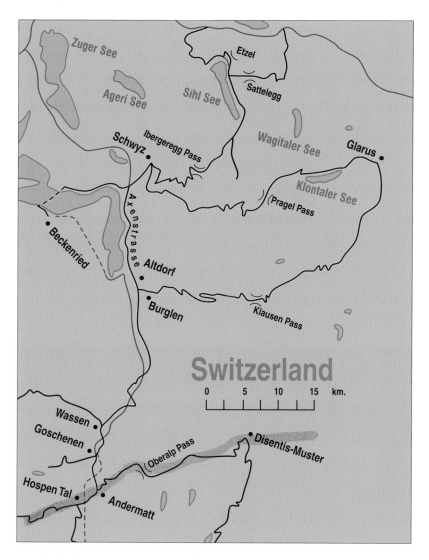

same name. Once down, the road passes through village after village, each with a 50 kilometer per hour speed limit. Recently, Glarus had a cantonal meeting, one of those very Swiss affairs, an open forum, and everyone debated spending millions of francs to build a more modern road around the villages. The new road was voted down. So we're stuck with the slow route through the villages.

Down below the Klausen in the town of Glarus, the road to the **Pragel Pass** intersects, but the pass is so small and remote that there's no sign for it. Watch for a sign pointing to the left, west, to **Klon Tal** or **Klon Taler See** (*Tal* added to a German word means valley).

The road is two lanes as far as the lake, Klon Taler See, where there's a modern terrace restaurant and hotel called **Hotel Rhodannenberg.** The rest of the road over the pass is one paved lane and has a feel like maybe nobody's ever been there. But a long period with no oncoming traffic doesn't mean there isn't a logging truck around the next corner. The asphalt is smooth but has a significant lip on each edge. It follows the lake for several kilometers, where there are triangular warning signs advising drivers to look out for frogs. Across the lake are sheer vertical cliffs of almost a thousand meters. Spectacular. Looks like Lake Louise at Banff in Canada.

Signs along the road with lengthy passages in German say that this part of the road is not open to traffic on weekends. The same signs greet the rider coming from the other direction across the pass at **Muota Tal,** the valley on the other side. Muota Tal leads down to **Schwyz,** the town the country's named after. (Heading for the Pragel from Schwyz, follow the signs to Muota Tal, as there are none for the pass.)

At **Ibach,** next to Schwyz, the main road passes the **Victorinox** factory, one of the "original Swiss Army Knife" factories. Showrooms have everything for sale. Down a little lane near the factory is a BMW dealer. From Schwyz, the main road back toward Altdorf and Andermatt is called the **Axenstrasse**

From the Oberaare road, the marvel of the Grimsel's alignment is apparent. The Aare River is dammed at regular intervals, creating *Stausees*, lakes created by a dam, like this one for hydroelectric power plants. (Trip 1)

On the inside of a 180 on the Klausen Pass is the attractive Hotel Posthaus Urigen. It advertises itself as a motorcycle meeting place.

because it was carved by ax from the steep cliffs around Lake Luzern, Vierwaldstatter See.

Until recently, the Axenstrasse, hanging on the east side of the Vierwaldstatter See, was the only way around the lake toward the St. Gotthard. Now, there's a four-lane Autobahn tunnel through the cliffs on the other side of the lake, where before there was no road of any kind. (Following the lake in the opposite direction, actually west, from Schwyz, there's a ferry across the lake to **Beckenried** and connections with the roads of the Berner Oberland, Trip 6. There's a good hotel at the ferry landing across the lake.)

A lesser pass, the **Ibergeregg,** 1,406 meters and heading northeasterly, starts in the middle of Schwyz, by the church. The view over Vierwaldstatter See from the restaurant at the top is great. Little-trafficked and heavily forested, the Ibergeregg comes down by a couple of lakes and a huge pilgrimage church at **Einsiedeln,** not far from Zurich. The church is of modest historic or artistic interest, but it is big.

Short of Einsiedeln, a one-lane road (with a few meters unpaved) crosses a handsome covered bridge and snakes over a woodsy ridge called **Etzel** coming down out of the forest to the town of **Pfaffikon** and to the congestion of **Zuricher See.**

An even less challenging pass called **Sattelegg,** 1,130 meters, loops east from the north end of Ibergeregg back toward Zurich See and civilization. Sattelegg has a pleasant restaurant, but an unpleasantly low speed limit.

West of Andermatt

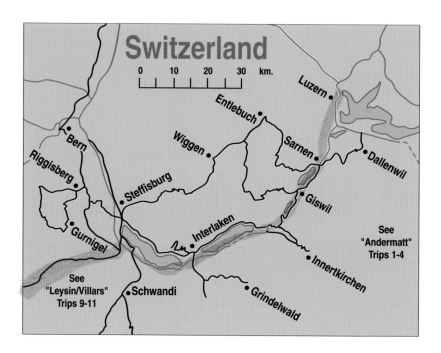

Switzerland

0   10   20   30   km.

Luzern •

Entlebuch •

Wiggen •   Sarnen •

Bern •   • Dallenwil

Riggisberg •

Steffisburg •   Giswil •

Gurnigel •   Interlaken   See
                                                     "Andermatt"
                                                      Trips 1-4

See   • Innertkirchen
"Leysin/Villars" •Schwandi
Trips 9-11   • Grindelwald

The Berner Oberland

West of Andermatt, west of the Furka and the Grimsel and the Susten, down-stream from the Aareschlucht, in the valley of the Aare River, is the town of **Interlaken.** It's in canton Bern, in the area called the **Berner Oberland,** the high mountain country south of Switzerland's capital, Bern.

Interlaken is between two lakes made by the Aare River, the **Brienzer See** to the east and the **Thuner See,** to the west. It has been host to every guided tour that hits Switzerland. It's the jumping-off place for cog train rides up the **Jungfrau** mountain. It's also a great place to buy a Swiss army knife or a watch from Bucherer or a cup of genuine English tea. On one cross street into the old part of town, there's a hardware store (**Eisenwaren**) with everything from hand tools to Swiss cowbells. The saving grace of this tourist trap town is the public parking in front of most of the shops, and the good riding in the nearby mountains.

All the Berner Oberland is in the valley of the Aare River which flows north to the Rhein from right here. From near the top of Grimsel Pass, this road climbs up on the high peaks that are the source of the Aare. Controlled by traffic signals at each end that permit traffic for a half hour in one direction at a time, the road leads up and over and down to a hydroelectric dam (Stausee) where there is a restaurant. (photo by Stacy Silverwood)

In Lauterbrunnen, the valley of waterfalls, you can stay right near the base of Staubach falls at the Jungfrau Hotel. (Trip 5)

The area is crawling with hotels. There are big ones and little ones, expensive and cheap, in the bigger towns, on lakes, and hanging on the mountainside above little villages.

The island village of **Iseltwald,** one potential home base, hugs the cliffs on the south shore of Brienzer See. To get there, take the Autobahn around the south shore of the lake and take the exit (Ausfahrt) onto Iseltwald. Tourist Office; CH-3807 Iseltwald; T 033 845-1201.

A choice hotel right on the lake where the lake steamer stops is the **Strand Hotel.** Upon exiting the freeway onto Iseltwald, there's a parking lot for tourists.

The road into the village is marked with the international "do not enter" sign. But the little white sign underneath reads to the effect of, "unless you have business." So ride on in and have some business.

Another village with hotels, restaurants, and rooms for rent is **Beatenberg,** on the cliff hundreds of meters above the north shore of the Thuner See. Follow signs from the north side of Interlaken. From the whole village, there are sweeping views of Thuner See below and the Berner Oberland mountains beyond, including the Jungfrau. Beatenberg is a good place to catch **Alpenglow,** the almost hot pink glow of snow covered mountains in the rising or setting sun.

On the opposite shore of Brienzer See from Iseltwald is an outdoor museum called **Ballenberg** with a collection of farmhouses from all parts of Switzerland. They're furnished and have costumed people working in and around them. There are two entrances (and exits), a lower one near the town of **Brienz,** and a higher one about halfway up the **Brunig Pass.** Park and walk in.

A steam cog train climbs from Brienz to a mountaintop restaurant called **Rothorn.**

On the north bank of the Aare River in Interlaken is **Hotel Goldey.**

The **City Hotel** is small and modern with underground parking just off the main drag in Interlaken, behind the post office and across a little plaza from the hardware store.

Right on the main drag in Interlaken is **Hotel Krebs** with a cafe overlooking the street, but with rooms and parking on the quiet backside.

West of Interlaken, on the south shore of the Thuner See at Faulen See, is the **Strand Hotel Seeblick.**

The Schallenberg is a non-commercial, non-tourist, motorcycle favorite. The cafe at the top has special parking for bikes and a prize second floor balcony from which to watch the developing scene below (Trip 6).

Trip 5 Switzerland's Yosemite ★

Distance *About 60 kilometers round trip from Interlaken*

Terrain *Curving valley roads*

Highlights *Spectacular cliffs, waterfalls, and glaciered mountains*

There's a dead-end valley 12 kilometers south of Interlaken so breathtakingly beautiful, such a joy to behold, that it's worth a detour. It's called **Lauterbrunnen,** valley of the waterfalls. The valley is narrower than Yosemite, and has at least as many waterfalls, one inside the mountain, called

The Lauterbrunnen valley, known as the valley of the waterfalls—Switzerland's Yosemite—is located just a few kilometers from Interlaken. It is possible to stay right at the foot of Staubbach waterfall, shown here. The witch's hat church steeple is typical of German-speaking Switzerland. This is the countryside where all the tourists have fondue, some expressing surprise that it isn't always cheese.

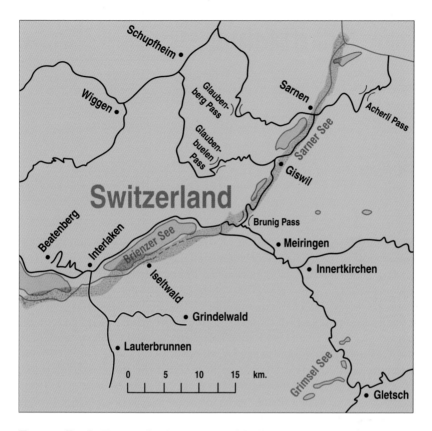

Trummelbach. Trummelbach has a sort-of incline elevator that takes visitors inside the mountain almost to the top. Winding and narrow stairs lead to viewing platforms of the water storm inside the mountain, and then back down to the bottom. Take at least your rain suit jacket. It's possible to stay in the valley. Two hotels are the **Schutzen** and the **Jungfrau.** The latter has a good indoor pool.

A cable car from Lauterbrunnen goes up to the top of the **Schilthorn** mountain to what is reportedly the highest revolving restaurant in the world. You may have seen it in a James Bond film.

The road to Lauterbrunnen intersects with a road into the next valley east. It leads in just a few kilometers to the village of **Grindelwald.** Grindelwald is pretty touristy, but it's at the base of the **Eiger,** the mountain face that Clint Eastwood played on in the movie, *The Eiger Sanction.* It's handy to know that the Eiger, another word for "devil," is separated from the Jungfrau mountain, "the maiden," by a mountain called "Monk."

There are several villages with hotels above Lauterbrunnen and Grindelwald accessible only by cog train or cable car.

There are plenty of hotels in Grindelwald.

Trip 6 North of Interlaken

Distance About 180 kilometers from Interlaken via Glaubenberg Pass plus about 40 via Acherli Pass

Terrain Sweeping and twisting through meadows and forests on five lower passes, some narrow, tight stuff

Highlights Bucolic motorcycle favorite roads, a couple of motorcycle cafes, mostly off tourist routes, Schallenberg (1,167 meters), ★Glaubenbuelen Pass (1,611 meters), ★Glaubenberg Pass (1,643 meters), Brunig Pass (1,008 meters), ★Acherli Pass (1,458 meters)

This loop offers pleasant, bucolic, often challenging, but not exotic riding off the main tourist routes. Alpine guidebooks don't mention these roads.

The **Schallenberg** road starts climbing from the town of **Thun,** at the west end of the Thuner See, the westerly of the two lakes that bracket Interlaken. From the north side of Thun, signs direct you first to **Steffisburg,** then to Schallenberg. (The English ear doesn't distinguish between "burg" and "berg," but technically the former is a fortified town and the latter is a mountain.) From the Autobahn, take the Steffisburg exit, which seems convoluted. Just follow the signs. At last, the road exits on a street, with signs to Schallenberg to the right.

A block beyond the Schallenberg sign is one of the largest motorcycle shops in Europe, **Moto Center Thun.** It's on the main road, but the entrance is a left turn before you get to it. The place is huge and attractive with Hondas and BMWs for sale and rent, with a large and well-equipped shop. Vast space is devoted to accessory display and sales. Downstairs is a bargain basement, and overlooking the road, a bike cafe.

Most Swiss don't know of little Acherli Pass. This view is of the south side, swooping down through green meadows toward Dallenwil.

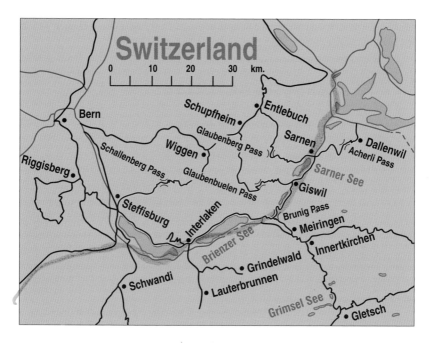

The Schallenberg road has open sweepers through farms that have no great commercial or tourist value, so it's a motorcycle favorite. The area is a bit less polished-looking than most parts of Switzerland. The cafe at the top, **Restaurant Gabelspitz,** is almost exclusively aimed at serving *Tofflers.* All the parking close by is for motorcycles. A choice second-floor balcony lets patrons watch the road and the parking lot activity.

The east side of the Schallenberg comes down to a village called **Wiggen.** From Wiggen, the trip heads east in the direction of **Luzern** for a few kilometers. Just at the edge of a town called **Schupfheim,** a road to the right leads south to a town called **Fluhli.** This is the **Glaubenbuelen Pass** road, sometimes called *Panorama Strasse.* From Fluhli, the road is twisting, paved, one-lane across the top with lovely views of lakes and mountains and forests. But it seems like only cows are looking at the panorama. There are no restaurants, no services. The Swiss will insist that Heidi came from eastern Switzerland, but the Glaubenbuelen looks like what Heidi country ought to look like. In the fall and spring the road may be full of cows heading to or from the high pastures, with floral headdresses in the fall. In either case, the lead cow will wear a big brass bell hung from an elaborate collar. Lesser cows have smaller bells and smaller collars, down to the least with tin sheet metal bells.

The pass road connects with the main highway between Interlaken and Luzern at **Giswil,** just in time to climb west over the **Brunig Pass** in the direction of Interlaken. (Looking for the Panorama Strasse from Giswil, the only hint is a sign on the main road pointing to Schupfheim. Look for the Giswil church which sits back on sort of a nob. The Panorama Strasse goes by it.)

To extend the trip, instead of going back to Interlaken over the Brunig, take the main road in the opposite direction toward Luzern. Then at **Sarnen,** head back north on the **Glaubenberg Pass.** More below.

The Brunig isn't high, but it *did* have some great sweepers that drew motorcycles from all around. A few years ago an avalanche took out most of the good sweepers and some vehicles with it. The replacement road does the job, but has less oomph. There remains one corner, a righthander going up from the east, that has a pull-out space that fills with bikes on good days. And the several restaurants and hotels at the top often host huge crowds of motorcyclists. Friday night is supposed to be *the* night on the Brunig. The **Motel Restaurant Brunig** always has a sport bike mounted on a post out front, changed from time to time. Across the road, the **Restaurant Silvana** has a big lot carved out of the mountainside, often packed with bikes. Its front tables are right on the road for good view and sound. From the top of Brunig, a dead-end road goes south a few kilometers to an area called **Hasliberg** with good views of the Aare valley, including Meiringen and Reichenbach Falls, described in Trip 1.

Parallel to and east of the Glaubenbuelen Pass (the *Panorama Strasse*) is another pass road called **Glaubenberg.** They must have named them to confuse us. Anyway, it's at least as high, even less used, and is also one lane across the top. Don't give up, the gravel part is only one kilometer. A restaurant/ski lodge named **Hotel Langis** on the south slope accommodates lots of motorcyclists during the summer. It's famous as a site where motorcyclists meet to make blood

Even though some of its famous sweepers were swept away by an avalanche, Brunig Pass has always been popular. The Motel Restaurant Brunig, atop the pass, is a *Tofftreftpunkt,* a motorcycle meeting place. Note the bike on the pole to the left of the Swiss flag.

From Brunig Pass, there are glimpses of green fields and Lungernsee.

donations (called "blut spenden" in German). The north end of the Glaubenberg is in the middle of a village called **Entlebuch,** a few kilometers closer to Luzern than Schupfheim, above. Its southeast side ends at **Sarnen,** a town at the end of a lake by the same name.

From Sarnen it's possible to cross the main road and catch an obscure pass called **Acherli** over the next mountain into the **Engelberg valley.** There are no signs for the pass, so follow the signs from Sarnen to Kerns and then to Sand. The only intersection in **Sand** is at the north edge of the village, and that's the pass road. Leaving Sand on the pass road there's a reassuring sign, **DALLENWIL,** the next town in the Engelberg valley. A couple of kilometers in the woods above Sand are gravel. Across the top and down the south side is one-lane, paved, open cattle range. There are electric cattle gates. The winding road through green vistas is lovely. It comes out on the main street of **Dallenwil.** Coming the other way, from the Engelberg valley there are no signs for the pass either. Just follow the main road into and through Dallenwil.

From the Engelberg road it's only a few kilometers on the Autobahn toward the **St. Gotthard** to **Beckenried,** where a ferry crosses the **Vierwaldstatter See** to the **Axenstrasse** and the roads of Trip 4. There's a fine hotel restaurant, **Sternen Hotel am See,** right at the ferry with a terrace overlooking lake and mountains. Ferries run about once an hour. A less romantic connection from Beckenried to the roads of Trip 4 is the Autobahn tunnel, four lanes, about five kilometers through the cliffs above Vierwaldstatter See. A marvel, but no view.

Or head back over the Brunig Pass to Interlaken.

The west side of the Brunig has a connecting road to the Susten and Grimsel Passes, the roads of Trip 1. Weekend bikers often head that way.

Trip 7 Gurnigel ★

Distance *About 120 kilometers, round trip from Interlaken*

Terrain *Lakeside road, then a climb through woods to high pasture*

Highlights *Handsome lakefront, woods, maybe military artillery, Gurnigel Pass (1,608 meters)*

Riggisberg, about 15 kilometers northwest of the town of **Thun,** is the access key to a loop west of the **Thuner See.** From Riggisberg, this loop heads south on back roads to the summit at a restaurant called **Berghaus Gurnigel.** The easterly leg of the loop is a full two-lane road. The westerly leg is partly one-lane and is a bit rough, although paved. Both are fun. Both have good views, as does the restaurant at the top. The restaurant terrace has views over the low mountains to the south, often used for military exercises.

In the fall, cows come down from the high summer pastures. The lead cow is usually decorated with flowers. Of course, it has the biggest bell. Coming at the cows, it's best to pull over and let them pass. Then enjoy the road well-sprinkled with cow pies. Approaching them from behind, the cow pies will give fair warning of what's ahead. But it is difficult to pass through the herd from the rear.

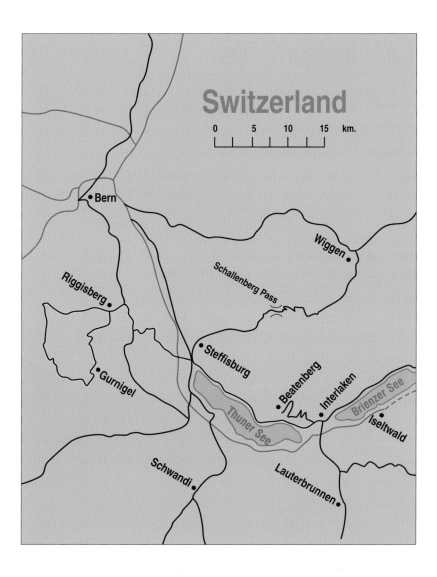

Switzerland

0 5 10 15 km.

Bern

Wiggen

Schallenberg Pass

Riggisberg

Steffisburg

Gurnigel

Beatenberg

Interlaken

Brienzer See

Thuner See

Iseltwald

Schwandi

Lauterbrunnen

Trip 8   Trimbach bei Olten   ★

Distance   *About 140 kilometers, one way from Interlaken*

Terrain   *Highway and Autobahn*

Highlights   *Thousands and thousands of motorcycles*

Friday night is the meeting night on **Brunig Pass,** but the biggest gathering of riders is usually on Thursday night at **Trimbach bei Olten** (Trimbach is just north of Olten), about 80 kilometers straight north of Interlaken, south of Basel, and west of Zurich. To get to Trimbach bei Olten from Interlaken, head north over the Brunig Pass and continue on the Autobahn past Luzern. Olten is just off the Autobahn, about halfway between Luzern and Basel. Or take the Autobahn from Interlaken to Thun and Bern and then to Olten.

A huge parking lot next to a modest Gasthaus named **Eisenbahn** (railroad) accommodates about 3,000 motorcycles, and on good nights they spill out over

On Thursday nights, thousands of motorcyclists gather for tire kicking at the Eisenbahn restaurant in the Swiss village of Trimbach bei Olten. Bikes fill the parking lot, and the rest spill over adjoining fields and roads.

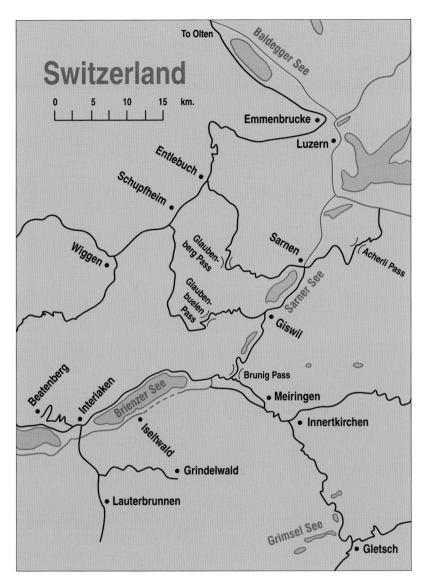

Switzerland

0   5   10   15   km.

To Olten

Baldegger See

Emmenbrucke •

Luzern •

Entlebuch •

Schupfheim •

Glauben-
berg Pass

Sarnen •

Acherli Pass

Wiggen •

Glauben-
buelen
Pass

Sarner See

Giswil •

Brunig Pass

Beatenberg

Interlaken •

Brienzer See

Meiringen •

Iseltwald •

Innertkirchen •

Grindelwald •

Lauterbrunnen •

Grimsel See

Gletsch •

neighboring fields. No events. No program. Only tire kicking. Special parking is reserved for any and all Harleys. The latest everything will show up, along with customized and restored bikes of all kinds. Every Thursday. Unfortunately, there aren't any recommended hotels nearby. There are a couple of serviceable ones in Olten.

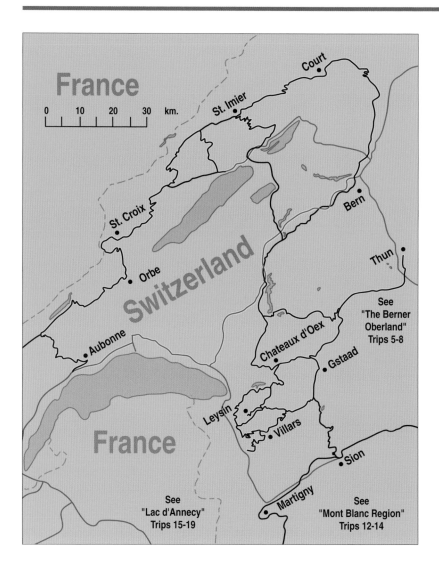

France

0 10 20 30 km.

Court

St. Imier

Switzerland

St. Croix

Bern

Orbe

Thun

Aubonne

See
"The Berner
Oberland"
Trips 5-8

Chateaux d'Oex

Gstaad

France

Leysin

Villars

Sion

See
"Lac d'Annecy"
Trips 15-19

Martigny

See
"Mont Blanc Region"
Trips 12-14

Leysin/Villars

Hung on a mountainside at about 1,200 meters, **Leysin** is a village with a view and a lot of hotels, and it's off the beaten track. It's in canton **Vaud,** and French, *s'il vous plait.* From most any point on the one road through town, from any balcony on any hotel, and from any terrace, there's a view across the **Valley of the Rhone River** (that started at the glacier on the Furka Pass) to the eternal snows of **Mont Blanc** and its neighbors.

Leysin is about six kilometers off the **Col des Mosses** road, the one road into Leysin, above the Rhone Valley town of **Aigle.** A cog train runs down the mountain from Leysin to Aigle.

A small family-run hotel near the top of the town, with views and good hearty cooking, is the **Hotel Mont Riant.** Another is **Hotel Colina.**

Since there's a Swiss hotel school in Leysin, there are many other hotels, some quaint and some more grand. In case you need a wash cloth, there's even a Holiday Inn.

An alternate to Leysin is **Villars,** a village hanging on an adjacent mountainside above Aigle at about 1,200 meters. It's signed from Aigle and from **Bex** and is the jumping off place for the **Col de la Croix.** A good hotel bet is the international style **Eurotel.**

Villars is home to a handy hotel guide for the budget traveler in Switzerland called E and G Hotels. "E" and "G" stand for Einfach and Gemutlich, which gets translated, "simple and cozy." It's published every year and lists about 175 or so modestly priced hotels all over Switzerland. Each listing has a color picture along with prices, hours, address, phone, and a clever symbol system that describes showers, pools, view, and other amenities. Naturally, a cheaper hotel in the city may prove less attractive than one of similar price in the country. The book is available at all Swiss tourist offices, or write **E and G Hotels,** Case Postal; CH-1844 Villars; T 024 495-1111; F 024 495-7514.

Trip 9 Simmen Tal and Jaun Pass

Distance *About 145 kilometers from Interlaken to Leysin via Jaun Pass; about 110 kilometers via Saanenmoser*

Terrain *Easy sweeping climbs over low passes*

Highlights *Picturesque villages and covered bridges, lush pastures, forest, medieval walled town and famous cheese factory (Gruyeres), Jaun Pass (1,509 meters), Saanenmoser (1,279 meters)*

The picturesque **Simmen Tal** (valley) feeds into the south shore of the Thuner See, just west of Interlaken. From the lake, the road up the valley winds past quaint wooden covered bridges and through small villages. Unfortunately, it's marked "no passing" (double white, not double yellow) for practically its whole length. And the many little villages are famous for strict enforcement of the speed limits.

Up the Simmen Tal about 15 kilometers from the Thuner See is a tiny one-building village called **Weissenburg** (don't confuse it with Weissenbach, farther upstream). The building is the **Hostellerie Alte Post** at Weissenburg, a joy for any antique connoisseur as well as anyone ready for a genuine Swiss meal. It's famous for serving coffee cream in chocolate cups that melt into the coffee.

The top of the Simmen Tal is called **Saanenmoser,** not much of a pass, but it leads right into one of Switzerland's classiest tourist areas: **Gstaad.** *Everybody* skis and plays tennis here, or at least the rich and famous are supposed to.

From Gstaad, it's straight over the **Col du Pillon** to **Leysin,** or from nearby **Saanen,** it's straight ahead over the Col des Mosses to Leysin. To **Villars,** take the **Col du Pillon** and **Col de la Croix** right into Villars. These roads are more completely described in Trip 10. The road up the mountain to Leysin is just about where the Col du Pillon road and the Col des Mosses road meet.

But should you choose the longer route over the **Jaun Pass,** the turnoff is out in the country, in a meadow, just outside the little Simmen Tal village of **Reidenbach.** Jaun Pass (yawn, not whawn) runs between the Simmen Tal on the east and **Gruyeres** on the west with views of the Simmen Tal. It's an easy climb and there are restaurants at the top of the pass.

Gruyeres, on the west end of the Jaun Pass, is a preserved old walled city on a hill. No vehicles. It's worth the short walk in to visit. Bikes can park right by the city gate. Too many restaurants offer almost any concoction or most any kind of berry with the thickest, richest cream imaginable, cream that comes from the cheese factory for which the town is known. On through plaza and shops of the walled village is a castle, for which an entry fee is charged. The factory is at the

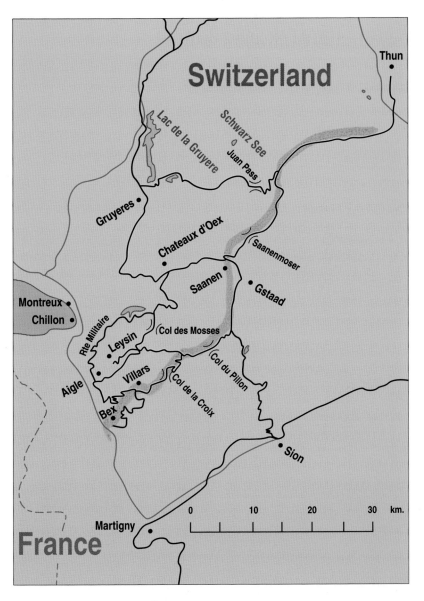

bottom of the hill and is open to visitors in the morning. Do the town rather than the cheese. In case you hadn't guessed, Gruyeres is French speaking.

South from Gruyeres is the **Col des Mosses,** leading to the road to Leysin, or on to Aigle and Villars.

Trip 10 Three Cols and a Route

Distance *About 144 kilometers from Leysin*

Terrain *Fun sweepers over lower passes, mostly modern highways, modest height and difficulty*

Highlights *Well-known resorts (Gstaad, Chateau d'Oex), log village (Saanen), German/French culture border, Col du Pillon (1,546 meters), ★ Col de la Croix (1,778 meters), Col des Mosses (1,445 meters), Route Militaire*

The **Col des Mosses** climbs out of the Rhone Valley from **Aigle,** past a handsome private castle, and past the dead-end road to **Leysin.**

Chateau d'Oex (sounds like "shat oh decks") and **Rougemont** are attractive tourist towns at the north end of the Col des Mosses. The highway now bypasses both villages. The medieval church at Rougemont is worth a stop if you're passing by. Although the village is French speaking, the church is of Germanic style, because the diocese was controlled from nearby Germanic Saanen.

Rougemont has a comfortable log hotel restaurant that's called **Hotel de Commune.**

An interesting and fun alternate route parallels the Col des Mosses from Aigle. It's a military road and is open only on Saturdays, Sundays, and holidays. The south end, out of the valley village of **Corbeyrier,** climbs through handsome vineyards, then some narrow, steep hairpins and a twisting, one-way-at-a-time tunnel.

The north end cruises by a lake, then over many bridges. Some pass roads number the hairpins. This one numbers the bridges: forty some. Unfortunately, part of the road has a low speed limit.

Heading to Les Diablerets from Col de la Croix on a morning after an early fall snow.

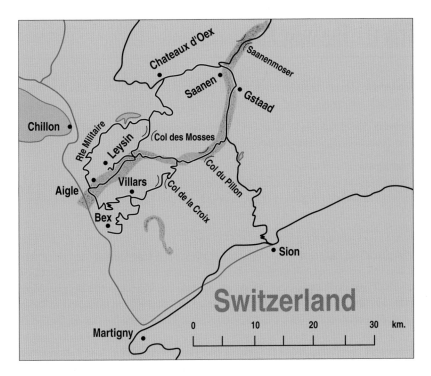

At the lovely log house village of **Saanen** (also the westerly base of the Sannenmoser) the road heads south for **Gstaad,** and then starts climbing the **Col du Pillon** through the village of **Gsteig,** which has one of the nicer Germanic-Swiss church steeples, shaped much like a witch's hat.

As the name Col du Pillon implies, the top of the pass is in French-speaking Switzerland. In the few kilometers between Gsteig and the top of the pass, the buildings and menus change from Germanic to French.

The attractive restaurant at the top of the Col du Pillon, with a terrace viewing the highest peaks in the area, is called **Les Diablerets.** So are the peaks. So is the next town. At the next town, Les Diablerets, the **Col de la Croix** road heads southwest. Somehow, the Col de la Croix is uncluttered, with sweeping turns and sweeping views. It has gotten rough in spots. The Col road comes down to the village of **Villars,** one of the few Swiss towns that is anxious to sell condos to foreigners.

At Villars, the Col de la Croix road forks. One leg, the main road, heads for the Rhone Valley at Aigle. The other, the nicest, winds down to the valley at **Bex,** following much the same route as the trolley-train, (mind the tracks) through chalet-filled villages and vineyards with views across the Rhone to the high Alps around **Mont Blanc.** From either road, it's just a few kilometers back up the Col des Mosses road to Leysin. Looking for the Col de la Croix from the Rhone Valley, follow signs to Villars from either Bex or Aigle.

Trip 11 The Swiss Jura

Distance *About 390 kilometers round trip from Leysin or Villars, about half on autoroute (freeway), about 200 kilometers from or to Col de la Faucille*

Terrain *Some autoroute, farm land, lower wooded passes with narrow, non-tourist roads, French culture*

Highlights *Good views of Lac Leman, Lac du Joux, Lac du Neuchatel, famous Castle of Chillon, Col du Mollendruz (1,180 meters), Col de Marchairuz (1,447 meters), ★Col de l'Aiguillon (1,293 meters), Col des Etroits (1,152 meters), Vue des Alpes (1,283 meters), Col du Chasseral (1,502 meters, toll), Weissenstein (1,279 meters), Col du Mont Crosin (1,227 meters)*

The **Jura** is a range of mountains just northwest of **Lac Leman** and the lower Rhone River. About half the Jura are in the French-speaking part of Switzerland and half are in France. They're pretty mellow compared to the rugged Alps, more like the Smokies in the U.S. This trip covers all the good riding in the Swiss Jura, all reachable from the Leysin/Villars base. The French Jura are in Trip 16.

Or maybe stay at a spectacularly sited mid-point hotel, **La Mainaz,** just in France at the Swiss border, high in the Jura overlooking **Lac Leman** and **Geneve.** From the hotel room, you can see all of Geneve, the **Jet d'Eau,** a major portion of the lake, and beyond that, **Mount Blanc** itself. The hotel is all by itself on the **Col de la Faucille,** just twenty minutes from the Geneve airport. On one side of the hotel are the Swiss Jura, the French on the other. **La Mainaz** is a *Relais de Silence . . .* a quiet hotel, but motorcyclists have enjoyed it.

Arcing west from Leysin and Aigle for about 100 kilometers, the north shore of Lac Leman harbors the major cities of French-speaking Switzerland: **Montreux, Lausanne,** and at the west end, **Geneve (Geneva).** Suspended above the lake, sometimes on spectacular viaducts, an autoroute (freeway) whisks right by the **Castle of Chillon** (made famous by Lord Byron's poem) on the east end of the lake to Geneva on the west end.

The Castle of Chillon is a real medieval castle that seems to rise right out of Lac Leman. It can be visited from the lake shore road below the autoroute, just east of the city of Montreux. One American visitor was overheard wondering, "Why did they build this nice castle so close to the railroad tracks?"

To get to these passes, it's best to avoid traffic along the lake shore road by taking the autoroute west toward Geneve (Geneva), past Lausanne, exiting at **Aubonne,** then climbing northwest over the **Col de Marchairuz.** The restaurant atop Marchairuz has a hand washing machine. It's been in place for years yet seems unique. Put your hands in the opening. First warm water. Then soap. Then more warm water. Then warm air. North of the col, the road descends to the **Lac du Joux.**

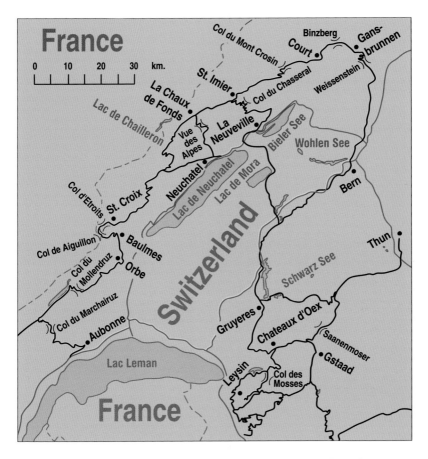

Follow the lake shore east, then up the low **Col du Mollendruz.** Just across the top head east to **Orbe,** then northeast to **Baulmes,** a pleasant small village nestled in a nook of the mountains. Into and through Baulmes is the **Col de l'Aiguillon** road. It climbs through forests and into meadows, a little road where no tourist has gone . . . at least not many. It meets a more main highway near the French border. Go east, staying in Switzerland, over the **Col des Etroits** to a town called **St. Croix,** then on east to **La Chaux de Fonds,** where a jaunt south goes over the **Vue des Alpes,** then merge with the autoroute to **Neuchatel** and follow the autoroute east under (that's right, under) the city of Neuchatel exiting at **La Neuveville** beside **Bieler See.** Climb north over the toll pass, **Col du Chasseral,** through **St. Imier,** and on northeast over the **Col du Mont Crosin,** then east toward **Moutier.** Just past **Court,** continue east to **Gansbrunner,** over a mountain called **Binzberg** in German and **Graitery** in French. At Gansbrunner, head south over **Weissenstein.** (Or cross the same mountain on the narrow Balmberg road a few kilometers further east at Welshenrohr. No tourists for sure.) From **Solothurn,** it's Autobahn back to Leysin/Villars.

CHAPTER

3

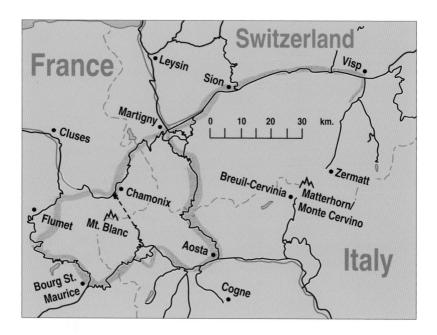

Mont Blanc Region

The **Rhone Valley** makes a 90-degree bend at a pretty good sized Swiss town called **Martigny.** Quite French. It's where two pass roads head out to encircle the eternal snows of the highest mountain in the Alps, **Mont Blanc,** 4,807 meters (15,779 feet!). From Martigny the **Col de la Forclaz** road heads toward France, and the **Grand St. Bernard** road heads toward Italy.

Martigny, or any of the villages hung on the mountains around it, are good bases for the Mont Blanc trip. Right where the two pass roads come together in Martigny is hotel **La Porte d'Octodure;** *Malhereusement,* it's a Best Western!

A little village called **Les Marecottes,** atop a spectacular road just eight kilometers from the Martigny town square, has a variety of hotels that have served motorcyclists well. Go northwest from the square, over a covered wooden bridge, and keep climbing. The road climbs a traverse overlooking the Rhone Valley, then crosses to the north side of the **Gorge du Trient** on a high bridge. From that point on, the road barely hangs on the cliff edge overlooking the gorge. A train up the gorge goes through to France. The road doesn't. Les Marecottes is near the end of the road. One hotel is called **Aux Mille Etoiles.**

From the autoroute in the Rhone Valley, the pass roads are signed via a bypass road that misses downtown Martigny.

The trips in this chapter are accessible from Leysin or Villars.

On the northwest side, the Col du Pre leads through some of *le plus joli* vistas in France (Trip 13).

Trip 12 Valley of the Rhone

Distance *About 160 kilometers between Martigny and Andermatt, one way; about 110 kilometers between Martigny and Tasch (Zermatt), one way; about 100 kilometers between Martigny and Simplon Pass, one way*

Terrain *Fairly straight valley road and sweeping mountain climbs on good modern highway*

Highlights *Sweep up a finger valley toward the Matterhorn, over a high mountain pass (★ Simplon, at 2,006 meters), some concrete roofed highway*

From the high passes at **Andermatt**, the Rhone Valley makes a pretty straight shot down to **Martigny.** The higher eastern part of the valley, called the **Goms,** is an amusing ride through log cabin villages. The lower part is more commercial and boring. It does make a functional east-west connection, about 150 kilometers long, with such high mountains on both sides that there's hardly any way out. From the **Grimsel Pass** back by Andermatt, there's no through road going north until the **Col des Mosses** by **Leysin.** It is possible to put a bike or car on a train and take it through a tunnel toward **Interlaken.** Switzerland is slowly extending an autobahn/autoroute easterly up the valley.

Two dead-end roads north make for interesting escapes into high valleys: **Lotschen Tal** climbs up to the glaciers behind **Lauterbrunnen** (turn off at the signs for the train tunnel to Goppenstein), and the **Col du Sanetsch** from **Sion** almost makes it across the top to **Gsteig,** but doesn't.

One road out of the Rhone Valley to the south toward Italy, the **Simplon Pass,** starts at **Brig,** 50 kilometers below the Furka. The Simplon is one of the major passes of the Alps between Italy and France, through Switzerland. The first major Alpine train tunnel went under the Simplon to carry the Orient Express. Both sides of the pass road are in Switzerland, with good quality sweepers to the summit on both sides. The north side has an amazing "S" curved poured concrete suspension bridge. On the summit is a giant stone eagle monument and a couple of serviceable restaurants. One regular menu item is goulash soup, a spicy, meaty specialty of the Germanic Alps that tastes something like chili.

An elaborate two-lane (on-coming traffic) freeway and tunnel now lead from the Goms around, through, and under Brig, with well-signed connections for the Simplon Pass.

(For good road connections from the south side of the Simplon, see Trip 32, "Simplon Pass".)

Several dead-end valleys go south from the Rhone Valley. The most famous valley is **Matter Tal** to **Zermatt** and the **Matterhorn,** but no vehicles are allowed into Zermatt. The Rhone Valley turnoff for Zermatt and the Matter Tal is at **Visp,** into a newly constructed tunnel that by-passes some commercial clutter.

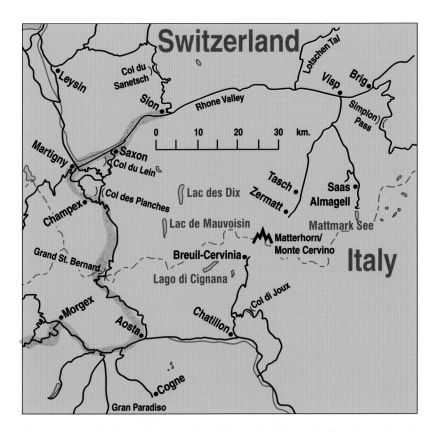

From the tunnel, it's a fine sweeping ride up the Matter Tal as far as **Tasch,** where one of the biggest parking lots in Europe accommodates tourists taking the cog train the rest of the way to Zermatt. There is underground and indoor parking at Tasch. Outdoor bike parking is available right next to the train station.

The village of **Randa,** just below Tasch, bears witness to the terror of the Alps. In recent years a whole mountain collapsed into the valley, burying everything—the stream, parts of the village, the road and railroad—under granite boulders. The road and railroad now go around the site.

About ten kilometers up the Matter Tal from Visp, there's an intersection. The west fork continues to Tasch and Zermatt, while the east fork goes all the way up to the towns of **Saas Fee** and **Saas Almagell.** The road to the former is interesting, with glaciers right at hand, but it's a walk-around-only village. Motorcycle parking is free.

Just downstream from Visp in the Rhone Valley, without a sign, everything changes from German to French: architecture, menus, bread, even cars.

Visible from the autoroute near **Sion** are castles and vineyards and airstrips with airplane hangars in the mountainsides. The autoroute by-passes Sion, the capital city of canton Wallis, only here it's French and the canton is called Valais.

Trip 13   All Around Mont Blanc   ★ ★

Distance   *About 300 kilometers from Martigny*

Terrain   *Circle the greatest mountain in the Alps, Mont Blanc; from low valleys with some congestion, climb to empty mountain roads; three major Alpine passes and several lesser ones; some narrow, tight, steep hairpins*

Highlights   *Three countries, famous passes and ski resorts, Roman ruins, plus some quiet, remote, twisting stuff,* ★*Col du Grand St. Bernard (2,469 meters),* ★*Colle San Carlo (1,971 meters),* ★*Col du Petit St. Bernard (2,188 meters),* ★★ *Cormet de Roselend (1,922 meters),* ★*Col du Pre (1,703 meters), Col des Saisies (1,633 meters), Chamonix, Col des Montets (1,461 meters), Col de la Forclaz (1,526 meters), Col des Planches (1,411 meters), Col du Lein (1,656 meters), Champex (1,486 meters)*

Three amusing little roads start near **Martigny.** Just toward downtown a few hundred meters from the **Hotel La Porte d'Octodure,** a tiny road, the **Col des**

The single lane Col de Pre road crosses the Barrage (Dam) de Roselend, and climbs, affording fine views of Mt. Blanc in the distance.

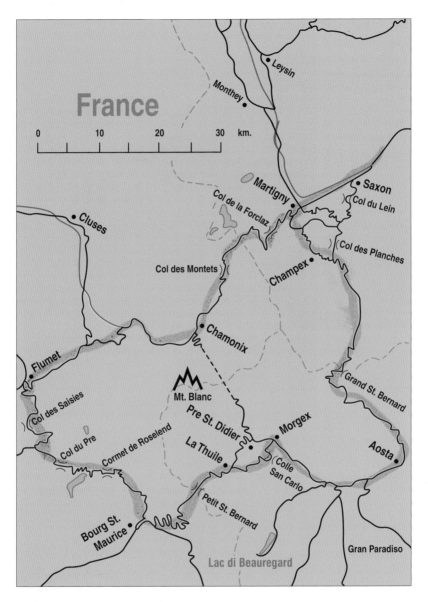

France

0   10   20   30   km.

Leysin

Monthey

Martigny

Saxon
Col du Lein

Col de la Forclaz

Cluses

Col des Planches

Col des Montets

Champex

Chamonix

Mt. Blanc

Grand St. Bernard

Flumet

Col des Saisies

Pre St. Didier

Morgex

Col du Pre

Cormet de Roselend

La Thuile

Colle San Carlo

Aosta

Petit St. Bernard

Bourg St. Maurice

Gran Paradiso

Lac di Beauregard

Planches, climbs up the mountainside. It isn't high, but it does lead up and over to a high resort at **Verbier,** 1,390 meters. Up the **Grand St. Bernard** a few kilometers, at **Les Valettes,** another small road makes a twisting climb up to a mountain lake village called **Champex.** The road goes through and winds back down to the Grand St. Bernard road at **Orsieres,** where an interesting dead-end valley road, **Val Ferret,** heads up toward some glaciers at 1,705 meters.

Just a few kilometers up and out of Bourg St. Maurice, the south slopes of the Cormet de Roseland seem to have entered a never-never land.

The third amusing little road is the **Col du Lein,** crossing the mountain behind Martigny between **Saxon** in the Rhone Valley and the Grand St. Bernard road near **Sembrancher.** Saxon is about ten kilometers east of Martigny, and the turnoff is from the center of the village, marked **Col du Len,** not Lien. Sembrancher is 12 kilometers up the Grand St. Bernard road from Martigny. The little col road climbs to about 1,600 meters, one lane, with about four kilometers unpaved.

There are two St. Bernard Passes, a Grand (big) and a Petit or Piccolo (little) St. Bernard. The big one goes between Martigny, Switzerland, and **Aosta,** Italy. It's where the dogs are. The little one goes from Aosta in Italy to France. There's a statue of St. Bernard on both of them.

The Grand St. Bernard Pass is fairly commercial and has high-speed sweepers so well engineered that it's hard to realize how quickly you're up among the glaciers. But it goes by tunnel into Italy. Motorcycles want to stay on the pass road, so turn off just after entering the tunnel, where a sign, COL, points to the right. Sometimes the col is labeled OUVERT, open, on the Swiss side, but the border crossing just over the col is closed. Sometimes it's closed with huge concrete blocks. The restaurant on the Swiss side is French. It will have sandwiches (try a croque-monsieur, grilled ham and cheese) and plates of cold cuts (assiette); the Italian, fresh pasta and salad and cappuccino. Most of the dogs around are stuffed toys. On the Italian side, the 14 kilometers between the pass and the Italian entrance to the tunnel are fairly challenging and wild. Approaching the pass from Italy, the pass road leaves the tunnel road just before a long viaduct that leads to the tunnel entrance. There's a place to change money at the complex of offices just across the viaduct. Euros are needed for cash purchases in Italy, Swiss francs in Switzerland. The rest of the route down into Aosta has commercial traffic.

Aosta center has some significant **Roman ruins,** an arch, walls, and a theater. On the east end of town, past the airport, is a very large motorcycle shop called **America.** It does not sell Harleys. It does fit tires quickly.

Even though it's in a fabulous Alpine valley, Aosta has a lot of traffic and smog, alleviated recently by the newly completed **Monte Bianco** autostrada that bypasses the town taking most trucks and busses with it.

There is a serviceable hotel in Aosta. **Hotel Valle d'Aosta** is on the east end of town (see Trip 14 for riding in the vicinity of Aosta). An exceptionally attractive hotel, the **Miramonti,** is at **Cogne,** the end of a road south out of Aosta into the **Gran Paradiso National Park.** Cogne, and the hotel furnished with lovely and comfortable antiques, are worth a special trip. The hotel's working language is French. Another hotel, carefully more business-like, is at **Chatillon,** miles east (downstream) of Aosta. It's called **Relais du Foyer.** Located well above the valley on the north side, it is near the road that climbs to **Monte Cervino,** the **Matterhorn** (see Trip 14 for more about the roads near these hotels).

To get to the **Piccolo St. Bernard Pass** from Aosta, follow the signs to **Courmayeur** and the Italian entrance to what used to be the longest vehicle tunnel in the world under Mont Blanc. Commercial truck traffic to the tunnel is terrible. An elaborate autostrada is under construction, but . . . . Fortunately, motorcyclists need not go through the tunnel. From the smog-filled highway there are occasional glimpses of Mont Blanc, huge and white, before the turnoff at the village of **Pre St. Didier,** 30 kilometers from Aosta, where the Piccolo St. Bernard goes south and leaves the traffic behind.

Or better yet, before the Piccolo St. Bernard turnoff at Pre St. Didier, there's a long cut over an obscure pass called the **Colle San Carlo.** It's recently been improved with new retaining walls and pavement. Escape the traffic early by turning up the Colle at a village called **Morgex.** The pass isn't marked. The sign is to **Arpy,** a town on the pass. After a great climb twisting through the forests, the road descends into the village of **La Thuile,** on the Piccolo St. Bernard road.

The rest of the Italian side of the Piccolo St. Bernard is a delight. Often the road cuts through deep banks of snow well into mid-June. The only village, **La Thuile,** has a good ristorante called **Grotto,** and another called **Les Marmottes** just across from the little and only parking lot in town. Try tortellini carne in garlic and walnut sauce.

On the French side of the col, at **La Rosiere,** are a couple of pleasant restaurants. Several hairpins below La Rosiere is a shortcut in the direction of the **Col de l'Iseran** (Trip 17), signed for the village, **Montvalezan** (D84).

Some American motorcyclists have noted that French road repair crews use a lot of gravel, often marked with a portable sign that profiles a pre-World War II Citroen spraying rocks from its wheels. Gravel piles can spoil the French side of the Grand St. Bernard.

One of the *plus joli* (prettiest) roads in France, the **Cormet de Roselend** (sounds like "core may"), starts at **Bourg St. Maurice** at the base of the Petit (it's *petit* in France, not *piccolo*) St. Bernard. Find it (D902) heading north from the east end of town. The road has no commercial or even ski activity. Early in the season, it may be marked *ferme* (closed) because of snow. Give it a try. Very possibly a bike can get through. Parts are only one lane wide and bumpy, but it feels like no one else was ever there. Near the top should be herds of handsome red-brown cows, source of the famous cheese that comes from the other side of the mountain at Beaufort.

On the north side of the Cormet is a beautiful lake with a couple of satisfactory mountain restaurants. The northerly one is a bit more substantial in building and menu. The lake results from a dam (*barrage* in French) with a road across the top that leads to another pass of no significance except views so wonderful that even the most enthusiastic rider will pause to look. It's mostly one lane wide, paved, and is called **Col du Pre.** A restaurant on it called **la Pierra Menta** is justly proud of it's "tartelettes aux myrtilles" mountain blueberry tarts, and its terrace with views of mountain meadows, the lake, and in the distance, a very white **Mont Blanc.**

On over the col, the road winds down through open pastures surrounded by snowy peaks into **Beaufort,** the town of cheese fame.

Three kilometers below Beaufort is the turnoff for the **Col des Saisies** (say coal day sigh zee) heading up and north (D218). Cross-country skiing events for the **Albertville Olympics** were held on the col and there's a lot of ski-oriented development. It's a north-south pass, with the north end daylighting at **Flumet,** a little village on the main valley road between **Albertville** and **Chamonix.**

But wait. There's a more fun and more beautiful way up the Col des Saisies. The signed road three kilometers down from Beaufort (D218) heads up a finger valley in the direction of **Hauteluce.** But just one kilometer further downstream is a sign for a village called **Villard.** Go into Villard (D123) and keep climbing, back and forth switchbacks up the face of the mountain with views for miles and kilometers. The road eventually makes it up to the col and joins the main road. Just across the col, at a mini-traffic circle, there should be a sign for **Crest Voland,** a little village down on the edge of the mountain. It's a fun alternative to the main road into Flumet.

From the Swiss side of the Col du Grand St. Bernard, the restaurant in sunny Italy is almost at hand. Across the border in those buildings there will be cappucino and fresh pasta.

Coming into Chamonix on the road from Flumet all traffic gets funneled onto an autoroute that marches up the valley on stilts out over the top of everything. Finally, at Chamonix, the huge glaciers of Mont Blanc come into view. And the tunnel entrance to Italy. Chamonix is a summer and winter tourist center with all the accommodations and traffic to prove it. One of the most exotic cable car rides (*telepherique* in French) in the world goes from Chamonix to the **Aiguille du Midi** on the Mont Blanc massif. From the main highway through the city, an underpass takes you to the parking lot of the cable car. The ride up is exciting if the weather's clear.

Most of the traffic is going through the tunnel to Italy, not to Switzerland. For Switzerland, follow the signs to **Argentiere** and **Col des Montets,** a hardly noticeable pass, and on to the Swiss border.

The Swiss side of the border crossing has all kinds of services, including money exchanges. Across the border there's a turnoff to a town called **Finhaut.** A road climbs through Finhaut to dead-end at a lake called **Emosson** at 1,930 meters. The road's good and there's a restaurant with a terrace and view of the whole Mont Blanc massif.

Back at the foot of the mountain, the road on to Martigny climbs over the **Col de la Forclaz.** The Martigny side of this col has a couple of restaurants with good views of the Rhone Valley and surrounding vineyards.

CHAPTER
4

Trip 14   Val d'Aosta

Distance   *About 78 kilometers from Martigny to Aosta, one way, plus about 50 kilometers from Aosta to Breuil (the Matterhorn, called Monte Cervino in Italy) one way, plus about 25 kilometers from Aosta to any of the valleys in the Parco Nazionale Gran Paradiso, one way*

Terrain   *Once out of the Aosta valley, quiet, twisting narrow roads into high forgotten valleys surrounded by glaciers*

Highlights   ★*Breuil, as close to the Matterhorn as a road goes (2,006 meters), glaciers and peaks of Gran Paradiso National Park,* ★*Col di Joux (1,640 meters)*

Just west of **Aosta,** on the traffic-jammed highway to **Courmayeur** (the Mont Blanc tunnel), three roads dead-end south into the **Parco Nazionale Gran Paradiso.** The closest to Aosta is **Val di Cogne,** the next is **Val Savaranche,** and the third, **Val di Rhemes.** They quickly leave traffic and civilization behind. Each twists and climbs into high Alpine valleys.

Val di Cogne is a good base for hikers and climbers and offers beautiful views of Mont Blanc and the Gran Paradiso. At the top of the valley, surrounded by the

The back side of the Matterhorn, the Italian side, where it's known as Monte Cervino, is best viewed across little Lago Bleu at Breuil.

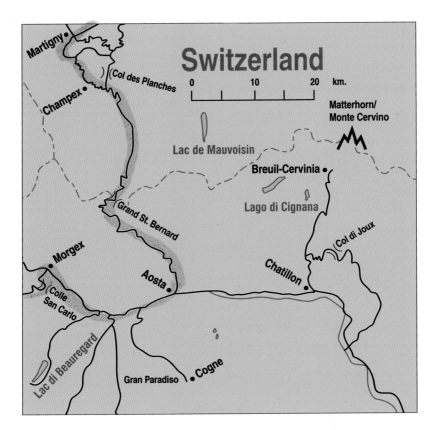

Gran Paradiso mountains, is the village **Cogne,** at 1,534 meters, a painstakingly preserved mountain village, and the home to an exceptionally lovely **Hotel Mirimonte.** The village is much as Zermatt would like to be.

Twenty-six kilometers from Aosta, going east on the autostrada toward Torino, is **Chatillon,** a town hung on the north slopes of the valley and the base for two good roads, and it has a nice hotel as well, **Relais du Foyer.** One road climbs north up to 2,006 meters, the very base of the Matterhorn. Of course, in Italia, it's Monte Cervino. The village up there, **Breuil,** has a lot of ski hotels, usually closed in the summer.

Just short of Breuil is a little lake, **Lago Bleu.** Hike up over a little slope for a picture to treasure, Cervino reflected in the lake.

Easterly from Chatillon through **St. Vincent,** the **Col di Joux** road makes a nice loop. From St. Vincent it climbs over to the next valley where a road, not nearly as interesting as the one to Monte Cervino, climbs to **St. Jacques** at 1,689 meters. Just west of the top of the Col di Joux is a restaurant with views to die for: the whole Aosta Valley west to Mont Blanc, er, Monte Bianco. The owner studied English in Buffalo! Coming the other direction, the col and St. Jacques are signed from the autostrada exit at Verres.

CHAPTER

4

See
"Leysin/Villars"
Trips 9-11

Switzerland

Geneve

Martigny

Cluses

Brenaz

Annecy

Italy

Albertville

Chambery

Bonneval

St. Jean

Grenoble

See
"The Gray Alps"
Trips 22-23

See
"Grenoble Heights"
Trips 20-21

France

0   10   20   30   km.

Lamure

Lac d'Annecy

In France, south of **Mont Blanc,** are some of the highest passes and wildest country of the Alps. Exciting to explore. The '92 Olympics at **Albertville** highlighted some of them. France alone of the Alpine countries has good, prominently marked route numbers. (Ns are national roads; Ds are departmental roads. Department road numbers may change from one town to the next.) The only trouble is, the numbers disappear in cities where there are sure to be many confusing intersections. As you approach a city in France, there may be signs like POUR FLUMET SUIVRE ALBERTVILLE, "for Flumet follow Albertville." So there won't be route number signs, but there will be signs for Albertville. And France has a lot of roundabouts, always preceded by a sign, VOUS N'AVEZ PAS LE PRIORITE. Entering the roundabout "you don't have the priority." Any vehicle to the left does. But once in the roundabout, you have the right of way and can go around as many times as it takes to check signs and plot an escape. Remember, signs may point at the road as well as, or instead of, the direction of travel. In France, freeways are called "autoroutes." Some have tolls.

Although they're pretty well developed for winter sports, the French Alps seem to close down during the summer season. Facilities, almost endless in number and variety elsewhere in the Alps, are a bit harder to locate in France, and some pass roads aren't open until late in June.

But facilities are always open at **Lac d'Annecy,** one of the loveliest lakes in the Alps, just a few kilometers northwest of Albertville. Passes south of **Lac Leman** lead to **Annecy,** as do the autoroutes south from **Geneve** and west from **Chamonix.** The French province that includes Annecy and most of these good passes is **Haute Savoie.** Its flag looks almost like the Swiss flag, a white cross on red. On Savoie's flag, the white arms of the cross reach the edge of the flag.

The town of Annecy, at the north end of the lake, has all services, including a variety of large and helpful motorcycle shops, even Harley. Annecy has a colorful walking old town with little canals, and a smart modern lake front promenade and beach. The whole city presents a very clean, neat, pleasing aspect.

Hotels for all tastes are located around the lake. On the eastern shore is a village called **Talloires** (say Tal whar). There are some pricey places like **George Bise,** and **Le Cottage,** fairly pretentious. The owner of nearby **Hotel le Lac** is a biker and he also owns a ski hotel high in the Val d'Isere. Next door is the **Hotel la Charpenterie,** attractive and more modest, and **Hotel Beau Site.**

A couple of good and reasonable hotels can be found east of Annecy at **La Clusaz** where the **Col des Aravis** meets the **Col de la Croix Fry; Alp Hotel** and **Hotel Sapins.** Don't get confused. This town is la Clusaz and north of it on the autoroute is Cluses.

Trip 15 Lac d'Annecy

Distance *About 230 kilometers from Martigny to Annecy, one way*

Terrain *Sweeping and twisting over seven non-commercial passes*

Highlights *Farms, forests, high meadows, some narrow roads, ski resorts, Pas de Morgins (1,369 meters), Col du Corbier (1,237 meters), Col des Gets (1,163 meters), ★Col de Joux Plane (1,712 meters), Col de la Colombiere (1,613 meters), Col des Aravis (1,486 meters), Col de la Croix Fry (1,467 meters), Col de Joux Verte (1,760 meters)*

Several passes south of **Lac Leman** make fun connections between Switzerland and the high roads of the French Alps. On most of them there is no traffic. Start out of the Rhone Valley in Switzerland on the **Pas de Morgins.** From the town of **Monthey,** just a few kilometers downstream from Martigny, it climbs through pleasant Swiss countryside and crosses into France at the top. The operator of the motorcycle shop in Monthey is an enthusiast who has biked all over the world, including North America and Baja.

Coming down into France below the town of **Abondance,** the little pass road of **Col du Corbier** (D32) heads up and south into a wonderful set of switchbacks on the northeast side. It leads to the next valley and the road up the **Col des Gets.** To the east of Gets is another little pass road called **Col de Joux Plane** (D354). It's a one-lane road that twists up from the town of **Morzine** on the north to

Annecy's old city is one of quaint canals and shops.

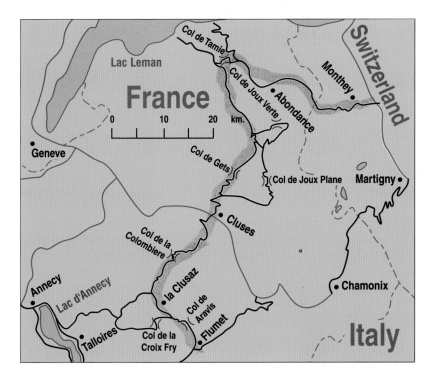

Samoens on the south. It's not conspicuously marked at either end, but it's popular with French and Swiss motorcyclists and is worth the effort to find it. A restaurant at the top is called **Relais des Vallees.**

A high loop out of Morzine to **Super Morzine** (that's its name) climbs easterly to the **Col de Joux Verte** (D338) at 1,760 meters and comes down at **Montriond** about five kilometers downstream from Morzine where it started. The northerly leg is through rustic country.

The whole loop adds about 30 kilometers.

All this leads down to a fairly large city, **Cluses,** on the autoroute to Chamonix. Signing through Cluses is circuitous.

Across the autoroute from Cluses, the **Col de la Colombiere** (D4) leads up and over the mountains toward **Annecy** through **St. Jean de Sixt** and **Thones. Colombiere** is a noncommercial play road. Oil spills have been noted, though. There is a restaurant at the top.

From **Flumet,** on the loop around Mont Blanc (north end of the Col des Saisies (Trip 13), the **Col des Aravis** (say are uh VEE) goes up and over toward Annecy. The Col des Aravis has a nice restaurant with a terrace view of Mont Blanc. Just down a little on the north side of the Col des Aravis, near the ski resort of **la Clusaz,** the **Col de la Croix Fry** heads up and west (D16). It's a good road with little traffic leading over to the town of Thones and the main road to Annecy. From it, a shortcut to **Talloires** turns south at **Bluffy** (D169).

Trip 16   The French Jura

Distance *About 210 kilometers from Annecy to Col de la Faucille, one way*

Terrain *Mostly small rural roads, some rough, pleasant mountain vistas*

Highlights *Walk in gorge, Grand Colombier (1,531 meters), Col de la Faucille (1,320 meters), Col de la Givrine (1,229 meters), Col de Richemond (1,060 meters)*

Just west of **Annecy** (and the autoroute) through **Lovagny** are the **Gorges du Fier** and a fine looking castle named **Montrottier.** You can park and walk through the gorge, not the castle.

Continue on across the Rhone Valley to **Culoz,** and climb the steep ascent of the **Montagne du Grand Colombier.** There's a rustic restaurant near the top at about 1,500 meters, **l'Auberge Le Grand Colombier,** with a view southerly over the **Lac du Bourget.**

Descending southerly from the Col de l'Iseran to the little village of Bonneval (Trip 17).

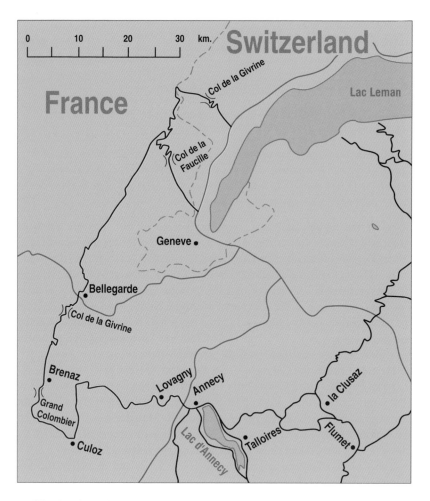

Wander along the Grand Colombier, northerly through **Brenaz,** and over the **Col de Richemond** which has a marker explaining that the col is named for World War II resistance martyrs.

Continue north across the autoroute near **Bellegarde,** where there are signs for **Col de la Faucille.** Climb a pleasant long valley then jog through some woods over the Col de la Faucille (1,320 meters) (see Trip 11 for Hotel La Mainaz, dramatically sited on the col). Geneve, Lac Leman, Swiss autoroutes are just over the col.

An alternate route, just before the Col de Faucille, is to turn north, crossing into Switzerland after a couple of kilometers over the **Col de la Givrine** (1,229 meters). The col road and the border crossing meet in a triangle, but you have to go around two sides of it to get across the border.

To continue in the Swiss Jura, see Trip 11.

CHAPTER
5

Trip 17 South of Lac D'Annecy ★★

Distance *About 250 kilometers round trip from Annecy*

Terrain *From commercial valleys to mountain highs on every kind of paved road, limited facilities*

Highlights *Ski resorts, one of the highest and loneliest roads of the Alps* ★★ *Col de l'Iseran, 2,769 meters, Col de la Forclaz (1,150 meters),* ★ *Col de la Madeleine (1,984 meters), Col du Glandon (1,951 meters), Col de la Croix de Fer (2,068 meters), Col de Tamie (902 meters)*

Some of the highest and most awesome passes of the Alps are south of **Albertville,** but their lower slopes are less forested and the heights seem grayer. In fact, they are often called the **Gray Alps.** Civilization seems further removed.

In addition to the main highways linking **Lac d'Annecy** with Albertville to its south, it's possible to take one of several low but interesting passes. **Col de la Forclaz** (same name as the pass out of Martigny, Switzerland) climbs right up the mountainside out of **Talloires.** In just a few kilometers, the restaurants at the summit provide views of the lake and of Talloires far below, as well as lunch, hang gliding, and parasailing. From the south end of the col, head for **Faverges.**

From **la Clusaz,** the **Col de la Croix Fry** leads to Faverges.

From Faverges, the pleasant little **Col de Tamie** heads south. It connects to N90, a toll-free autoroute south of Albertville, missing the city traffic. Head east, upstream on N90 in the **Isere Valley** to **Bourg St. Maurice** where the climb up the **Col de l'Iseran** starts in earnest. (You could get to Bourg St. Maurice by crossing over the Cormet de Roselend, a bit longer, and much twistier.)

The **Col de l'Iseran,** named after the Isere River and its valley, the Val d'Isere (the river is L'Isere in French, so it sounds like "lee zayer," and the pass sounds like "coal duh lee zay RAHN"), is one of the highest in the Alps. The valley is where all the skiing events took place in the **Albertville Olympics**. The col connects the upper reaches of the Val d'Isere with the next valley south, the **Val d'Arc** which sort of parallels it. Both flow to the Rhone.

The ski center at Val d'Isere, about 86 kilometers from Albertville, looks naked and uninviting in the summer, with its concrete highrises set in big gravel parking lots, and most everything closed. Above the ski center though, the road climbs and climbs through beautiful and ever-wilder looking country. As the deep snows melt in the early summer, the meadows are carpeted with flowers.

Cross the col—the mountains look even starker and wilder—into the Val d'Arc. The first village, **Bonneval,** has a couple of small hotels. One is the **Bergerie** where a big poster of Marilyn Monroe presides over the dining room. Further down, at **Lanslebourg,** a few more services are available and the **Col du**

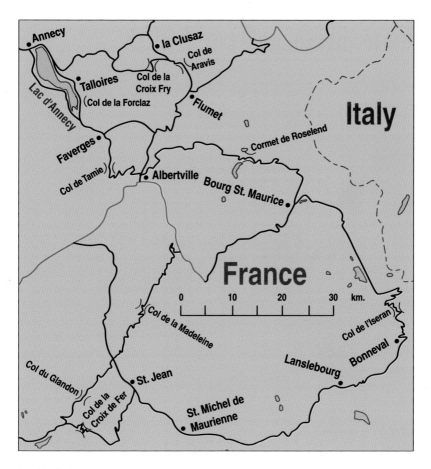

Mont Cenis heads up south to the roads of Trip 22. A good hotel at Lanslebourg is the **Alpazur.**

Further down the Arc, at **St. Jean de Maurienne,** turn south and climb up the twisty **Col de la Croix de Fer,** which bends west and meets the **Col du Glandon.** There's a small restaurant atop the Croix de Fer with views of gray granite peaks and a long valley with a little village.

Head back north on the Col de Glandon road to the Arc valley at **La Chambre.** Just cross the main valley road and head up north on the **Col de la Madeleine.** The south side of the Col de la Madeleine is fairly modern alignment with ski resorts. There's a restaurant at the top. The north side is narrow and more rugged. A good lunch stop on the north side is the **Hotel du Grand Pic** at a village called **Celliers,** at about 1,300 meters. Near the north end of the Col de Madeleine, almost back in the Val d'Isere there's a village quaintly named **Pussy.** It's not far back to Albertville and Lac d'Annecy. The **Col de Tamie** makes a good connection, bypassing Albertville.

CHAPTER

5

Trip 18 Straight South over Three Cols

Distance *About 175 kilometers from Albertville to south of Grenoble*

Terrain *High mountains, twisting high pass roads, some narrow, few services*

Highlights *Almost a straight shot across three mountain ranges from Val d'Isere to Val d'Arc, to Val da la Romanche, to Val du Drac; from Albertville to south of Grenoble, Col de la Madeleine (1,984 meters), Col du Glandon (1,951 meters), Col d'Ornon (1,371 meters)*

Three passes line up, north to south, each with narrow, fairly rugged north slopes. Start about 20 kilometers up the **Val d'Isere** autoroute from **Albertville** (N90) at an exit (sortie) marked **Col de la Madeleine.** Wind up the narrow col past the turn to **Pussy.** The top of Madeleine has a good restaurant with views to **Mont Blanc.** Down the south side past ski facilities cross the Arc river and the main valley road at l**a Chambre,** and start up the **Col du Glandon.** At the top it meets the **Col de la Croix de Fer** (Trip 17) then works its way down south past large reservoirs, into a gorge and back up around it, to the main road in the **Val de la Romanche** (N91). Four kilometers upstream along the Romanche, at l**e Bourg d'Oisans,** the **Col d'Ornon** (D526) starts its climb up south and over to **Valbonnais** and **la Mure** and the routes of Trip 21.

This trip could be combined with Trip 19, below, for a round trip of about 300 kilometers.

The Col d'Izoard, between Briancon and Guillestre, has strange formations (Trip 22).

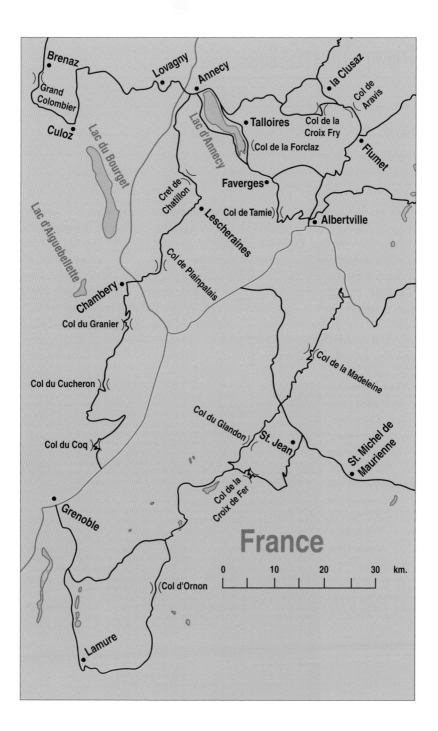

France

0   10   20   30   km.

Trip 19   The Crest Route South

Distance   *About 150 kilometers, one way*

Terrain   *Rural roads, little traffic*

Highlights   *Cret de Chatillon (1,699 meters), Col de Plainpalais (1,174 meters), Col du Granier (1,134 meters), Col du Cucheron (1,139 meters), Col du Coq (1,434 meters), Massif de la Chartreuse*

The **Cret de Chatillon** road starts right in **Annecy.** From the lakeside in Annecy, head uphill, west. The second round about should have a sign for **Semnoz** to the south. That's the one (D41). Immediately, you're out of traffic in a forest. After winding through the forest, the road comes out on a mountain crest where there's a restaurant with a terrrace view across lake and mountains to **Mont Blanc.** Then it's down through some hairpins and through several villages to one called **Lescheraines** where a road starts to climb up the **Col de Plainpalais** (D912). South, across the col, the road comes down to **Chambery,** a pretty good sized city. Follow the main road (not the autoroute) toward **Grenoble** a few kilometers and pick one of several roads (like D12A) climbing the **Col du Granier,** only

The international sign, a red circle with a horizontal white line, means traffic is coming the other way, toward you. In this instance on the Col d'Allos in France, a construction worker is using it to control traffic around work in progress.

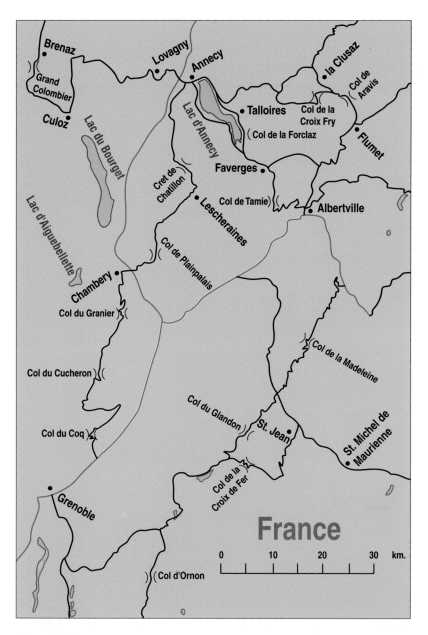

about 20 kilometers up. The col has a pleasant restaurant and a wood carver. Down through a gorge and on up over **Col du Cucheron,** (D512) skirt the **Chartreuse Massif.** Just past the village of **St. Pierre-de-Chartreuse,** the **Col du Coq** climbs east up over the massif and wends down to **Grenoble** . . . a big city.

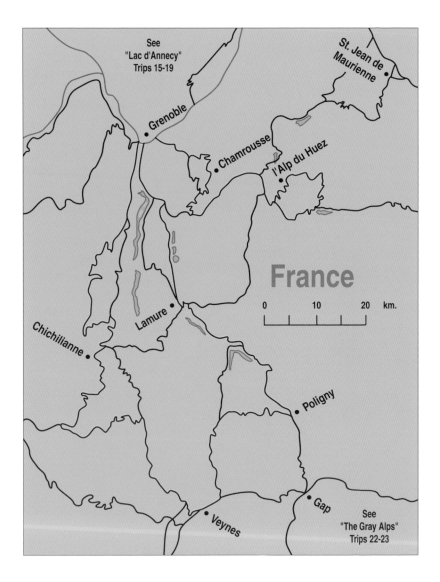

See
"Lac d'Annecy"
Trips 15-19

St. Jean de
Maurienne •

• Grenoble

• Chamrousse

l'Alp du Huez •

France

0   10   20   km.

Chichilianne •

Lamure •

• Poligny

• Gap

See
"The Gray Alps"
Trips 22-23

Veynes •

Grenoble Heights

Grenoble is a city surrounded by mountain massiffs, each worth exploring. To the north is the **Massiff de la Chartreuse** (Trip 19). To the east is the **Chamrousse,** and beyond that, **l'Alpe d'Huez,** famous in the **Tour de France.** To the south is the **Vercors Massif.**

An autoroute comes into Grenoble from the northeast and exits to the northwest, looping south of the old city. The first exit (sortie) on the northeast side of the loop has a cluster of chain hotels. One, the **Ibis,** is a little nicer than a Motel 6, others are even more modular than Motel 6. In fact Motel 6 is owned by the same French company, the Accor Group, that owns Ibis. Quite serviceable. (There are over 500 Ibis hotels around France).

At the other end of the loop around the old city, the northwest side, is an exit (sortie) named **Fontaine.** Fontaine is a suburb and it's main street, on the south side of the autoroute, has a line of motorcycle shops.

Many sources tell of the history and wonders of Grenoble, an Olympic city. Here, we'll concentrate on roads, some of which have already been described in Trips 18 and 19.

On the west side of Grenoble, the suburb, Fontaine, has a motorcycle shop row.

Trip 20 Chamrousse

Distance *About 170 kilometers round trip from the Grenoble area*

Terrain *Nice sweepers through forested mountains; some arduous switchbacks*

Highlights *Forest roads, famous climb of Tour de France, Chamrousse (1,650 meters), Col Luitel (1,262 meters), l'Alpe d'Huez (1,860 meters), Col de Sarenne (1,989 meters)*

The **Chamrousse** road is a high scenic loop to a ski resort. To find it, take the autoroute sortie for **Uriage** on the east side of the **Grenoble** (D524). From Uriage, a handsome residential area and spa, the Chamrousse loop starts (D111). One of the hotels at the top is called the **Hermitage** (rhymes with garage).

Looping clockwise, the descent meets the tiny **Col Luitel** road which works it's way down south to the valley of the **Romanche river** (N91). Turn east, up-stream, through the **Gorges de la Romanche.** A couple of kilometers past **le Bourg d'Oisans** is the turn for the famous switchback climb to **l'Alpe d'Huez**

All over the Alps, businesses, especially restaurants and hotels, are anxious for motorcycle business. This one is near the intersection of the Nufenen Pass road with the Furka Pass at Ulrichen (Trip 2).

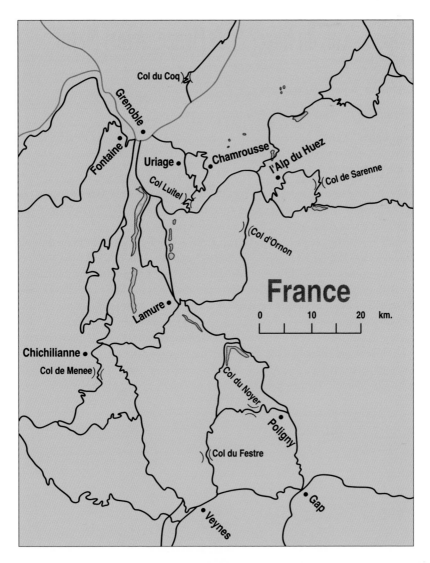

Col du Coq

Grenoble

Fontaine

Uriage

Chamrousse

l'Alp du Huez

Col de Sarenne

Col Luitel

Col d'Ornon

France

0   10   20   km.

Lamure

Chichilianne

Col de Menee

Col du Noyer

Poligny

Col du Festre

Gap

Veynes

(D211). At the top, on through l'Alpe d'Huez, the road climbs up further over the **Col de Sarenne,** leaving the ski resorts behind. It narrows, and a bunch of deep, rock-paved cross-gutters welcome you to remote pastures of sheep. It then works it's way down to the valley of the Romanche at a nondescript intersection with N90.

The **Col du Lautaret** and the roads of Trip 22 are 25 kilometers further up-stream. Grenoble is downstream.

Trip 21   Cols du Noyer & de Menee, Vecors Massif

Distance   *About 250 kilometers*

Terrain   *Fairly rugged, very lonely passes connected by a few more traveled*

Highlights   *A sense of exploring tiny roads, with some wonderful views. Col du Noyer (1,664 meters), Col du Festre (1,441 meters), ★Col de Grimone (1,318 meters), ★Col de Menee (1,457 meters)*

Take the road south toward **Gap** from **Grenoble** (N85) past **le Mure** (Trip 18) as far as **Poligny** where there are signs for the **Col du Noyer** (D17) to the west. Almost aimlessly, the road from Poligny wanders through farms and farm yards for several kilometers before starting the persistent climb back and forth up the col. Views across the farms to the high Alps beyond are wonderful. Across the col, the road comes down a little way into the village of **St. Entienne** and then down more through the **Defile des Etroits,** before climbing southerly over the **Col du Festre** to meet a main east/west road (D994). Heading west just a couple of kilometers (toward Veynes) and then north toward Grenoble (N75) leads in 26 kilometers to the intersection with the **Col de Grimone** road (D539). Climb westerly over the col and encounter the marvels of the **Gorges des Gats**—Incredible formations, pierced occasionally by tunnels as the road fights to share the gorge with its stream. Before **Chatillon** (aren't there a lot of these?), a one-

Nobody rides Col du Noyer, even though it affords sweeping views of the high Alps.

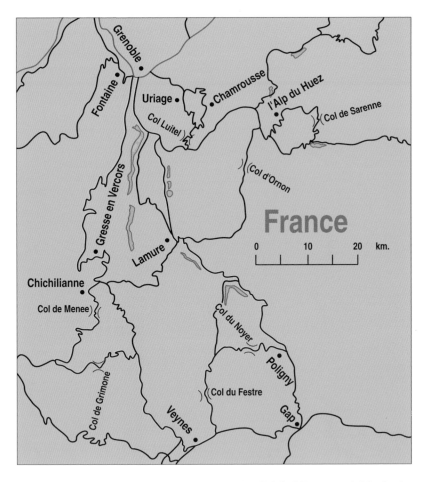

kilometer-long shortcut leads to **Mensac** on the **Col de Menee** road. North, the Col de Menee climbs to the **Vercors** massif through fairly open country. The route is marked "difficult" on some maps and has been used in vintage car rallies. A tunnel at the top leads to a much more forested world on the north side.

A real delight is a hotel on the north side of the Col de Menee in a tiny village with the musical name of **Chichiliane.** Actually, the hotel and the village are just off the col road, and are signed. The hotel is a restored 14th century chateau with turrets and a massive door and winding stone stairs. Plumbing is a bit more modern. The food is wonderful. There's an outdoor swimming pool and an art collection. It's called **Chateau de Passieres.**

Back on the main road (N75), eight kilometers toward Grenoble, is **St. Michel,** where a wonderful road climbs west into the Vercors and works its way toward Grenoble. Along the way, it passes through **Gresse-en-Vercors,** home to a hotel proud of its cuisine, **Hotel Chalet.**

CHAPTER

6

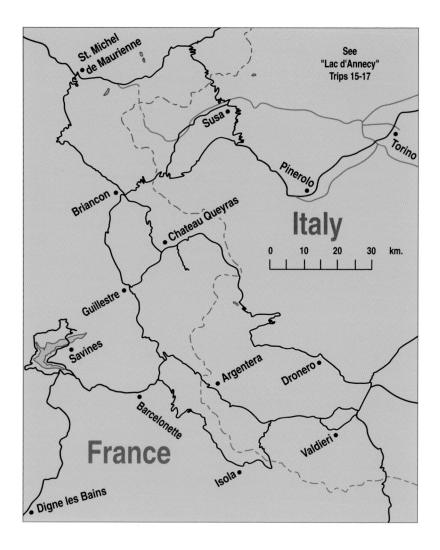

St. Michel de Maurienne

See "Lac d'Annecy" Trips 15-17

Susa

Torino

Pinerolo

Briancon

Chateau Queyras

Italy

0   10   20   30   km.

Guillestre

Savines

Argentera

Dronero

Barcelonette

Valdieri

France

Isola

Digne les Bains

The Gray Alps

A succession of kings and emperors pushed the French border east across the southern Alps at the expense of Italy, so that much of the high country is in France today. A few minor passes cross down into Italy. The countryside is bleak and the few towns are walled fortresses, left over from the defense budgets of past centuries. Here are some of the highest passes in the Alps, several of which are known today as the **Route des Grandes Alpes.** The first Napoleon is supposed to have used some of these cols when he landed in France from exile on the Mediterranean island of Elba. Taking these highest roads, he escaped detection until he was ready to pounce on Paris. It must have been quite a trip in 1815. We know that 100 days later, he was defeated at Waterloo and got shipped off a bit farther than Elba.

While the northern Alps abound in tourist accommodations, restaurants and hotels are few and far between in the southern Alps, and often closed. The small village of **Guillestre,** at 1,000 meters, offers the best amenities. It's one of those fortress towns with stone works that boggle the mind, left over from Louis XIV. Guillestre is south of **Briancon** and east of **Gap,** and the base of two passes on the Route des Grandes Alpes, the **Col de Vars** and the **Col d'Izoard. Les Barnieres** is a good modern hotel with a good restaurant, even tennis and a pool in season. No English!

A little closer to the center of Guillestre and a bit less formidable is **Hotel le Catinat Fleuri.** To an American eye, it looks more like a U.S. style motel, with a parking lot in front.

A huge stone fortress, **Mont Dauphin,** of Louis XIV's time, dominates the valley at Guillestre. Cross the moat, ride through the gates, and check it out.

Why not stay at the highest hotel in the highest village in the Alps? Upstream, east of Guillestre, in the **Parc Regional du Queyras,** is a rustically preserved village called **St. Veran** at 2,257 meters. At the village limits is a NO VEHICLES sign, except those on business. You have business. Past the little village church there should be a sign pointing up to the **Chateau Renard** above the village. English spoken. The owner's wife is from Tasmania. To get to St. Veran, head up the **Col d'Izoard** and turn east at the fortress, **Chateau Queyras.** A couple of kilometers past the fortress, turn south to **Molines** and then St. Veran (see road description for Trip 19).

Trip 22 Around Guillestre ★★

Distance *About 250 kilometers*

Terrain *High, rugged mountains and roads, limited facilities*

Highlights *Exotic wild scenery, ★★Col d'Izoard (2,361 meters), Col de Montgenevre (1,850 meters), into Italy, Sestriere (2,033 meters), Col de Finestre (2,174 meters), Col du Mt. Cenis (2,083 meters), Col du Telegraphe (1,578 meters), ★★Col du Galibier (2,645 meters), Col du Lautaret (2,058 meters)*

East from **Guillestre** the **Col d'Izoard** road (D902) enters the **Parc Regional du Queyras** following the gorge of the Guil river. The road twists and tunnels through the gorge (this part of the road often seems to have gravel on it, not always conveniently placed) and climbs to a fork at a fortress on a mountain, the **Chateau Queyras.** The north fork is the Col d'Izoard. The right leads to **St. Veran** and Trip 19. The Col d'Izoard snakes up through very strange formations and barren gravel, an area called the **Casse Deserte,** to a summit with an obelisk monument, and winds down past a refuge with minimal facilities dating from Napoleon III, coming down right into **Briancon,** a pretty good sized city with another fortress.

Loop through the city to get on the main road and take the road east to Italy (N94) and the **Col de Montgenevre,** only 15 kilometers up.

Then, six kilometers down into Italy, the road splits. A south leg climbs to a ski resort, really a pass, called **Sestriere,** then goes down toward Torino, passing **Fenestrelle** where there's a tempting climb north on a partly paved pass road, the **Col de Finestre,** which comes down near **Susa.**

The highest hotel in the highest town in the Alps is Chateau Renard above the village of St. Veran, France.

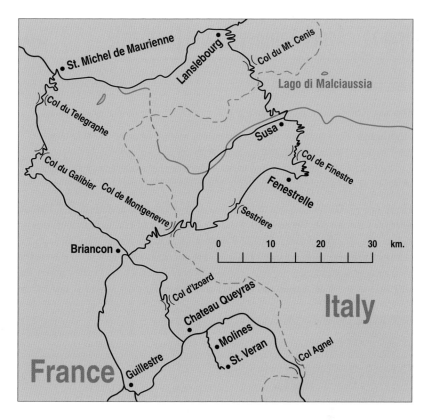

Or, the north leg goes directly to Susa (passing a toll tunnel at Bardonecchia that goes back into France) and by-passing Sestriere and the Col de Finestre. At Susa, a pass road climbs back north into France, passing along a lake, over the **Col du Mt. Cenis** and down into the **Val d'Arc,** just below the **Col de l'Iseran** at **Lanslebourg,** Site of **Hotel Alpazur** (Trip 17).

There are two parallel east-west roads through Susa, a few blocks apart. The **Col de Finestre** and the **Col de Montgenevere** are signed from the southerly one. The Col du Mont Cenis is signed from the northerly one. The Col de Finestre rates a brown sign a bit east of the centro, city center.

Head downstream, west, in the Val d'Arc (N6) as far as **St. Michel de Maurienne,** where one of the wildest passes of the Alps (D902) climbs right up south, the **Col du Galibier.** Before tackling the wonderful high stuff, the road climbs the **Col du Telegraphe** to a village, **Valloire,** Where there's a hotel called le **Relais du Galibier.** From Valloire begins the real climb over the Col du Galibier. Coming down the south side of the Col, there are views of the junction below with the top of the **Col du Lautaret,** which is an east-west road.

From the junction (N91), it's an easy ride on down to Briancon and Guillestre.

Trip 23 Agnel, Sampeyre, and Lombarde ★★

Distance *230 kilometers*

Terrain *Little roads over high passes*

Highlights *Four high passes, two unknown, seldom traveled ★★Col Agnel (dell'Agnello, in Italian) (2,744 meters), ★★Col di Sampeyre (2,284 meters), Col de Larche (Maddelena in Italian) (1,996 meters), Col de Vars (2,111 meters), ★★Col de Lombarde (2,351 meters), Madonna di Colletto (1,304 meters)*

Head out of **Guillestre** on the road to **Col d'Izoard,** and turn at **Chateau Queyras** toward **St. Veran** (D5). (There's a rough dead-end road that climbs up behind the Chateau fortress to 2,257 meters.) Before St. Veran, turn through the village **Molines,** which doesn't believe in street repair. Not to worry. Above the village is smooth narrow asphalt, climbing very high in a broad valley above the tree line to the **Col Agnel** and the Italian border. This little road is one of the

Col du Noyer is a wild climb on a narrow road. No busses for sure.

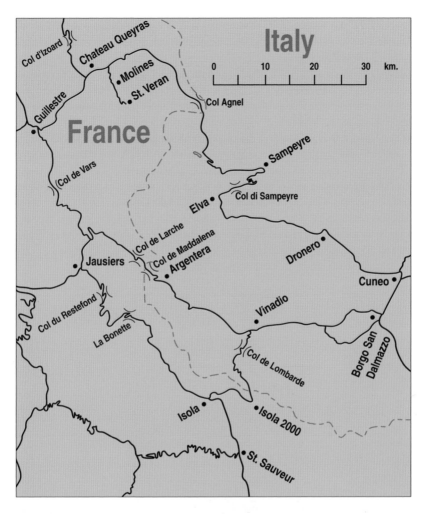

highest in the Alps. Sometimes, back at Molines there's a FERME, closed, sign. But the road is opened for the **Giro d'Italia bicycle race** very early in June. So go for it. Down below the pass, in Italy, there may be a bar across the road, but just join the locals driving around it.

Down about 35 kilometers into Italy at a village called **Sampeyre,** there's a pass of the same name, **Col di Sampeyre,** even less traveled, heading up and south. There's an interesting metal sculpture at the top. Then down the south side at the village, **Elva,** there's a little church with a very fine Renaissance fresco. What's it doing here? The ristorante in Elva will lend you a key to the church while it prepares your very Italian lunch. The descent south from Elva is spectacular. And the artist must have come through this gorge 400 years ago.

Back on the valley road, below Elva and the gorge, head downstream to **Donero,** a town about out of the mountains with tree shaded streets. Then south to **Borgo San Dalmazzo,** avoiding **Cuneo,** a fair sized city to the east. At Borgo, head west to France on the **Col de Maddalena** road. There are a couple of ways to cross into France from Borgo. Most traffic signs point southerly to France and Monaco through the Col de Tende tunnel. If that's not your intention, be sure to head west toward **Argentera,** a village near the border on the Col de Maddalena. If you should find yourself on the road to **Valdieri,** which is a dead end valley parallel to, but south of the Argentera road, not to worry. At the village, Valdieri, there's a good little pass road going north called **Madonna di Colletto.** It crosses north and comes down on the road for Argentera. Once you cross into France from Argentera, Col de Maddalena is called **Col de Larche.** There are a couple of good bends on the way down to the valley road which it joins just south of the Col de Vars and north of **Jausiers.** Head back over the **Col de Vars** for Guillestre and St. Veran.

(Roads south are in the next section, Some High Stuff)

Spray-painted signs for bicycle racers on the Giro d'Italia cover the pavement on Passo Mortirolo (Trip 38).

A group of bikers pauses near the little monument atop the Col di Sampeyre, Italy, looking at those French peaks in the distance. Recently the Madonna on the monument lost her head.

Or, instead of crossing back into France on the main Col de Maddalena road, connecting to the Col de Vars, it's possible to cross the border on a seldom traveled high pass, the **Col de Lombarde,** which ties in with the south end of the passes in Trip 25. West from Cuneo toward the French border on the Col de Maddalena road, after the village of **Vinadio,** the narrow Col de Lombarde heads south. It is a lot of fun on the Italian climb to the summit. (At about 2,000 meters elevation, the road straight ahead dead ends. The pass road cuts back to the left.) A few kilometers down into France, the road enters a ski resort called **Isola 2000,** apparently the elevation. On into **Isola,** in the valley below, the road is aligned to get busloads of skiers up to Isola 2000. The lower Isola is on the south end of the **Col du Restefond,** which leads north to the Col de Vars.

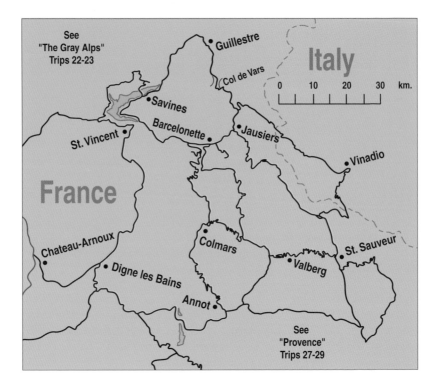

See
"The Gray Alps"
Trips 22-23

Italy

• Guillestre

Col de Vars

0   10   20   30   km.

• Savines

Barcelonette

St. Vincent •

• Jausiers

France

• Vinadio

Chateau-Arnoux

Colmars

Digne les Bains

Valberg

• St. Sauveur

Annot

See
"Provence"
Trips 27-29

Some High Stuff

South over the **Col de Vars** from **Guillestre** is the high valley of the **Ubaye River** where there's a town, **Barcelonnette,** surrounded by high Alps. North of town, only a few trails climb a kilometer or two up the steep slopes. But south of Barcelonnette, several twisting pass roads scale the peaks of the **Parc National du Mercantour.** And east eight kilometers is **Jausiers,** gateway to the **Col de Restefond** and **la Bonette.** Downstream, west along the Ubaye are pass roads seldom explored offering marvelous vistas of lakes and mountains.

It's possible to stay in Barcelonnette. Would you believe, the main hotel is called the **Azteca,** famous for its Mexican decor. But no Mexican food. In fact, no restaurant.There are hotels in nearby mountain villages. For instance, eight kilometers southwest and up on the mountainside is **Pra Loup** with a hotel called **Prieure de Molanes.** Just four kilometers up south is the village **la Sauze.** (Note that in French, "at la Sauze" becomes *au Sauze.*) *Au Sauze* are the **Alp Hotel** and the **Hotel Soleil et Neiges** (Sun and Snow).

After a long day's ride, some bikers took a little back road into la Sauze. Armed with nice web page pictures of the Alp Hotel, they asked for it, only to be told, "I don't think you want to go there." Seems the poor owner had just fallen to his death from a high window. "Not to worry," said a lady, "my hotel, the Soleil et Neiges, will be open tonight at 6:30 and I will have rooms." Well, she did open at 6:30, and she did have rooms. After a fabulous dinner, the bikers were still the only guests. Strange. And why 6:30? Aha. By 9 p.m., the place was packed with an office party from Nice.

Hardly anyone finds their way to the top of the Col des Champs.

Trip 24 Three Highs ★★

Distance *140 kilometers*

Terrain *High rugged mountains and roads*

Highlights *Seldom traveled narrow mountain roads through wild mountains.*
★Col de la Cayolle (2,327 meters), ★Col des Champs (2,087 meters), ★Col d'Allos (2,240 meters)

The road south from **Barcelonnette** forks a couple of kilometers above town. The tine to the west climbs the **Col d'Allos.** The easterly tine climbs the **Col de la Cayolle.** Each is a narrow, exciting road climbing opposite sides of a gorge into the **Mercantour Park.** Each road barely clings to the cliffs above the gorge. Over the top of the Col de la Cayolle about six kilometers down, at **Estenc,** there's a fine restaurant in a stone building called **Relais de la Cayolle.** Farther

The turnoff for obscure little Col des Champs is well marked with flags at St. Martin-d'Entraunes. The turn is south of the top of the Col de la Cayolle.

down the south side of the col at **St. Martin,** there's a connecting pass road, the **Col des Champs.** It climbs west from the town of **St. Martin,** connecting it with **Colmar,** over on the south side of the Col d'Allos. The intersections in both towns are well marked. From St. Martin, the Col des Champs road is fairly well defined, climbing past jagged peaks. But once across the top, above the treeline, the road on down to Colmar has many deep paved drainage ditches and lots of gravel trailing off the slopes.

Still in the woods of the Col des Champs over Colmar a view site has a marker entitled "Un peu d'Histoire," a little history, with a map of Colmar and its fortifications. Seems in the early days of Louis XIV, Colmar was on the border, so Louis ordered it fortified. Then, after a couple of battles, Louis annexed the surrounding area, so Colmar was no longer a border town. However Louis' armies did it, it's probably more fun today on a bike. It's interesting to walk inside the walls of old Colmar. Colmar and the Col d'Allos mark the headwaters of the **Verdon river** (see Trip 28).

Take the Col d'Allos back to Barcelonnette.

Trip 25 La Bonnette ★

Distance *about 200 kilometers*

Terrain *Very rugged, barren mountains and a road oft called the highest in the Alps.*

Highlights *Exotic wild scenery. Col du Restefond (2,678 meters) ★★la Bonnette (2,862 meters), Col de la Couillole (1,678 meters), Col Valberg (1,668 meters), ★Col de la Cayolle (2,327 meters)*

About eight kilometers east of **Barcelonnette** at a village called **Jausiers,** the **Col du Restefond** road begins its struggle up the pass, which may not be open until mid-summer. It isn't a commercial route. Near the top, there's a loop road called **la Bonette** which might be the highest paved road in the Alps. It climbs up around a peak to a high point where many seem to have been unable to restrain

This rock marks the highest point on the highest road in the Alps, la Bonette (2,862 meters). It's a loop off of the Col du Restefond.

themselves from leaving a mark of their visit. Near the loop junction are two arrow signs. One pointing north reads PARIS. One pointing south reads NICE.

From the col it's about 50 kilometers south, past some abandoned military
buildings, a village or two, the **Col de Lombarde** road at **Isola** (Trip 23), on
down to **St. Sauveur.** There, instead of contiuing on to Nice, turn sharply down
across a river, for the **Col de la Couillole.** It really twists up a red rock gorge,
past a medieval village hung on the cliff, **Roubion.** The road comes down in a
valley and then climbs up again over the **Col Valberg.** At Valberg there's the **Hotel Le Chalet Suisse** that advertises itself as having winter sports only 80 kilometers from Nice.

West of Valberg, at **Guillaumes,** is the **Col de la Cayolle** road, heading north
to **Colmar, Barcelonnette,** and **Guillestre.**

Trip 26   Around Lac De Serre-Poncon

Distance   *About 285 kilometers*

Terrain   *Some tiny, tight roads, some open sweepers*

Highlights   *Little, low passes with amazing views of lakes and mountains and fields; rural France, one major pass, Col d'Allos (2,240 meters), Col Lebraut (1,110 meters), Col de Pontis (1,301 meters), Col St. Jean (1,333 meters), Col de Maure (1,346 meters), Col de Toutes Aures (1,120 meters), Col de la St. Michel (1,431 meters)*

Westerly from **Barcelonnette** the main road follows the Ubaye river in a pleasant sweeping fashion (D900). Just west of the village, **le Lauzet,** about 24 kilometers from Barcelonnette, turn down northerly along and across the river (D954). In about six kilometers, a tiny road starts steeply north, signed for **Pontis.** Near the top there are sweeping views of lakes and mountains. The Pontis road comes back down, north, on D954. At **Savines** it joins N94. Take N94 north across a long bridge, then, for fun, take a little road up the mountain north to **Puy Sanieres.**

A rest stop on the Col des Champs above the village of Colmar provides a great view of the walled village. A plaque entitled, "A little history," tells how Colmar was fortified under Louis XIV, and then sort of abandoned when adjoining areas were annexed to France and it no longer was on the border (Trip 24).

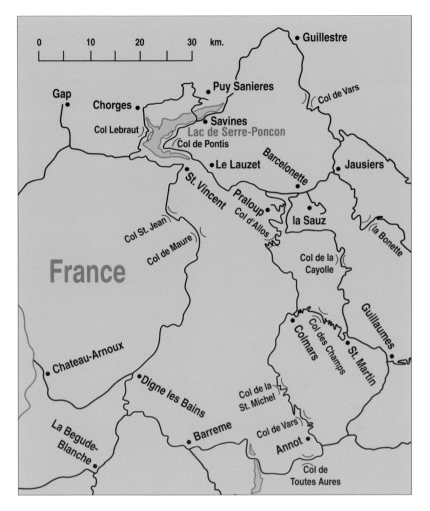

From Puy Sanieres, D9 wends through remote meadows back down to N94 at **Chorges.** Cross under N94 on D3, climbing over **Col Lebraut** to a view cafe, then down to D900. Take it easterly to a junction at **St. Vincent** where it continues a climb south over the **Col St. Jean,** then on south over the **Col de Maure** to **Digne-les Bains** (say DEEN yay) where there's the **Tonic Hotel.**

From Digne, take N85 south, not west, about 30 kilometers to **Barreme** where N202 heads east around a lake and over the Verdon river (see Trip 28) and over the **Col de Toutes Aures.** East of Toutes Aures, near **Annot,** D908 heads back north, making a dramatic climb over the **Col de la St. Michel** down to the valley of the Verdon. Upstream, north, the road leads to **Colmar,** the **Col d'Allos** and Barcelonnette.

123

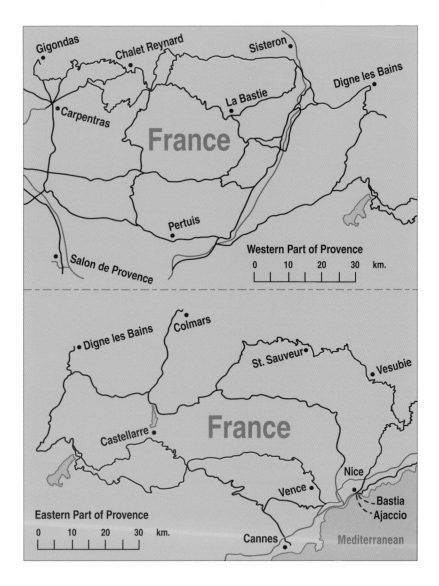

Gigondas

Chalet Reynard

Sisteron

Digne les Bains

Carpentras

La Bastie

France

Pertuis

Salon de Provence

Western Part of Provence

0   10   20   30   km.

Digne les Bains

Colmars

St. Sauveur

Vesubie

Castellarre

France

Nice

Vence

Bastia

Ajaccio

Eastern Part of Provence

0   10   20   30   km.

Cannes

Mediterranean

Provence

Provence in France conjurs up romantic notions and stories enough to fill a thousand books. It's where the southern end of the Alps meets the sea . . . the Mediterranean. And it *is* different. Instead of gray stone houses with gray slate (or metal) roofs, provincial houses are beige stucco with rosy tile roofs. There are indeed fields of lavender. Markets are full of blue and yellow linens. It's usually drier, sunnier, than the Alps to the north. This is the Provence of the mind's eye. It includes several political divisions.

Should you be checking out this Provence, the one in the travel books, the one in the mind's eye, there are some roads to enjoy, too.

A likely base in the east near Nice and Monaco is **Vence,** a city almost atop the first range of mountains, about 15 kilometers from the Mediterranean and about 25 from Nice. It has a lively provincial marketplace, a chapel designed by Matisse, a coastal climate, and it's not too far from the **Grand Canyon du Verdon,** a major motorcycle destination. A good modern hotel with parking and a pool is the **Mas de Vence.**

Nice is a big city with motorcycle dealers of all brands. (Moto Deschamps, BMW, Kawasaki, and Bimota, has proved very helpful to travelers.)

To the west, not far from Avignon and Aix and the Rhone River and vinyards, not to mention the major motorcyle destination, **Mont Ventoux** (always on the Tour de France), the village **Gigondas** is just into the foothills from **Orange** (say oh RAWNGH). And there, hidden in the trees, is **Hotel Les Florets.**

There a lot of roads in Provence. Here are some of the best.

Ride in the mountains all day, relax by a Mediterranean beach in the evening.

Trip 27　Twisting to Vence

Distance　*About 120 very kinky kilometers*

Terrain　*Low mountains, but very convoluted pass roads*

Highlights　*Col St. Martin (1,500 meters), Col de Turini (1,604 meters), Col de Braus (1,002)*

The south end of the **Col de Restefond** described in Trip 25 is at **St. Sauveur** where that trip route headed west over the **Col de la Couillole.** From St. Sauveur, there are some fairly direct roads to Nice and Vence. But here is the twisty way.

Despite its age, Hotel Vittoria on the Italian side of the Splugen Pass (Passo Splugo) is a welcome refreshment stop (Trip 36).

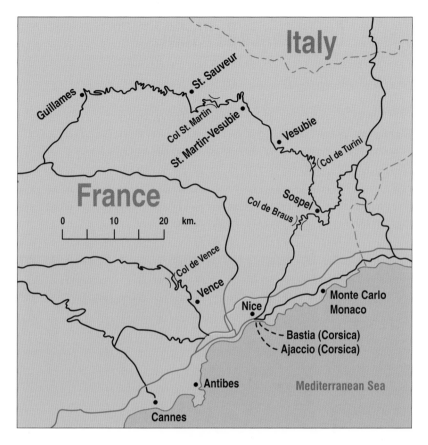

Just four kilometers south of St. Sauveur is a junction. Turn up east over the **Col St. Martin** (D66) to **St. Martin-Vesublie.** Vesublie is a river. Then south, downstream 13 kilometers to another junction. Turn up east (D70) across the **Col de Turini** and then south to **Sospel,** a pretty good sized town. North from Sospel, one road climbs to Italy via a tunnel, the **Col de Tende.** The one to Nice and Vence wiggles southwesterly up the **Col de Braus,** and then winds down to Nice, about 40 kilometers away. There are few services between Sospel and Nice. From Nice, take the autoroute or coast road west about 15 kilometers to **Cagnes,** where there are signs for Vence.

Trip 28   Grand Canyon du Verdon

Distance   *About 240 kilometers, round trip from Vence*

Terrain   *Low mountains, rural roads, some very twisty*

Highlights   *Grand Canyon, Corniche Sublime, Col de Vence (963 meters), Col de Luens (1,054 meters), Col d'Ayen (1,032 meters), Cirque de Vaumale (1,201 meters), Col de Clavel (1,060 meters)*

Don't expect the Grand Canyon of Arizona or the Copper Canyon of Mexico. But this **Grand Canyon du Verdon** has good paved roads that go around and through it.

Many roads in the Alps slink through narrow, twisty gorges.

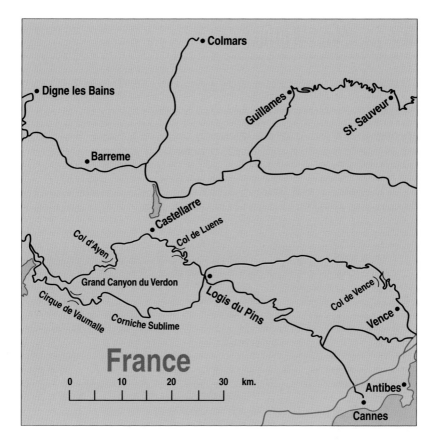

The **Col de Vence** road climbs north out of Vence (D2) over the col and then heads west all the way to **le Logis du Pins,** where a main road (N85) climbs northwesterly over the **Col de Luens** to **Castellarre.** Cross over the Verdon River, and head for its famous canyon (D952).

The Verdon flows mostly from northeast to southwest. This route is on the north side of the canyon. Parts of the road wind down a bit into the canyon. It's kind of like looking from the south rim in Arizona, the high walls are across the river. A loop road (D23) goes down deeper. There are tunnels and viewpoints. At the west end of the canyon, a large lake comes into view. It's possible to turn back along the lake (D957) and a few kilometers later, turn up the famous **Corniche Sublime** (D71) which twists quite laboriously back east along the south rim to **Comps,** where a road (D21) heads back to le Logis du Pins and the road to Vence.

Should one way be enough, it's possible to go north 50 kilometers from the west end, by the lake where the north side road meets the Corniche road, to **Digne-les-Bains** (say DEEN yay) where a very satisfactory hotel is the **Tonic.**

Trip 29 Mont Ventoux

Distance *About 200 kilometers from Gigondas*

Terrain *Good mountain roads, rural fields, and villages*

Highlights ★*Mont Ventoux (1,909 meters), Gorges de la Nesque, Povincial village Sault, Col de l'Homme Mort (1,212 meters), Col de Macuegne (1,068 meters)*

From **Gigondas,** a road (D90) works through a jagged mountain called the **Dentelles (laces) de Montmirail** to **Malaucene,** the beginning of the climb up the west side of **Mont Ventoux** (D974).

Friendly hotels and biker stops await you atop nearly every pass in the Alps. Invariably, there are also many other motorcyclists.

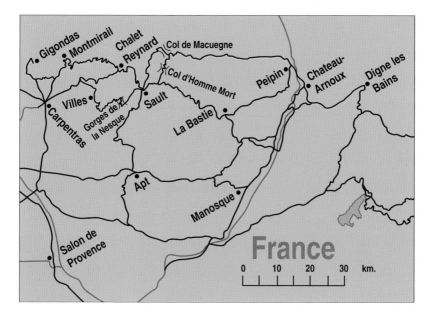

Mont Ventoux isn't a pass. It's a mountain almost 2,000 meters high not too far from the Mediterranean and close to the tourist centers of Aix and Avignon (North of Aix and Northeast of Avignon). The three roads to the summit are often used to test cars and brakes. One of the three, the one from the west (from Gigondas and Malaucene), is usually featured in the **Tour de France.** It's a steady climb with mostly open sweepers, a few tighter than others, through several climate zones. A sort of missile-looking pylon marks the windswept top. There's a cafe just below the summit. Then, a few kilometers down to the east, there's a junction and a restaurant, the **Chalet Reynard.** South from the Chalet, the road down (D974) is tight but banked like a race track for 15 kilometers. At the bottom of the mountain, a few jogs south across little fields lead to a village called **Villes,** gateway to a twisting, climbing, and scenic ride through the **Gorges de la Nesque** (D942). At the east end of the gorge road is an interesting provincial village, **Sault.**

Meanwhile, the road east from the Chalet Reynard wends more roughly down to Sault. Sault sits atop an embankment, with views back to Ventoux. Some may need to stop and shop.

From Sault, two pass roads loop further east through very rural landscapes. **Dead Man's Pass** (Col d l'Homme Mort) is northeast from Sault (D63). It meets the **Col de Macuegne** (D542) which heads back to Sault.

Sixty rural kilometers east of Col de Macuegne is **Digne-les-Bains** and the **Hotel Tonic.**

South of
Andermatt

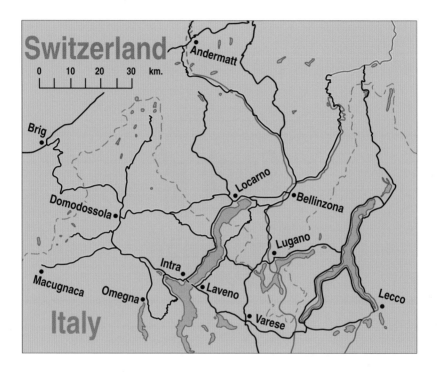

Lago Maggiore

If it gets a bit chilly or misty up in the high county, just do what the Swiss do: head for **Lugano** or **Locarno,** down in that Italian-speaking, pasta-eating part of Switzerland called **Ticino.** It's only an hour or two away. Hawaii, it's not. But around the lake shores there are real, if dwarf, palm trees, and oleander and hibiscus blooms—probably in pots—even while the snowy mountain peaks are still in sight. And there are some pretty good roads to get there on.

Locarno is on the north shore of a long, large lake called **Maggiore.** Part of the lake is in Italy, the rest in Switzerland. Lugano is on a smaller lake called Lugano, a bit southeast of Locarno. Why must the names sound so much alike? To confuse us.

Locarno, on **Lago Maggiore,** is small, sunny, and closer to the mountains than Lugano. It has hotels on the lake, on the hills, and in neighboring villages.

Right on the lake in Locarno is the **Beau-Rivage.** Rooms with a view of the lake are a bit more than "garden views". Just a few blocks uphill and down in price is a plain, practical hotel, **Hotel Carmine.** Across Lago Maggiore from Locarno, about 20 kilometers around the north tip of the lake, is **San Nazzaro,** where a modest hotel, **Albergo Consolina,** is squeezed on the water's edge and has great views across to Locarno and the Alps beyond from the dining room and some of the guest rooms (the back rooms are close to a train track).

From Lugano, the southernmost Swiss city, almost surrounded by Italy, the border crossing in the direction of Lago Maggiore is signed **PONTE TRESA.** At Ponte Tresa there's a pleasant waterfront hotel restaurant called **del Pesce.**

From the high Alps there are three pass roads leading down to Lago Maggiore: from Andermatt, the **St. Gotthard Pass;** from the Rhone Valley, the **Simplon Pass,** and from **Graubunden** and the Rhine Valley, the **Passo del San Bernardino.**

Trip 30 Passo San Gottardo

Distance *About 100 kilometers from Andermatt to Locarno, one way*

Terrain *Modern pass road and valley autostrada*

Highlights *Quick way to get down out of the mountains, Passo San Gottardo (2,108 meters)*

From central Switzerland, that is, cantons Zurich, Bern, Luzern, and Uri, north-south Passo San Gottardo is the link to warmer, sunnier Ticino on Lago Maggiore. Of course in these cantons it's called St. Gotthard Pass, and from Andermatt the top is just a few sweeping kilometers up and above the tree line.

Through the years, the pass road provided major commercial connections and so was regularly improved for higher speeds and weather protection. Now, the pass road itself is superseded by the long tunnel under the pass. Hurrah.

At the top of the pass, just 12 kilometers from downtown Andermatt, there's a mini diamond interchange providing access to the cluster of buildings that have always provided shelter and sustenance to travelers on the pass.

Parts of earlier, more torturous alignments remain and some are traversable, like the link on the south slope, often called the Tremola, that starts down near the cluster of buildings. Its sweepers and hairpins hug the mountainside, supported by rock walls. And it has fine cobblestone pavement.

On the south slopes of Passo San Gottardo a view point overlooks the town of Airolo way below. Multiple ramps in Airolo connect the San Gottardo road with the Nufenen Pass and the long vehicle tunnel which goes under Andermatt. In the distance, the Swiss "Autostrada" leads toward Lugano, Lucarno, and Milano.

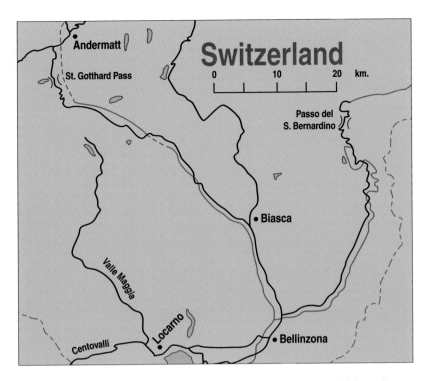

Meanwhile, the higher speed road heads down from the mini interchange through concrete snow sheds and tunnels with a couple of sweeping turns cantilevered in space, occasionally crossing and intersecting the old Tremola road.

About halfway down there's a view point with a little shop. The whole Ticino river valley, ringed by snowy mountains, is below. And the little village called Airolo where the pass road joins the autostrada as it emerges from the tunnel, all in an amazing collection of bridges and ramps.

Head down the valley on the autostrada, past the Nufenen Pass connection at Airolo, and the Lukmanier Pass connection at Biasca, joining the autostrada from the San Bernadino Pass at Bellinzona.

A few kilometers south of Bellinzona, the autostrada begins to climb on stilts over the next range of mountains toward Lugano, Lake Como, and Milano.

There's signed exits for Locarno and Lago Maggiore, leading to a pretty busy standard highway, lined with commercial development, and decorated every little ways with roundabouts that keep traffic crawling.

Approaching Lago Maggiore, the road splits, one branch to Locarno, on the north shore of the lake, and the other branch to the south shore with San Nazzaro, Indemini, and Passo Alpe di Neggia.

Getting through Locarno to Valle Maggia, the Simplon Pass, and Val Cannobina used to be a nightmare of congestion. Now there's an autostrada tunnel under the whole town.

CHAPTER
10

Trip 31 Passo del San Bernardino

Distance *About 105 kilometers from Chur, in the Rhine Valley, to Locarno, one way*

Terrain *Tight, twisting, narrow mountain pass road, followed by high speed swooping across huge bridges to autostrada*

Highlights *Rustic cafe on top of pass, exhilarating swoops, Passo del San Bernardino (2,065 meters)*

From the **Rhein** (we spell it Rhine) valley in **Graubunden,** the **San Bernardino Pass** (in Ticino, Passo del San Bernardino) makes a direct and good ride connection to **Locarno.** The pass road is a sweeping, high-speed, two-lane Autobahn

From the upper slopes of the Great St. Bernard Pass road, on the Italian side, riders can see the completely enclosed "dark" highway tunnel as it daylights across a valley. Tunnel users never know they're on a bridge, out of the tunnel (Trip 13).

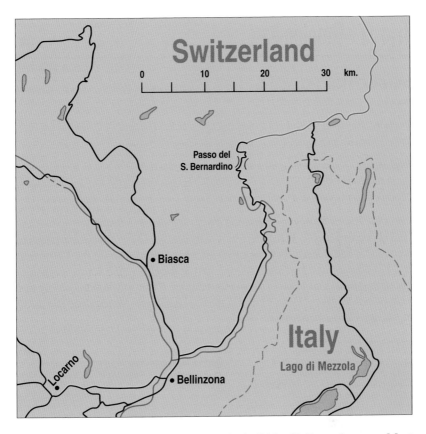

most of the way from Chur in Graubunden in the Rhine Valley to Locarno. Most of the way it's possible to dodge back and forth, keeping to pieces of non-Autobahn roads. There's an all-weather tunnel under the highest peaks, but there's a twisty, attention-demanding road up over the pass, above the tunnel, that's a motorcycle delight. A restaurant on a lake at the top makes a great stop, and a regular *Tofftreffpunkt*. Dine rustically upstairs if it's not comfortable sitting out.

The south side of the San Bernardino is on a magnificent series of sweepers with high arched bridges carrying the road back and forth over the valley below.

Near **Bellinzona** the San Bernardino road joins the San Gottardo autostrada.

CHAPTER
10

Trip 32   Simplon Pass   ★

Distance   *About 100 kilometers from Brig in the Rhone Valley to Locarno, one way*

Terrain   *High pass with high speed sweepers in Switzerland; Val Cannobina in Italy is narrow and tight*

Highlights   *Narrow and tight and fun, used by locals only, leads to lakefront road; Simplon Pass (2,006 meters), a major pass between Italy and Switzerland; charming Centovalli and Val Cannobina, Swiss Army may be on maneuvers*

From the Rhone Valley, the **Simplon Pass** (Sempione in Italian) is in Switzerland all the way across, then enters Italy at its southern base. From here, there are a couple of fun connections back to Switzerland and Locarno: the **Centovalli** and **Val Cannobina.** Just after entering Italy at the base of the Sempione, before the Italian industrial town of **Domodossola,** the Centovalli road heads up and east toward **Malesco.** From Malesco, the road heads into Switzerland and down to Locarno. A pleasant route.

The roads in the Alps are challenging, and some are even marked so, but not necessarily for motorcycles. This pass, the Col de Champs, is narrow, and it is paved, and it does have many drainage cross gutters that are best not taken at speed.

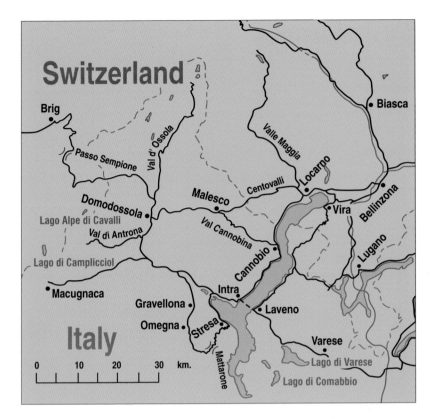

For a more challenging ride, head up and around Malesco's village church (not the big domed basilica on the edge of town which, incidentally, has a gruesome collection of pictures of vehicle accidents) and up over a narrow pass, the **Valle Cannobina** road. Near a tunnel at the top, right on the edge of a lush, green, peaceful gorge, are some small memorial markers commemorating Italian partisans killed by the retreating Germans at the end of World War II. The road works down in a one-lane-wide collection of twisties through green forest to Lago Maggiore at an Italian town called **Cannobio.** From Cannobio it's a short ride north along the lakeshore to Switzerland and Locarno. (Lakeshore traffic can be tedious, and this little jaunt, however nice the views, may be all that's needed to illustrate the point.) Both the Centovalli and the Val Cannobina roads have rustic places to stop for refreshment.

CHAPTER

10

Trip 33 Valle Maggia

Distance *Valle Maggia, about 120 kilometers round trip from Locarno*

Terrain *Small, twisty roads into remote, high villages surrounded by giant mountains*

Highlights *To explore where no one goes, try these dead-end valleys*

A couple of kilometers out the **Centovalli** road from Locarno, it splits. The **Valle Maggia** road goes north and climbs through quiet villages with stone houses and roofs of huge stone slabs. The road narrows to work up switchbacks to high Alpine lakes where it dead-ends, 50 kilometers from town. Nobody there.

Over toward the base of **Passo Sempione,** on the Italian side of the border above **Domodossola,** the **Val d'Ossola** climbs north almost to the **Nufenen Pass** in Switzerland. There's a *rifugio* near the lake at its top. (*Rifugios* are Italian in-

Even though spring days are warm and long, last winter's snows are still deep in the high country. Here, a snowblowing plow has opened the road.

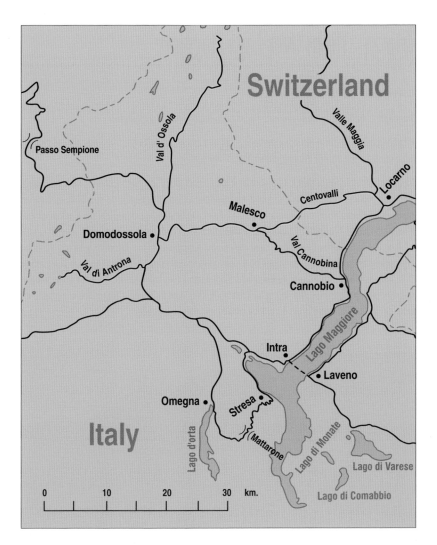

stitutions, usually staffed by a resident family to serve Alpine travelers and workers.)

South of Domodossola, at **Villadossola,** a wild little road climbs the **Val di Antrona.** There's a rifugio there, too.

Trip 34   Highs Over Lago Maggiore

Distance   *220 kilometers*

Terrain   *little mountain roads right behind the lake congestion*

Highlights   *A pass no tourist sees, Passo Alpi di Neggia (1,395 meters), ferry across the lake (toll), Mattarone (1,491 meters)*

On the east shore of the lake, south of Locarno, still in Switzerland, at **Vira,** take the steep little road uphill signed **INDEMINI.** That's a town at the Swiss-Italian border. Getting there, it quickly leaves houses behind and winds up and over the **Passo Alpi di Neggia.** There's a restaurant atop the pass with views to the north of Lago Maggiore, Locarno, and the snow-capped Alps. Border guards will be surprised to see you. You may be their only customers for the day. In Italy, ride down to the lake at **Maccagno** and south along the lake shore to **Laveno,** where there's a ferry across the lake to **Intra** on the west shore. There are a couple of ferries an hour, and the ride takes about twenty minutes.

Motorcyclists enjoy playing on the open sweepers of the east side of the Susten Pass.

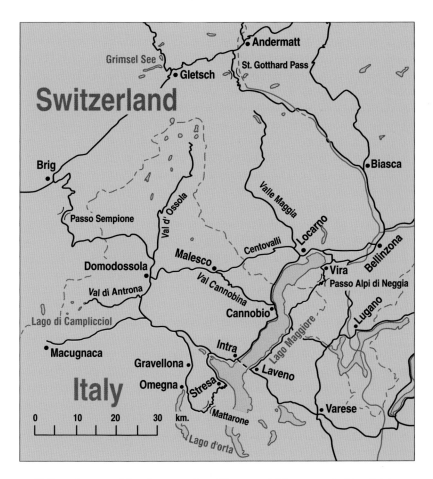

Follow the west lake shore south to **Stresa,** a fairly congested tourist town. Once there, head inland on cobbled streets, west for **Mattarone.** It's signed. You're quickly in the woods. At the top there's a cable car and a restaurant. There's also a toll. Head down west to the next lake, **Lago d'Orta,** and then north to **Omegna.** Might as well take the autostrada from **Gravellona** to **Piedimulera** where there's a dead-end road up the **Val Anzasca** to a ski resort, **Macugnaca,** separated by **Monte Rosa** from Zermatt, Switzerland.

Back in the valley, take the **Malesco** road from Domodossola to Switzerland.

CHAPTER
10

East of
Andermatt

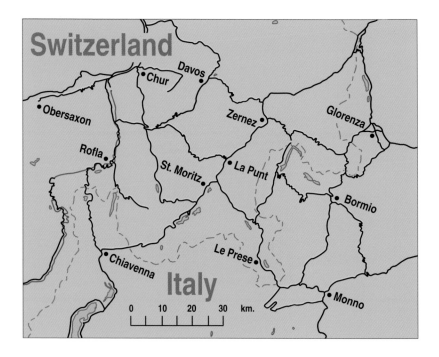

St. Moritz

East of Andermatt, over the **Oberalp Pass,** is the biggest and wildest of Swiss cantons, **Graubunden.** home of world-famous winter sports, **St. Moritz, Davos,** and more. Part of Graubunden is in the **Rhein Tal** (Rhein Valley) draining toward the **North Sea,** and part of it is in the **Inn Tal,** usually called Engadin, running toward **Innsbruck,** the **Danube,** and the **Black Sea.** A few parts in the south run into Italy and the Adriatic. Getting back and forth between these valleys across great mountain ranges makes for some good roads and good riding.

St. Moritz, in the high Engadin (valley of the Inn), is higher than a lot of passes, at 1,822 meters. Even though it's high and cool and famous, St. Moritz and its neighboring resort villages are a logical base for exploring the great roads of Graubunden. Most facilities are available. Its reputation as the old-time playground of royalty means that there are old-time posh establishments, but there are plenty of places for ordinary bike riders. **St. Moritz-Dorf** (the German word for "village" is *Dorf*) is on the north slopes of the Engadin, up the mountainside from St. Moritz on the main valley road.

Right in the center of the Dorf, facing one of the few outdoor eating plazas (one of the few level places in St. Moritz), is the **Hauser Hotel.** Right behind the Hauser is **Hotel Crystal.** Both are modern and touristy.

Traffic through and near St. Moritz is encouraged to use the main valley road below the Dorf, but there is a good high road running east and west from the plaza at the Hauser Hotel.

For a real experience in how a Swiss hotel can coddle, and at about the cost of a modest hotel in the city, treat yourself to **Hotel Le Prese** in the village of **Le Prese,** south of St. Moritz, on the other side of the **Bernina Pass,** and almost completely surrounded by Italy. An old building that's been modernized, Hotel Le Prese is guaranteed to make everyone feel luxuriously cared for. There's a large outdoor pool. Almost all guests are annual regulars, with hardly a foreigner (non-Swiss) among them. Since there's a dress code, the management may discreetly arrange a table with heavy linen and silver in the handsome bar room.

Escape St. Moritz down the Engadin (northeast) about 12 kilometers to **Zuoz,** with cobblestone streets and beautiful quaint houses, some hundreds of years old, with shops, banks, and cows. The main valley road bypasses the town on the south bank of the **Inn River** leaving **Zuoz** high—1,716 meters—on the north. In Zuoz is the **Post Hotel Engiadina,** complete with an outdoor pool for the brave.

Pontresina is a lovely village just six kilometers east of St. Moritz with a fine new hotel. The **Bernina Pass** road skirts the village. The old main street through Pontresina, now bypassed, is one way, uphill, and on it is **Hotel Allegra.** Very contemporary.

Trip 35 Vorderrhein (the 'Front Rhine')

Distance *About 150 kilometers from Andermatt to St. Moritz, one way*

Terrain *Narrow cliff-hanging road to major mountain highway*

Highlights *Brief glimpse at a Switzerland no tourist sees*

The summit of the **Oberalp Pass** is just a few sweeping kilometers up from **Andermatt.** Then there's a pretty quick and tight descent as far as **Disentis,** followed by a long ride down the **Vorderrhein valley** (the "front Rhine") toward **Chur,** the capital of **Graubunden,** and the next good roads. Along the way, the Rhein goes through one of those *schluchts.* The highway has to go up and around to the north of the Schlucht through the ski resorts of **Laax** and **Flims.** But there's a neat alternative. Chiseled out of the cliffs on the south side is a tight,

Across the top, Albula is almost a moonscape, and just a few kilometers from St. Moritz. (Trip 37)

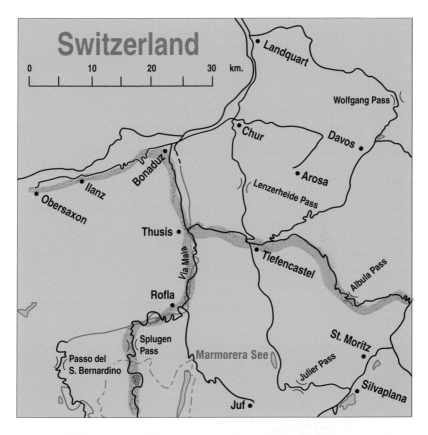

narrow, cliff-hanging road known only to locals and exploring motorcyclists. It's easy to catch at **Ilanz** by crossing into the village from the highway and heading east, downstream, at the village square. The east end of the road is at **Bonaduz,** on the main routes to **St. Moritz.** From Bonaduz, the main road goes to **Tiefencastel** and then over the **Julier Pass.** (For more information about these roads, see Trip 36.)

To extend the exploring, there's more high road paralleling the main one. Turn south off the main valley road about 20 kilometers upstream (west) of Ilanz. (At the time of the turnoff, the main road is briefly on the south bank of the Rhein.) It's marked **"Obersaxon,"** which is a region, not a town. The road climbs through high meadows with views over the whole valley, then comes down to the main square in Ilanz.

Trip 36 Hinterrhein (the 'Back Rhine')

Distance *About 170 kilometers from St. Moritz, plus 50 to Juf*

Terrain *Narrow, tight, steep climb, hairpins, and tunnels on Splugen; challenging, modern mountain highway on Maloja and Julier*

Highlights *Audacious mountain road, awesome gorges, rustic rifugio, highest village in Switzerland, Maloja Pass (1,815 meters),* ★★ *Splugen Pass (2,113 meters), Juf and the Via Mala,* ★ *Julier Pass (2,284 meters)*

Heading upstream (southwest) through the **Engadin** valley from **St. Moritz,** past some nice lakes, you don't feel like you're climbing. Then, suddenly, you come upon a real switchback downhill, the **Maloja Pass.** You're already at the top. The Maloja heads down through some pleasant Swiss villages, one of which has such a narrow street that there's a traffic signal at each end to let vehicles pass one way at a time. The road heads over the Italian border. A bit into Italy, in the larger town of **Chiavenna,** there's a little traffic circle (watch for the brown

Maloja Pass only has one side, down, westerly from St. Mortiz into Italy at Chiavenna. Or up only, if you're heading to St. Moritz from Chiavenna. It does sport a center line. But look, it's not double. Go ahead! Pass that bus.

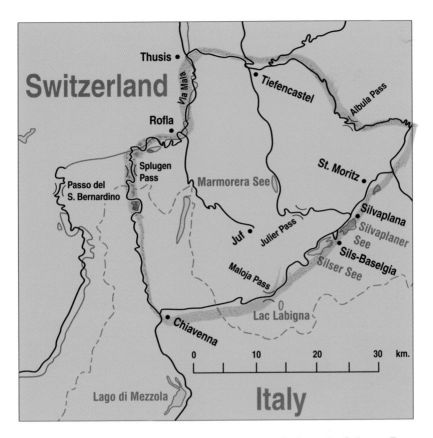

sign, PASSO SPLUGA) and the beginning of a wild climb up the **Splugen Pass** back toward Switzerland. (For roads south of Chiavenna, see Trip 46.)

The pass road often just barely hangs on a cliff, often hairpins in a tunnel, often works through stone snow shed tunnels that seem hardly helmet high and must have been built a century ago. Yet after snaking through stacks of cliff-hanging hairpins and one-way tunnels, in typical Italian fashion, the road ends in villages with people and trucks and buses, all using the road as their only connection to the world.

Short of the top of the pass, just below the face of a Mussolini-massive stone dam, is a typical Italian mountain rifugio, called **Rifugio Stuetta,** a fun place for a lunch, cappuccino, or good Italian hot chocolate. In a rustic wood-paneled room with a tiny bar, the host family will see that some kind of food, usually pasta and salad just waiting to be made, is available to refresh a weary traveler. It's a good place to remember that *bolognese* is meat sauce and *pomodoro* is tomato sauce, that oil and vinegar is the salad dressing of Italy, and that *formaggio,* cheese, will probably be Parmesan. Almost all remote Italian passes have these

Climbing up from Chiavenna, the Splugen Pass road hangs precariously to mountain slopes alternating between hairpins and tunnels, or sometimes both at once.

CHAPTER
11

154

inns, staffed by a family in residence, which provide shelter and food to road workers and travelers. Invariably, there's one clean, though small, toilet.

Many cafes in Italy serve no meals, but they may have panini, a grilled sandwich, or toast and gelato.

Higher and just a few switchbacks below the summit is the village **Monte Spluga,** at 1,908 meters, with a small, rustic hotel only 150 years old, **Hotel Vittoria.**

Back in Switzerland, the road pulls one of the most amazing and oft-photographed series of ladder switchbacks in the Alps. The road goes back and forth so often on the alluvial mountain slope that you can pass by the same vehicles going in the same direction time after time.

Ten kilometers over the border into Switzerland, the pass road meets the high-speed **San Bernardino Autobahn,** a two-lane freeway. This is the valley of the **Hinterrhein,** the "back Rhine," to go with the **Vorderrhein,** the "front Rhine" leading down from the Oberalp.

Just ten kilometers down the Autobahn from the Splugen, an Autobahn Ausfahrt (exit) called **Avers-Rofla** leads to an adjoining Schlucht, and a Tofftreffpunkt at **Gasthof Roflaschlucht.** Opposite, a winding and deserted road leads south up to **Juf,** the highest permanent town in Switzerland, at 2,126 meters. You'll find no tourists on this road.

Farther down the Autobahn, just before the Vorderrhein and Hinterrhein meet, is the **Via Mala,** the "bad way." The Autobahn sweeps through the gorge of the Via Mala in tunnels and bridges that make it easy to miss the narrow, deep gorge that for centuries was the "bad way." Take the Via Mala Ausfahrt and look down on what a frightening journey it must have been.

Below the Via Mala at **Thusis,** take the road toward **Tiefencastel** and the **Julier Pass.** The first part is another engineering tour de force, sweeping through an impossible gorge, playing back and forth at times with the **Glacier Express** train. Tiefencastel, wedged into a tiny valley, has gas, hotels, and a church typical of Romansch style: square stucco bell tower with an octagonal belfry topped by a dome.

The Julier road starts in Tiefencastel and climbs long, snaking up a gorge, then by a lake. Facilities at the top are good only for a postcard. Because the Engadin around St. Moritz is so high it's not far down to them from the top of the Julier into **Silvaplana,** a town with cute hotels and restaurants, and on into St. Moritz.

Trip 37   Albula Pass Connections ★★

Distance   *About 190 kilometers from St. Moritz*

Terrain   *Four high passes and one medium high pass*

Highlights   *Cute Romansch villages, views of Glacier Express trestles, ski resorts,* ★★ *Moonscape on Albula Pass (2,312 meters), Lenzerheide (1,547 meters), Wolfgang Pass (1,631 meters),* ★ *Fluela Pass (2,383 meters), Arosa (1,775 meters)*

Right in the middle of a little village called **La Punt,** 12 kilometers down the **Engadin** (north) from **St. Moritz,** is the **Albula Pass** turnoff. It looks like a street of no significance between two buildings. The Albula is a back road. It climbs quickly above the tree line and then dips and jogs and weaves across a wild, rocky no-man's land to the summit, where there's a pleasant restaurant, before starting down through lovely remote Romansch villages. Sometimes, it barely squeezes through a gorge, or barely hangs on a cliff.

While the **Julier Pass** is considered the main auto road into St. Moritz, the train takes the Albula. Several of the bridges used by the **Glacier Express** along the route are famous on postcards and travelogues. Around the town of **Bergun,** the train makes several climbing loops inside the mountain, and below **Filisur,** the train crosses a gorge on a high stone arch viaduct, only to disappear at a right angle into the sheer granite cliff face.

The Albula leads down to **Tiefencastel,** quite a crossroads in its narrow gorge. The Albula Pass meets the Julier Pass to continue the main connection toward **Thusis** and the rest of Switzerland, working through another gorge also used by the railroad. Another road out of Tiefencastel climbs north over **Lenzerheide.** And there's a shortcut road across to **Davos,** base of the **Fluela** and **Wolfgang Passes.**

For some reason Lenzerheide is never called a pass, even though it's always listed as one. It's where the book *Heidi* is supposed to have taken place. It is very pretty country, but not exotic. The area centers around **Chur,** the canton capital, a large city with motorcycle shops and services, but the Lenzerheide road stays on the hillside above Chur and connects directly to the **San Bernardino Autobahn.**

East above Chur is **Arosa,** a well-known ski resort, accessible only by a very twisty road that follows the arc of a mountain stream called **Plessur** for 30 kilometers. Arosa, at 1,775 meters, is the end of the road. It's necessary to go into Chur to catch the Arosa road.

A 15-kilometer jaunt north on the Autobahn brings the rider to **Landquart** and the **Wolfgang Pass** road to Davos. Just short of the summit of the Wolfgang Pass is **Klosters,** where some members of the British royal family have been

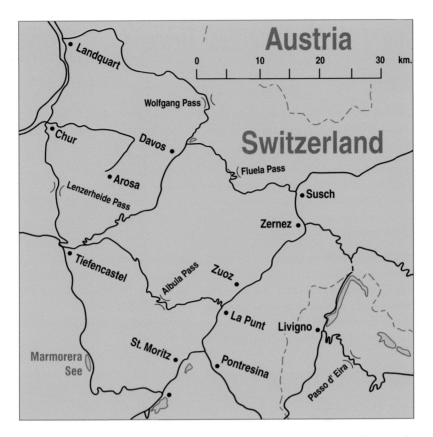

known to ski. A most spectacular bridge is under construction along this stretch, part of a plan to bypass Klosters. It looks like something designed by Disney.

A couple of kilometers over the Wolfgang is Davos, with a one-way loop street that makes for an easy return to the Fluela Pass road. The Fluela, which has a pleasant, rustic restaurant at the top, crosses back to the Engadin below **St. Moritz.**

Once, 500 motorcyclists, on a rally sponsored by Michael Krauser, paraded through Davos past a reviewing stand with some notables, while the Davos town band played and replayed Queen Liliuokalani's "Aloha Oe," "Farewell to Hawaii."

CHAPTER
11

Trip 38 Italian Connections, Stelvio ★

Distance *About 230 kilometers*

Terrain *Endless tight hairpins on Stelvio, one of the highest passes in the Alps; a short unpaved section on Umbrail Pass, and a challenging modern pass road on Bernina Pass*

Highlights *Good sweepers over ★ Bernina Pass (2,328 meters) into Switzerland's farthest corner; a major motorcycle goal, the ★★ Passo dello Stelvio (Stilfser Joch) (2,758 meters), with restaurant terraces, and hotels, vendors on top; Swiss national park, Umbrail Pass (2,501 meters), Ofen Pass (2,149 meters)*

The **Bernina Pass,** south from **St. Moritz,** swoops down and around, bypassing **Pontresina,** a popular resort. Then after climbing the first switchbacks, and just over some railroad tracks, there's a view point with the best views of **Piz Bernina** (the highest peak of the area) and its glaciers. The restaurants at the top are serviceable. Just across the top is an intersection with a border crossing into the isolated Italian valley of **Livigno** (see Trip 39).

Motorcyclists pass themselves coming and going many times when working up the Stelvio.

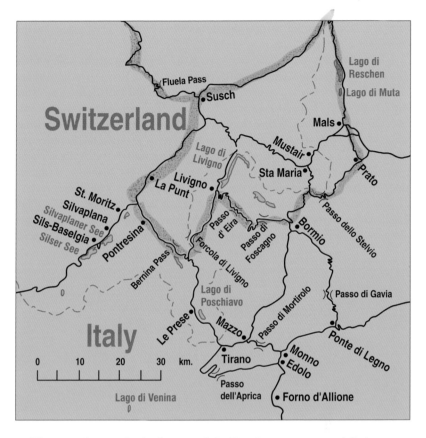

The sweeping southerly descent of the Bernina stays on good Swiss pavement. Below the town of **Poschiavo** is the little village of **Le Prese,** notable to bikers because of the train tracks that go down the middle of the street—well, almost the middle. It would be easier if they stayed in the middle. At the downhill end of the village, just as the tracks pull off to the side, is the **Le Prese Hotel.** Stop for lunch or refreshment on the lakefront terrace.

Recently an avalanche took out the road around the lake, below the hotel. Travelers had to take a boat across the lake until a precarious wooden ramp could be built. The ramp served until the permanent road could be rebuilt.

The Italian border is just a few kilometers on, with a steady parade of Italian cars crossing into Switzerland, tanking up on less expensive Swiss gas, and making a U-turn back to Italy. Not a bad idea.

Just into Italy is the Italian town of **Tirano,** where a turn north by the big yellow church starts the climb to the most famous motorcycle destination in the Alps, the **Passo dello Stelvio,** known in German as the **Stilfser Joch** (say yoke.) At 2,758 meters, it's one of the highest pass roads in the Alps. Every motorcyclist has to climb it. The collection of stalls, shops, restaurants, hotels, and even a bank at the top of the Stelvio probably does violate environmental sense, but the convenience is unmatched.

Italy is building a two-lane freeway up the lower part of the valley from Tirano as far as **Bormio,** but the road over the pass above Bormio can only be described as *laissez faire* Italian determination. It seems like half the hairpins in the Alps are on the Stelvio, 40 or so on each side. And they are hairpins, with practically zero inside radius. Where there's room, the road may be almost two lanes wide, but much of the time, one narrow lane seems to strain the limits of the slope. In some places, the hand-laid rock retaining walls have obviously been pushed beyond their limits, and the road has slipped a bit down the mountainside. The Italian solution is to bridge the gap by pouring asphalt in the crack.

The Stelvio clearly illustrates the problem of mountain road building and maintenance. Surrounded by high cliffs, the alluvial slope is the only possible place to hang a road. And the alluvial slope is inherently unstable. The alterna-

From a small border station on the Bernina Pass in Switzerland, a good Italian road leads into duty-free Livigno, an Italian valley almost surrounded by Switzerland, where everything, including gasoline, is tax-free.

Hairpins connect the traverses on the northeast side of Stelvio. (Trip 38)

tive, often used elsewhere in Italy, is a tunnel deep inside the mountain. But that surely spoils the view.

There's a road sign repeatedly seen in Italy: LAVORO IN CORSO, "work in progress." It perhaps should read "work needs to be in progress."

Whether it's sunny or foggy or snowy or rainy, there are always bikes on Stelvio. It's a must-stop for lunch or cappuccino or just tire-kicking. The post-card vendors know their market: there are plenty of cards showing the road, some with bikes in the hairpins. Skiers are permitted and there's summer skiing on the glaciers. There are even a couple of hotels on the top: **Hotel Stilfser Joch** (also known as Passo dello Stelvio Hotel) and **Stelvio Hotel Perego,** recently re-modeled.

The northeast side of the Stelvio is equally exciting. It is often marked *chiuso,* "closed," but traffic is usually going around the barricade.

Just short of the top of the Stelvio, on the southwest (Bormio) side, is a border crossing back into Switzerland. This is the **Umbrail Pass.** From the border crossing it's all downhill. A reasonable portion of it is not paved, but is maintained in good condition. It goes down to the main Swiss road in the handsome Romansch village of **Santa Maria,** where the **Ofen Pass** climbs back toward the Engadin.

A fascinating alternate route to Santa Maria is to continue on across the Stelvio and, at the Italian base town of **Prato,** head north on a beautiful side road past the **Castle of Lichtenburg** to **Glorenza** (and the German is Glurns), a very attractive walled village with cafes and shops. From Glorenza, it's 20 kilometers to the Swiss border and the Ofen Pass road.

Just north of Glorenza (in Italy) there's a wonderful hotel in the village of **Mals.** (It's actually on the Reschen Pass road.) With spacious rooms, views of the valley and mountains from every one, including the indoor pool, **Hotel Garberhof** is a good base for exploring the Passo dello Stelvio.

The endless supply of roads in the Alps includes lots of twisting and climbing. These hairpins on the east side of the Passo dello Stelvio in Italy regularly entertain riders.

There's always a crowd on the top of Passo dello Stelvio. It isn't pretty, but it's exciting—sort of a motorcycle Mecca. There's skiing all summer on nearby glaciers so there are hotels and even a bank on the pass.

Just inside the Swiss border, above Gloranza, is the Swiss village of **Mustair.** Right on the road is a small church dating from the time of Charlemagne, famous for some of the earliest frescoes in Europe. Most of the frescoes tell the story of John the Baptist. The main ones focus on the gruesome aspects: tied up before Solome, then his head on the platter, etc., in the almost comic-book art style of the Middle Ages. The parking lot is across from the church, but bikes can usually park on the sidewalk by the gate.

Santa Maria has **Hotel Stelvio,** a good hotel just above where the Umbrail Pass comes down into town. It has good parking, WCs, an outdoor terrace, and goulash soup.

The **Ofen Pass,** heading back toward the Engadin and St. Moritz, passes through the **Swiss National Park.** The park area seems very arid by Alpine standards, looking much like western parks in the U.S. From the Ofen Pass road, there's a one-way-at-a-time toll tunnel back into Italy and the Livigno valley (Trip 39). The small, narrow tunnel is several kilometers long. Traffic signals control the direction of traffic flow.

Trip 39 Duty-Free Livigno & Passo di Gavia ★

Distance *About 230 kilometers*

Terrain *Rugged, high, challenging mountain roads*

Highlights *Forcola di Livigno (2,315 meters), Passo d'Eira (2,210 meters), Passo di Foscagno (2,291 meters), Passo dell'Aprica (1,176 meters), a high valley of Italy where everything is tax-free, including gasoline; also one of the Alps' more famous challenges, the ★★ Passo di Gavia (2,621 meters), ★Passo di Mortirolo (1,896 meters), unknown to most map makers*

Just over the **Bernina Pass** from **St. Moritz** is a border station, open during the day, into Italy. It opens to a nicely paved Italian Alpine pass road, **Forcola di Livigno,** that descends to an Alpine curiosity, the duty-free high Alpine valley of **Livigno.** The valley is pretty well surrounded by Switzerland. The only Italian road out is up over two passes. Everything in Livigno is tax-free, including gas.

Free enterprise has not treated Livigno with gentleness. It's a hodgepodge. Most of what merchants think visitors should buy won't fit too well on a bike. Hotels and restaurants are adequate, but nothing special.

Besides the road from the Bernina Pass, there are two other ways out of Livigno. Straight down the valley, through the town and out the other side, a road winds around a lake to the toll tunnel back into the **Swiss National Park.** It's a one-way-at-a-time tunnel, controlled by lights (Trip 29).

The other way is through Italy, a bumpy 50-kilometer trip over two passes, the **Passo d'Eira** and the **Passo di Foscagno,** that few tourists or visiting motor-cyclists see. These pass roads lead to **Bormio,** the base of the **Passo dello Stelvio** and also the take-off point for **Passo di Gavia,** one of the higher roads in the Alps. Follow the brown signs for the Gavia in downtown Bormio.

From Bormio, the first 15 kilometers of the Gavia are standard highway. Then the fun begins. Much of the south side of the Gavia is very narrow and has just seen its first asphalt, maybe three meters wide. It hangs on little ledges with tight hairpins supported by flimsy old rock walls with hardly a piece of string or a tree branch for a guard rail.

This is another of those roads where "chiuso" (closed) probably means "travel at your own risk." Even when the road is closed, the rifugios near the top may be open, but there are no other services on the 35-kilometer crossing to **Ponte di Legno.**

Ponte di Legno is on a main east-west highway. Head west in the direction of **Edolo.** (Edolo is a few kilometers north of Trip 46.)

About five kilometers before (east of) Edolo is the turn for a fantastic little road used on the **Giro d'Italia** bicycle race, but otherwise forgotten, **Passo di Mortirolo.** No maps show this road correctly. It is paved but narrow, and goes

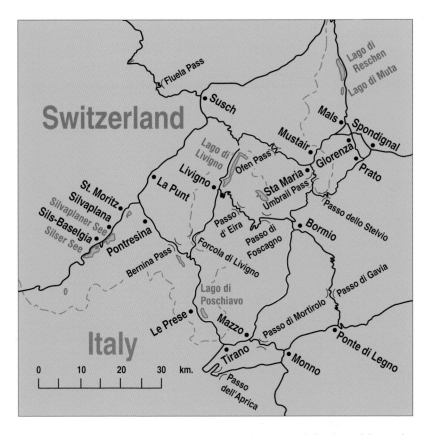

across the mountain between the villages of **Monno** and **Mazzo**. In Mazzo, its north end, it's signed PASSO DI MORTIROLO. At the other end, near Edolo, the only sign is MANNO. At the top, a small road leads west, while the pass road zig-zags down, one lane of narrow pavement covered with painted slogans for the bicycle racers. Mazzo at the north end is in the Adda valley. Downstream, west, is Tirano and the entrance to the Bernina Pass. Upstream, east, is the Passo dello Stelvio.

Should you choose to continue on through **Edolo,** instead of Passo di Mortirolo, the **Passo dell'Aprica** is straight ahead. The Aprica isn't high but has some ski hotels and restaurants right on the road through town. The west side of the Aprica has sweeping views of the **Adda Valley** which leads toward **Lake Como**. But before that, about seven kilometers below Aprica, just after a tight curve that reverses the traverse, a little sign saying STAZZONA points at a little road into the woods that works down the mountain to the main road toward **Tirano.**

At Tirano, the big yellow church marks the gateway back to Switzerland, Le Prese, the Bernina Pass, and St. Moritz.

CHAPTER
11

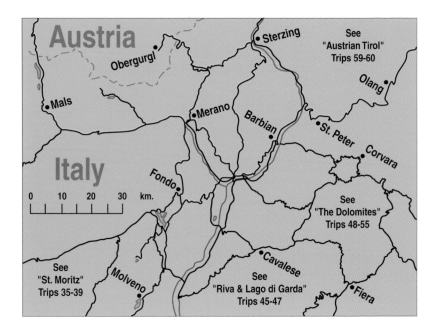

Austria

Obergurgl

Sterzing

See
"Austrian Tirol"
Trips 59-60

Olang

Mals

Merano

Barbian

St. Peter

Corvara

Italy

Fondo

0   10   20   30   km.

See
"The Dolomites"
Trips 48-55

See
"St. Moritz"
Trips 35-39

Molveno

Cavalese

See
"Riva & Lago di Garda"
Trips 45-47

Fiera

Sud Tirol

Handsome is the word to describe **Merano,** Alto Adige, also known as Meran, **Sud Tirol.** Giant trees shade its streets. A mountain torrent, the **Passiria** in Italian, **Passeier** in German, regularly used for whitewater racing pours through its heart. Flowered promenades with coffee houses and *gelaterias* (ice cream parlors) follow the edge of the torrent. Its little medieval section has narrow arch-shaded streets lined with shops selling everything: bananas, nuts, pastries, leather goods, toys, the latest fashions. Behind the shops are beer gardens with the best Austrian and Italian food. Mountain peaks surround the town, lower slopes laden with apples and pears and vines. It's been the favorite spa of kaisers and kings. Yet Americans never stop in Merano. Say "Merano" to an American travel agent and you will be corrected, "You mean Milano." No, Merano.

Merano is one of those places that has become Italian instead of Austrian only in the twentieth century. Much of the culture is both Austrian and Italian, and most everything has a name in both languages. You'll find pasta right beside Wienerschnitzel on many menus.

The mountainsides are lined with hotels. **Hotel Augusta** is a handsome yellow structure in a sort of Austrian Victorian style, secluded in a shaded garden just off the promenade.

The giant old time hotel "spa" of Merano is the **Kurhotel Palace.** It looks like a palace, sitting well back from the street. It has huge halls and lots of gilt, only slightly faded. In low season prices are reasonable, especially for rooms facing the town. There's an outdoor-indoor pool with an electric eye to open the glass door between them as you swim up to it. Across the street is a shady park with a statue of the Empress Elizabeth, wife of Franz-Joseph. (Remember, she was assassinated in Geneve by a guy wielding scissors.) Coat and tie required at dinner!

Up the Passeier 20 kilometers is **St. Leonhard** (San Leonardo, in Italian), a village with several good Tiroler style hotels, like **Hotel Stroblhof.** It's right on the main street where all the bikes pass.

Thirteen kilometers west of Merano in the direction of Reschen Pass and Stelvio, just past the village of Naturns, a great road called **Schnals Tal** (Val Senales) climbs north toward the glaciers. The road's another alpine wonder. At the top of the road, a cable car takes skiers up to summer skiing on the **Similaun Glacier** where the multi-thousand-year-old ice man was recently found.

Up the mountain east of Merano is **Hafling,** famous for the small horses called Haflingers. From Hafling, a small road hangs on the mountain south to **Bolzano** (in Bolzano, follow signs to **Jenesian** to reach Hafling) (see Trip 43).

Merano is a delight to be in, but it can be a pain to ride through. Brown signs do mark routes through town to the nearby passes.

Trip 40   Timmels Joch   ★★

Distance   *About 100 kilometers round trip to top of the pass*

Terrain   *Some congestion near Merano, narrow twisting climb, dark tunnel, on Italian side; more moderate on Austrian side*

Highlights   *Exhilarating views of glaciated peaks, connection to Austrian Tirol and Germany (toll),* ★★ *Timmels Joch (2,509 meters)*

Hairpins and traverses on the south side (Italian) of Timmels Joch demand attention. In the distance, the peaks called Giogaia de Tessa.

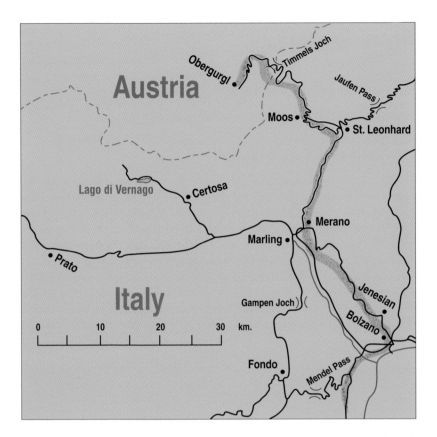

The raging river through **Merano** is the **Passiria** (Passeier in German). Follow it upstream, north from Merano, 20 kilometers to **St. Leonhard** (San Leonardo in Italian), at the base of the **Timmels Joch.** On the way, the road passes the home of Andreas Hofer, a sort-of George Washington of the Sud Tirol (only he didn't win). The house is now a Gasthaus.

The Timmels Joch is the lower leg of the fork in the road at St. Leonhard. It's a secondary road, narrow, tight, and twisty, hanging over deep canyons with a horizon studded with snowy peaks, and with some dark, rough-bottomed tunnels at the top.

In St. Leonhard there's a little bridge across the river. You may take it and follow a mini-one-laner through the forests as far up as **Moos** where it rejoins the main Timmels Joch road.

Across the border at the top, on the Austrian side, there's a good restaurant. The road quality improves—as well it should, because Austria collects a toll. It leads in a few kilometers to ski areas at **Hochgurgl, Obergurgl,** and **Untergurgl,** then into a long, pleasant Austrian valley (see Trip 59 for a hotel in Vent Tal, below the "gurgl's").

CHAPTER
12

Trip 41 Reschen Pass

Distance *About 160 kilometers round trip to top of pass*

Terrain *Gentle climb on Italian side, a little more precipitous on Austrian side*

Highlights *Orchards and farms, toll-free connection to Germany, leads to Stelvio, Reschen Pass (Passo Resia) (1,504 meters)*

The main highway skirts around **Merano** on the west, then crawls up past the huge **Forst Brewery,** followed by about 50 kilometers of gentle climbing through lovely Sud Tirol country: farms and apple orchards by the road, substantial houses on the hillsides, snowy mountains in all directions, cute villages with hotels and restaurants and far too much traffic. Because the pass is low and toll-free, it's a favorite of Germans pulling house trailers (wohnwagens) with low-powered sedans. Significant effort is being made to bore tunnels through adjoining mountains in order to bypass the congestion in villages. For all this distance, the only intersecting roads wind into mountain valleys, and then end. One valley road to the north, just 13 kilometers from Merano, near **Naturno** (Naturns in German) makes a wonderous climb up among glaciers. Called **Val**

Sometimes fog plays around the road, like here on Timmels Joch.

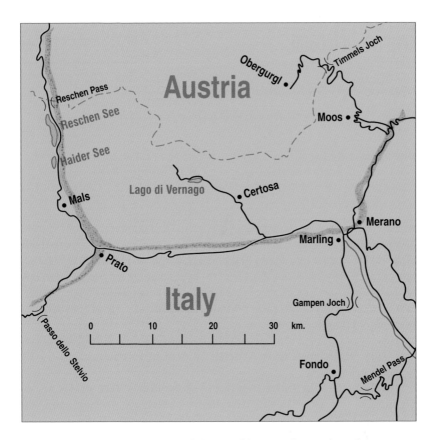

Senales (Schnals Tal in German), it has a cable car at the top that takes summer skiers to the **Similaun Glacier,** where the multi-thousand-year-old ice man was found.

The first through road intersection, about 50 kilometers upstream from Merano, is the well-marked turn for **Passo Stelvio,** the hairpin champ of the Alps, and a motorcycle favorite. A new intersection has just been opened west of the village, **Prato** (see Trip 38, Italian Connections).

Then nine kilometers further upstream is **Malles** (Mals in German), the turn for the walled village of **Glorenza** (Glurns), and Switzerland. **Hotel Garberhof** is near the intersection.

Above Malles the road zig-zags between concrete igloos, forts built by Austria to defend the pass from Italy in World War One. Just before crossing into Austria, the road passes a lake famous for its church steeple, all that shows of a submerged village.

Once into Austria, in the valley of the **Inn River,** downstream leads to the Austrian Tirol and Innsbruck, and upstream leads to Switzerland, the Engadin, and St. Moritz.

CHAPTER
12

Trip 42 Merano ★

Distance *About 170 kilometers*

Terrain *Steep climbs and descents with hairpins, some narrow roads, over four high passes.*

Highlights *Neat farms, forests, prosperous villages, Tirolian culture, ★ Jaufen Pass (Passo di Monte Giovo) (2,094 meters), ★ Penser Joch (Passo di Pennes) (2,214 meters), Mendel Pass (Passo di Mendola) (1,363 meters), Gampen Joch (Passo di Palade) (1,518 meters)*

At **San Leonardo** (St. Leonhard in German), 20 kilometers upstream from **Merano,** the road forks. The left tine, along the river, leads to **Timmels Joch** (Trip 40). The upper tine climbs **Jaufen Pass,** a tight and narrow road through forests that finally bursts out above the tree line. There are only sandwich shops on the top, and then a quick, steep descent into **Sterzing** (called Vipiteno in Italian). Sterzing is on the **Brennero-Modena Autostrada,** the major route between the cities of Italy and Germany.

Sterzing has an interesting but gotta-walk-in-to-see-it arcaded old street from the Middle Ages, similar to that in Merano, with many good restaurants. Try the four-cheese linguini.

The junction of the Jaufen Pass road with the **Penser Joch** road is before **Sterzing,** so it's not necessary to go into the town unless you want to check it out. The Penser Joch road is marked with one of those brown pass signs. It's a great twisting climb to the top, back up above the tree line, where there's a good rifugio restaurant. Then there's a long descent southerly, almost like a trip back in time, past flowering meadows and little villages and sturdy farmhouses. The valley, called **Saren Tal** (Val Sarentino in Italian), is completely Austrian in culture. Then some arched tunnels through a gorge and by a castle on a peak into **Bolzano,** a prosperous industrial city (see Trip 43).

Bolzano (Bozen in German) is at the bottom of the deep canyon used by the Brennero-Modena Autostrada. It's just a couple of hours north to **Munchen,** and less than that south to **Venezia.** Bolzano has good motorcycle shops.

Keeping to the west through Bolzano, follow the brown signs to **Passo di Mendola** (Mendel Pass), and the regular signs to **Eppan** and **Kaltern,** towns on the way.

Mendel Pass climbs along cliffs with views of the deep canyon, the autostrada and railroad in it, and the river that made it, the **Adige.** Then it climbs into park-like green forests. A good picnic area. The culture is very Austrian.

Just over the pass where it's Italian again, turn toward **Fondo,** and from there onto the **Gampen Joch** road. The Gampen Joch (Passo di Palade in Italian) climbs up, over, and down, with arched stone barriers on the edge of the pave-

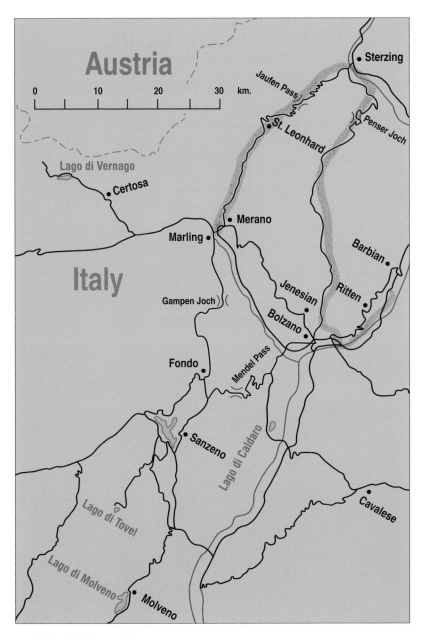

ment, typical of the Austrian Empire days. Toward Merano is the suburb **Marling** (Marlengo in Italian), with a good BMW dealer. Like many European BMW dealers, this one handles both cars and bikes.

Trip 43 One Lane Roads Across Sud Tirol ★★

Distance *About 240 kilometers*

Terrain *A couple of high passes, more modest heights, attention demanding narrow paved roads and the wonderful and handsome farming culture of the Sud Tirol. Weaving one lane mountain roads, some of them found in Trips 40, 42, 52, and 55, starting from the Austrian Ost (east) Tirol near Lienz, across Italian Sud Tirol to the Austrian Tirol near Imst. (Because the culture is Austrian, the German names for places are used here, even though the country is Italy. Where Italian names might be helpful, they're mentioned.)*

Highlights *Green forests, very neat farms with sturdy barns, and quaint villages all in park-like settings. Nothing flat. No busses. Plenty of facilities*

Take this route and discover the magic of the Sud Tiroler culture. For centuries the area was Austrian. At Versailles after World War I, it became Italian. Now, everything has an Italian name and the best map is the **Italian Touring Club (T.C.I.)** one called **Trentino/Alto Adige.** On the ground, everything is very

It's one way at a time on the Staller Sattel. All await the hour (the 1/4 of the clock face above the car that's green). Some of the bikes are planning to jump ahead of the car.

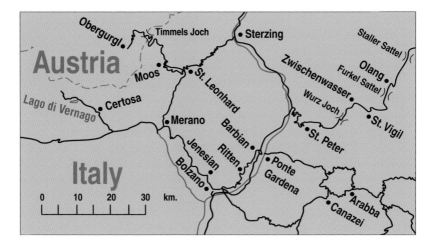

Austrian. Village churches have Austrian steeples, not Italian campaniles, restaurants have Wienerschnitzel rather than pasta. The flag of semi-autonomous **Sud Tirol** is red and white, remarkably similar to the Austrian flag. It is flown proudly from house, barn, and church tower on special days. The route description here is from east to west.

Start at the east end of the route, where the Sud Tirol meets the **Ost Tirol,** which happens to be the Austrian/Italian border, atop the **Staller Sattel** (NW of Lienz). It's one-way down into Italy for 15 minutes starting on the hour (on the half hour coming up from Italy) (see Trip 64).

Sweep down off the mountain. In about 23 kilometers, cross the main valley east-west road by jogging a few hundred meters west and then turning down through the village, **Olang** (Valdora, in Italian). Then you're climbing the one-lane **Furkel Sattel,** which after field and forest and a ski tow, comes down to **St. Vigil.** Turn downstream northwest (upstream dead-ends) to **Zwischenwasser** (Longega in Italian) where in a tight little valley our road meets the main north-south road. Turn south, upstream, toward **Corvara** for only one kilometer, then take the little bridge that crosses the adjacent stream, west, signed WELSCHELLEN. After about ten kilometers of one-lane, the road meets the one-lane "main" **Wurz Joch** road (Trip 52) coming up from St. Martin. Climb the sweepers and hairpins of the Wurz Joch, past the attractive rifugio at the top.

About eight kilometers west of the rifugio, the one-lane forks. The north tine goes down to **Brixen.** Take the south, the left tine, down to **St. Peter.**

At St. Peter is the Tiroler hotel restaurant **Hotel Kabis** with a plaza terrace just as the road hairpins around a building. (The area is called Vilnoss, Funes in Italian.) Here, as all across the Sud Tirol, the hotel and plaza will be full of locals in special Tirolian costume on Sunday morning.

From St. Peter it's but nine kilometers down west to the main valley canyon. Cross under the Brennero Autostrada, over the river, and go south, toward

Bozen for a whole eight kilometers of two-lane road. (Coming eastbound from the autostrada, be sure to turn north at St. Peter. The turn is signed WURZ JOCH. Straight ahead dead-ends.)

At **Ponte Gardena,** after eight kilometers of two lane, take the one lane west to and through **Barbian.** From Barbian, it's one lane southerly (two-way) traversing the edge of the mountain to Lengmoos. Along the way are some strange formations below the road: pointed peaks with rock caps.

Lengmoos has a popular restaurant terrace, the **Sporthotel Spogler.** From Lengmoos it's two lanes to **Klobenstein** where there's a good hotel, the **Dolomitenblick.** As its name suggests ("blick" is German for view), the hotel has views of the Dolomites, across the great canyon that contains the Brennero Autostrada way down below.

From Klobenstein, there's a two-laner down to Bozen in the valley. Don't take it. Take the one lane across the mountain to **Wangen,** a high point in the area with more views of field and forests and Dolomites. A hotel at **Ritten** is the **Berg Gasthof Plorr.** Then there's sort of a pass called **Oberinn** at 1,300 meters.

Twist down to **Saren Tal**—the Penser Joch road (Trip 42). Turn south downstream to Bozen. (Coming the other way, from Bozen, the turn up the mountain is marked "Ritten".)

In just about eight kilometers, after some tunnels, there's a castle on a pinnacle called **Runkelstein.** Just past Runkelstein, before Bozen, there's a turn up

No matter how many mountains you've seen, the first glimpse of the Dolomites takes your breath away. It's almost a religious experience. This first view is from Wurz Joch, a pass that climbs out of the great canyon of the Adige river.

The Italian side of the Staller Sattel is one way at a time as it winds down to beautiful Antholzer See (Lago d'Anterselva in Italian).

and west marked **"Jenesian"** (Genesio in Italian). Take it up the mountain, swooping through tunnels and loops, past Jenesian to **Molten** (Moltina in Italian). Stay up on the mountain heading north to **Hafling** (Avelengo in Italian). Between Molten and Halfling there's another pass of 1,357 meters at **Flaas.** From Halfing it's two lanes down to **Meran.** There's no way but to wend through Meran to the **Passer Tal,** the road to **St. Leonhard,** and the **Timmels Joch** (Trip 40).

St. Leonhard is a Tiroler style village lined with several hotels and restaurants and it's where the Timmels Joch road and the Jaufen Pass roads meet.

At the fork in the road, the easterly fork is the Jaufen. Take the westerly one, which seems to go down along the rushing river. It's the Timmels Joch road. Once down along the river, there's a bridge across it. Take it. This is the beginning of a remarkable one lane steep climb through forests to a community called **Moos.** From Moos, it's possible to cross the raging stream and continue the one lane climb up the Timmels Joch to Austria and the Tirol.

CHAPTER
12

Trip 44 Adamello Brenta National Park

Distance *135 kilometers, with an additional 40 into Lago di Tovel*

Highlights *Rural Italy with orchards and forests and views of the national park. Passo di Palade (Gampen Joch in German) 1,518 meters; Lago di Tovel (1,177 meters), a mountain gem with red water, peaks of the national park, Adamello Brenta*

Terrain *Comfortable two lane road, moderate curves*

The valley roads and autostrada connect **Merano** with **Riva,** to its south. This way is more fun.

Leave Merano through the town just southwest of it, **Lana,** and the **Gampen Joch** (Trip 42). Across the Joch, there's no more Sud Tiroler culture. It's pure Italian. From **Fondo,** head on south to **Sanzeno** where there's a pleasant Italian style hotel-restaurant, the **Albergo la Mela d'Oro** (the golden apple).

Next to the hotel is a rural church and beside it, a small war memorial monument in a contemporary style. Most every village in Europe has a war memorial honoring the local dead. This one recalls "the martyrs of the whole world." Nice thought. Southwest of Sanzeno, deep in the mountains of the **Adamello Brenta**

The old Devil's Bridge, the Teufelbrucke, in the Schollenen Gorge affords the best view of the Russian Monument carved in a nearby granite cliff. It commemorates a battle in 1799 when a Russian Army was temporarily trapped here by Napoleon.

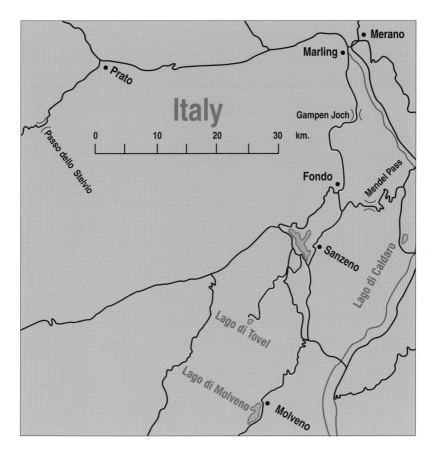

National Park, is a lovely secluded Alpine lake with unique red water reflecting the surrounding peaks.

To find it, go south of Senzano about four kilometers, then westerly about six kilometers to **Tuenno** where the road into the park and lake is marked. The road ends at the lake, about 12 kilometers upstream from Tuenno. There is a visitor's center, but no services. The park is reported to have bears.

Back at Tuenno, head south for **Molveno.** Since the main roads tend toward the Brennero Autostrada, it's necessary to avoid it by making several turns in a westerly direction back into the mountains toward Molveno. Molveno is a nicely sited Italian mountain-lake resort with hotels and restaurants well off the foreign visitor routes. There's the **Hotel Belvedere.** The road around the west side of Molveno's lake is not paved.

South from Molveno the main road hangs high on a cliff edge and then descends into **Ponte Arche** where there are signs for Riva.

To come the other direction, north from Riva, follow signs for Ponte Arche, the high road, and then on to Molveno.

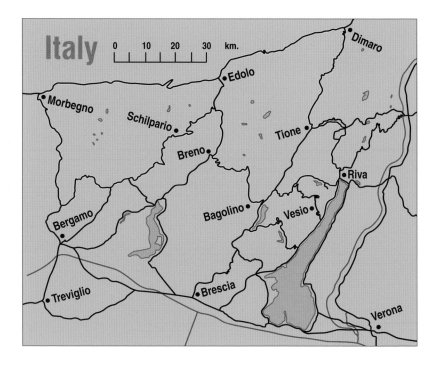

Riva and Lago di Garda

The south end of long Lake Garda, **Lago di Garda** (Italians are very casual about whether it's *del* or *di* Garda), is down in the flats of the **Po Valley** of Italy, near historic cities like Verona and Mantova. But the north end is up in the Alps, surrounded by giant vertical cliffs and snowy mountains. At the north point of the lake, surrounded by the cliffs of the Alps, is **Riva,** a small town and a beautiful destination.

Riva is a small lakeside resort, popular with Germans, and with all the amenities needed to serve the traveler—lots of shops, hotels, and restaurants stuffed inside some small fortifications of the Middle Ages. It is only 20 kilometers west of the Brennero-Modena Autostrada, and about 80 kilometers south of **Bolzano,** but a world away in spirit. It is signed from the autostrada at **Rovereto,** but it's a lot more fun to come down from the northwest, through **Tione** and over **Passo Durone.**

Riva sits at the north end of Lago di Garda, surrounded by high Alps and twisting roads. The road hugging the west shore of the lake is often in a tunnel chiseled through high cliffs that rise straight from the lake.

CHAPTER
13

Coming from the **Dolomites,** follow the route that goes down and around **Trento** from **Passo Manghen.** On the loop around Trento there are signs for Riva. Riva has a couple of motorcycle shops, and claims to be the "windsurfing capital of the world."

From Riva, there's a shoreline road around the west side of the lake that winds for miles through tunnels in the cliffs that rise a thousand feet or so out of the water. The road is in tunnels more than in daylight. Every driveway and intersecting road must be chiseled from the granite. Every spot where a wheel can fit has a restaurant or a hotel. One town, **Campione,** has a complete interchange tunneled into the adjoining mountain.

A scenic but cliff-hanging road used to climb west from Riva. It's closed now, replaced by a long tunnel.

Lake steamers and hydrofoils come into Riva at a pedestrian square with lots of gelaterias. This is where elaborate concoctions are to be consumed leisurely, taking time to indulge in that great European sport, people watching. The sport is European, but Italians are the champions.

Traffic doesn't loop in Riva. It sort of gets shoved away from the lakefront on roads that don't seem to be going in the right direction. Keep an eye on those round, blue signs with white arrows showing which way it's legal to go.

The main road climbing the cliffs from Lago di Garda to Pieve is either hanging on a ledge or tunneling through a mountain. Honking is okay on blind, narrow corners.

The balcony of the Hotel Paradiso hangs way out a thousand feet or so over Lago di Garda. It's worth a visit.

Right on the pedestrian square is **Hotel Sole,** completely modernized on the inside, with some rooms facing the lake. The piazza is not always open to vehicle traffic. Some fast talking and Italian arm waving might be called for to reach the hotel. Just don't hit a pedestrian. Next door on the lake is **Hotel Bellavista.** Approach it by vehicle from the other side.

More modest, facing the same plaza as the Sole is **Hotel Centrale.** A bit posher, but easier to park at, is the **Grand Hotel Riva.**

A modest hotel, beautifully sited high on the cliffs over Riva is **Hotel Panorama,** popular with German motorcyclists. Reach it via the **Lago de Ledro** road, turning to Pregasina just after exiting the long tunnel.

A well-known motorcycle journalist and connoisseur rates highly the cuisine at the hotel atop **Passo San Giovanni** (287 meters!) a couple of kilometers east of Riva on the main road connecting to the Brennero autostrada at Rovereto. And **Hotel San Giovanni** has rooms and a pool.

It's possible to stay way up atop **Monte Bondone,** northeast of Riva. The roads up are worth the trip. From Riva it's a sweeping dream. Down the far side to Trento it's too many hairpins to count. At almost 1,500 meters is **Hotel Montana.**

Or try the exotically sited **Hotel Paradiso** high atop the cliffs on the west side of Lago di Garda (Trip 45).

CHAPTER
13

Trip 45 Pieve and Passo di Tremalzo ★★

Distance *About 85 kilometers*

Terrain *Gentle lakeshore with tunnels, steep, very narrow gorge, and dark tunnels; steep, rocky, unpaved section between Vesio and pass, smooth sweeping asphalt around Lago di Ledro*

Highlights *Scenic lakeshore, exotic gorge and views from heights, rugged unpaved mountain climb, pass-top rifugio, ★★Pieve and Passo di Tremalzo (1,894 meters) and Lago di Ledro*

Sited on the tip top of the 1,000-foot cliff, straight up over the lake with a balcony cantilevered into space, is **Hotel Paradiso** at **Pieve.** And the road to it is an absolute must. Follow the west shore road south about five kilometers past **Limone,** where the road suddenly opens up with no houses or businesses in sight. Take the 90-degree turn into a tunnel. The road climbs out of the tunnel, makes several hairpins, and goes in another long tunnel—parts of it in full width, parts in tight, narrow curves—to reach a narrow gorge with overhanging cliffs, dripping water, a grotto to the Madonna, and a little monument to Winston Churchill, who must have painted there. Honk the horn on one-lane blind corners. Traffic is two-way, but there's space for only one lane.

The road circles around at a little opening in the cliffs and crosses over itself. At that spot is a good restaurant specializing in trout—pick yours out of the tank.

In another couple of kilometers, at the top of the cliffs, is the village of Pieve. The uphill road from the traffic circle at the gas station climbs past the town piazza, church, and school, and there's the Hotel Paradiso, down a long drive to the cliff's edge. Swimming pool, tennis, and food.

Once, a group of Americans at the Hotel Paradiso was supplied a menu in English. "What's this item, creamy noodle?" they asked. The hostess got out her Italian-English dictionary, which clearly translated "lasagna" into English as "creamy noodle." If you're lucky, they'll have "creamy noodle" as the first course.

If you stop just to look—and you should not miss it—buy something to eat or drink.

Passo di Tremalzo from Pieve became a dual-purpose legend when it was featured in *Motorrad,* the German motorcycle magazine. BMW was seen testing the GS models there. But it is now officially closed to motorcycle traffic. Some still risk official wrath and ride it. It's narrow, rocky, and unpaved, with hairpins hanging in space. A riding miscalculation could have very unsatisfactory results. It never was for uncertain riders, but all sorts of persistent street bikes have conquered it, most preferring to ride up rather than down it. From the rifugio at the top, down north, it's paved and open to all traffic. To find the pass from Pieve (not

184

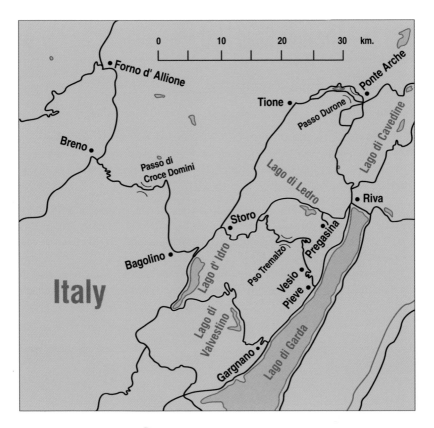

every intersection is marked), follow the signs from the gas station toward Vesio. The first several kilometers into a narrowing valley from Vesio are paved.

About halfway up, in a grove of trees, the pass road makes a hairpin into a fork going straight ahead, with some signs reading VIETATO, "forbidden." Whether or not it's forbidden, the straight-ahead fork isn't the right road.

The asphalt descent from the rifugio ends on the **Lago di Ledro** road. It swoops around the lake of that name, and starts to descend the cliffs into **Riva.** That's where the old road's been replaced with a 90-degree sharp turn into the mountain and a tunnel several kilometers long into the back side of Riva.

An alternate, much easier, and legal route crosses the mountains from the west shore of **Lago di Garda** at **Gargnano.** From the lake shore road, 12 kilometers south of the tunnel turn for Pieve, it crosses to **Lago d'Idro** from which roads lead north to **Storo** and the **Lago di Ledro** road back to Riva. The paved north slope of Passo di Tremalzo, open to all traffic, is signed from the Lago di Ledro road.

Trip 46   The High Road West

Distance   *About 230 kilometers to Morbegno*

Terrain   *Three narrow, steep, paved, high passes; and three less high*

Highlights   *Rushing streams and high meadows with no traffic, rustic rifugios,*
★★ *Passo di Croce Domini (1,943 meters),* ★ *Passo di Vivione (1,828 meters),*
Passo di Presolana (1,294 meters), Col di Zambla (1,257 meters), ★ *Passo di San*
Marco (1,992 meters)

A high route west from **Riva** uses remote passes known and used mostly by locals. Even those persistent explorers, German motorcyclists, seldom venture this
way. This route crosses three high ridges between several roughly parallel valleys running south out of the Alps.

Cross the first ridge via the **Lago di Ledro** road out of Riva, going through
the long tunnel, past the **Passo di Tremalzo** turnoff, and across to **Storo** in the
next valley.

Notice that there is no center line on the smooth asphalt of Passo Vivione—just two
big white lines marking the outside edge.

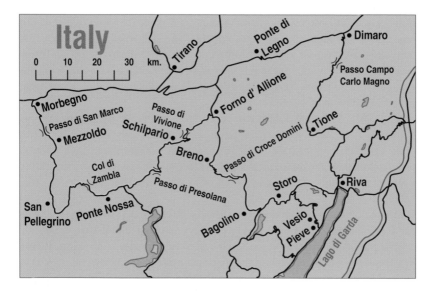

Storo appears a drab country village, but it has a first class coffee house that would do any city proud. It has marble and stained glass and comfortable booths and tables. It's at the main village intersection where a small road heads south.

From Storo, eight kilometers south on the valley road alongside a small lake, **Lago d'Idro,** the **Passo di Croce Domini** road intersects in a 170-degree right turn. After some heavy-duty climbing, you'll reach the mountain village of **Bagolino,** hung on steep slopes. It has a nice little piazza with a bakery/coffee shop. The outdoor tables have a view of the gorge and mountains, and the handsome colonnaded village church and campanile above.

From Bagolino, the Croce Domini road becomes one lane of dancing and climbing asphalt that runs beside torrents of water and rises out of the forests to cross the top above the tree line. The rifugio at the top serves refreshments in front of, or practically inside, a giant fireplace.

The dirt road south from the Croce Domini rifugio is not recommended. In fact, it usually has a dirt berm across it to discourage trespassing. West from the rifugio, the Croce Domini road has recently been rebuilt with elaborate concrete and rock retaining walls. It's still very narrow in spots. If the rifugio's family is absent, there are two albergos just a couple of kilometers down west.

Breno is a pretty big town at the western base of the Croce Domini. Coming the other way, looking for the Croce Domini road, turn into Breno. There are two turns up the pass; one with a fading sign is between two high walls enclosing fading villas. It goes staight up before twisting into the mountain. Apparently authorities prefer you to take a more circuitous route, more clearly signed, through a village called **Bienno.** The two routes merge further up the mountain. The valley north from Breno is surprisingly industrial (for a narrow Alpine valley), but it's only 20 kilometers to the **Passo di Vivione,** one of the most ignored delights

187

of the Alps. Passo di Vivione starts westerly at **Forno d'Allione** (which is just nine kilometers south of Edolo, see Trip 47). The pass road turns down across the valley stream, past a smelter furnace. Since *forno* means "kiln" and "furnace" as well as "oven," the turn is well named. In fact, the pass road is inconspicuous around and beyond the parking lot of the smelter. The pass is one-lane, paved, and devoid of traffic.

The little ristorante just across from the smelter is delightful. At this ristorante, the cook is also a wood carver, delighted to show off both his skills. (Take note that in all of Italy, the large noon meal, usually more than a lunch, is over by 2:00 p.m. and the kitchen is closed.) Because the pass has so little traffic, it's easy to assume you can play on all of its one lane. But there can be other vehicles.

There's a little rifugio at the top of the pass. Once it was seen flying an American flag. Around it are views of empty valleys and jagged mountain peaks.

The pass comes down on the southwest to **Schilpario,** a ski resort. Below Schilpario, resist the temptation to turn down into the deep valley. Rather, stay on the higher road which leads right up **Passo di Presolana,** in the direction of **Bergamo.** The road passes through a resort area popular with Italians, but unknown to most foreigners. There are several good hotels and ristorantes in towns like **Rovetta** and **Clusone,** but no English is spoken.

Five kilometers below Clusone, just below the village of **Ponte Nossa,** the **Col di Zambla** road climbs west, while the valley road continues to the large city of **Bergamo.** (Bergamo was home to Montessori and is home to Acerbis.) The Col di Zambla road comes down in the next valley by **Terme San**

The little rifugio on Passo Vivione was caught flying an American flag.

Passo Vivione has so little traffic that it's easy to stop and check wild flowers and wild streams.

Pellegrino. Terme means spa or "bad." This is the San Pellegrino of bottled water, often rated the best of bottled waters (better than Perrier?). The bottles and their plastic carriers and the trucks hauling it all will be in evidence. The spa itself looks well past its prime. The International Six-Day Trials were once held in the area.

   Passo di San Marco is a rarity: no other bikes. It's not marked. Follow the valley north from San Pellegrino, taking the forks toward the town of **Mezzoldo** (some maps erroneously show the pass from the area of a town called Cusio, but that's the wrong valley). The high road from Mezzoldo is the pass. It crosses over and comes down into the town of **Morbegno** in the **Adda Valley** (the valley that could be seen from Passo dell'Aprica, upstream from Lago di Como). From Morbegno, there are good connections into Switzerland via the **Splugen Pass** and the **Bernina Pass** (see Trip 36, Maloja Pass, Splugen Pass, etc., and Trip 38, Italian Connections).

CHAPTER
13

Trip 47 The Low Road West

Distance *About 210 kilometers to Morbegno*

Terrain *Three modest passes; occasional hairpins and grades, mostly main roads*

Highlights *Faster route west than Trip 31, more interesting than autostrada in Po Valley; Passo Durone (940 meters), Passo Campo Carlo Magno (Madonna di Campiglio) (1,682 meters), Passo del Tonale (1,883 meters), Passo dell'Aprica (1,176 meters)*

This south side of the Passo di Gavia has just been paved to almost one full lane width. It was graded dirt and rocks (Trip 39).

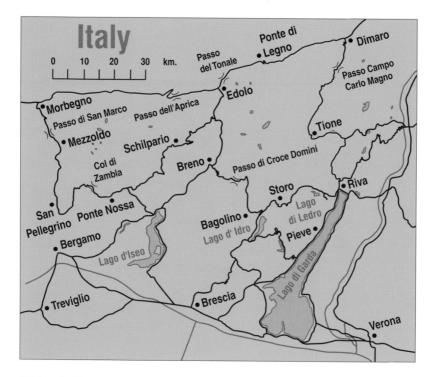

Taking the higher road north from **Riva** to **Ponte Arche** and over **Passo Durone** to **Tione** leads to the north-south **Passo Campo Carlo Magno** (that's Italian for Charlemagne) and the ski area **Madonna di Campiglio,** both in the woods, under the tree line.

At Dimaro, the pass road intersects the westbound road over **Passo del Tonale.** For some reason, there's a **Holiday Inn** at the corner. (East from the corner is Fondo and the roads of Trip 42.) Tonale doesn't hairpin so much as zig-zag in a fun climb. There's a World War I sacrario (cemetary) at the top, and several closed hotels waiting for snow and skiers. Down west it's a little more curvy to the intersection with **Passo di Gavia** (Trip 39) and **Ponte de Legno,** and further down, the intersection with **Passo Mortirolo.** There's a short tunnel into the pretty good sized town, **Edolo. Passo Vivione** (Trip 46) is just nine kilometers south. Remember, a sandwich is a sandwich, but a grilled sandwich is panini.

On the map, Passo Tonale and **Passo dell'Aprica** seem to line up almost straight east and west, with Edolo in the middle.

So, from Edolo, it's another zig-zag climb up west on the Aprica. Some believe that ristorantes on Aprica have the best hot chocolate in the world. Down west of the Aprica is the Adda valley, Morbegno, Tirano, and the roads outlined in Trip 39.

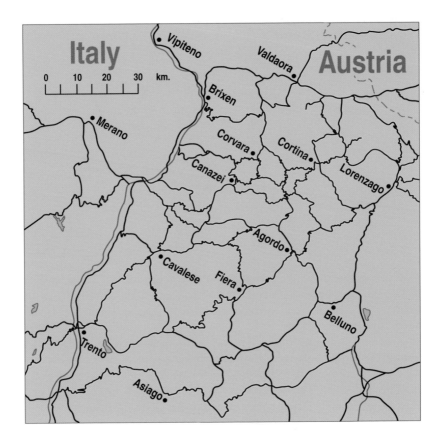

The Dolomites

The Italians call them Dolomiti, and the Germans, Dolomiten. Whatever they're called, the first view of the **Dolomites** will take your breath away. No matter how many mountains you've seen, no matter how many times you may have seen the Dolomites, that first glimpse—maybe as you emerge from a tunnel, or maybe as you accelerate out of a hairpin—will be an almost religious experience. The vertical massifs set in feathery green forests are duplicated nowhere. And there are more good roads than a good rider can cover in a week of hard riding.

Draw a straight line on the map between **Venezia** (Venice) and **Munchen** (Munich). There in Italy, just below the middle of that line, are the Dolomites. They're east of that giant canyon known as the **Brenner Pass,** the great divide made by the **Adige River** which is used as the major and lowest north-south route across the Alps.

There are good low-level routes around the Dolomites, so no one has to go through them to get anywhere. The only people there are there because of them. The Dolomites are a skier's and motorcyclist's dream.

The Dolomites are in Italy, with Italian laws, stamps, and money, but it was not always thus. Until World War I, they were in Austria, part of the Tirol. The Austrians were on the Germans' side in World War I, and the Italians were on the Allied side. The Austrian and Italian generals ordered up battles much like the horrible ones in France, only these were in the mountains. Little known in our history books are the costly battles fought between Austria and Italy in the Dolomites. Once one side or the other had charged up or down a mountain at great loss of life, they had to build a road to supply the dearly bought area. They built roads and tunnels that didn't seem to go anywhere except to serve some strategic need of the moment.

Now those roads make up a fantastic network for motorcycle exploring. Besides the roads, the war left only *sacrarios* (cemeteries) and some huge stone forts.

History doesn't indicate that the costly battles in the Dolomites decided anything, but at Versailles the victorious allies awarded the **Sud Tirol** (South Tyrol) to Italy. In the 1920s, some of the Tirol voted to return to Austria. The rest, including the great Dolomite range, is now known in Italy as the **Alto Adige.** Some of the World War I monuments and cemeteries (sacrarios) are mentioned on the trips here.

Vast areas of the region still remain Germanic. Many towns have Austrian-style buildings and food and are known by their German names. Typically, one side of a pass, usually the south and east side, will be completely Italian, while the next village, just a pass away, will be Austrian-Germanic. A quick clue: besides the pictures painted on the sides of the buildings, Austrian villages will have a church with a steeple, while an Italian town will have a church with a campanile.

Whether the village is Italian or Austrian, it'll have fresh pasta and great cappuccino. The Austrian ones will have Wienerschnitzel as well. A hotel or restaurant in either will have a dining room set with fresh linen and glasses, and another with bare tables. A meal may be available only in the room with the tablecloths, but there will always be a cover charge for sitting there. Noon time is siesta time and full meal time in Italy, and pasta is just the first or second course. (If pasta and salad is enough for lunch, make that clear, or the courses will keep coming.)

Cortina d'Ampezzo, usually known simply as "Cortina," is the most famous village in the Dolomites. It's spectacularly set on the eastern edge of the Dolomites and has been the site of winter Olympics. Regularly reviewed in travel magazines, it's the summer resort of choice for the wealthy of Milano. (It's a lot cooler than Milano.) Cortina's central pedestrian zone has pricey shops, and a department store with everything, called the **Cooperativa.** *The New York Times* once said something to the effect that the place to be seen is the bar of **Hotel della Post** in Cortina. Motorcyclists have been seen there, and also watching the scene from the narrow terrace in front of the hotel. It's a treat to have a drink, especially if the owner, S. Manijgo, is around to talk about the history of the valley. His family has owned the hotel for more than a century, and he has the photos to prove it. Cortina is nice, but expensive.

There's a figure eight loop, lying on its side, in the heart of the Dolomites just west of Cortina. The loop includes six major passes. Just as at Andermatt in Switzerland, it's possible to ride the figure eight and expand into the almost endless variations beyond it without ever coming down into lowlands or big cities.

Each of the villages on the trip has hotels and restaurants, many nicer, and all cheaper, than those in Cortina d'Ampezzo. The middle of the figure eight is **Passo di Campolongo,** only ten kilometers across. The towns at each end of the pass have good accommodations.

The south anchor of Passo di Campolongo is **Arabba,** a completely Italian town with good food and a variety of comfortable hotels.

Spacious rooms and a parking garage can be found at **Hotel Evaldo,** one of the several hotels in Arabba. It has a sauna and jacuzzi and makes a point of serving motorcyclists. Very friendly. Demi-pension dinners at the Evaldo include pasta (like tagliatelli or cannelloni), or aubergine (eggplant), or soup as the first course, then entrecote (steak) or veal, vegetables, salad bar, and dessert.

All of the hotels listed in the Appendix actively solicit motorcycle business. You will find the vast majority of their customers are on bikes. Note that "Gasthof" in German is often translated into Italian as "albergo," and calling a hotel a "Pension" has nothing to do with "demi-pension." It usually means that the hotel restaurant is for residents only.

No matter how wonderful the riding, the Dolomites can cause a rider to pause and look. Here they sport a dusting of snow.

Above Arabba on the Campolongo road is the **Hotel Olympia.** It's a nice place with a pleasant view and it solicits motorcycle business.

Ten kilometers north across Passo di Campolongo, at **Corvara** in **Badia** (usually called just "Corvara"), things are a bit more Germanic. Actually, signs may be in three languages, Italian, German, and Laden, the local dialect that is related to Romansch in Switzerland. A variety of hotels includes **Hotel Posta-Zirm,** an old-time place that's been modernized and has grown in all directions to include a lovely dining room, an indoor pool, and a ski lift at the side door. Dinners include an elaborate salad bar at the **Zirm,** a good place to mix the American custom of eating salad before the main course with the European one of having it afterwards. Breakfasts are bountiful by Euro standards.

Very popular with motorcyclists is **Pension La Fontana** in Corvara. Food in the attractive dining room may be about the best in the Alps. Bountifully and beautifully served. Prices are very reasonable. The road up the Passo di Campolongo goes right by it.

Right in the center of Corvara is the **Hotel Col Alto,** popular with some motorcycle travel groups.

In the fall you may see some *cacciatores* . . . hunters.

Trip 48   Dolomite Figure 8   ★★

Distance   *About 90 kilometers*

Terrain   *Climbs and descends with lots of hairpins and switchbacks; some cobblestones*

Highlights   *Six major passes encircle fantastic vertical massifs; many cafes and hotels. Includes:* ★*Passo di Valparola (2,192 meters),* ★*Passo di Falzarego (2,105 meters), Passo di Campolongo (1,875 meters),* ★*Passo di Gardena (Grodner Joch) (2,121 meters),* ★*Passo di Sella (2,244 meters),* ★*Passo Pordoi (2,239 meters)*

Passo di Valparola starts just downstream (north) of **Corvara** about five kilometers, at a village called **La Villa** in Italian and Stern in German. The handy signs for the passes are in distinctive brown color. Towns are in blue. The road goes southeasterly across a stream and climbs though several ski resorts. Near the top is the ruin of a massive World War I fort, set amidst a moonscape of Dolomite rocks and crags. A few kilometers south of the summit, the south end of the pass stops at the summit of **Passo di Falzarego,** with a couple of restaurants, a cable car to a neighboring peak, and a statue of an Italian World War I hero.

To the east, the Falzarego descends in hairpins past magnificent vertical formations toward **Cortina.** The figure eight goes the other way, westerly, in a se-

The west side of the Passo di Falzarego, part of the Figure Eight loop in the Dolomites, as seen from Passo Valparola. Those buildings are at the junction where the two pass roads meet.

ries of hairpins and tunnels. But not too far down. It hangs high on the edge of the mountain back toward **Arabba,** villages and fields a thousand meters below on one side, snow capped massifs on the other, a thousand meters up.

The area is known as the **Col de Lana,** a World War I battleground. Look way down in the valley below at a sacrario, cemetery, in the shape of a cross.

Along the edge of a tight hairpin is a World War I stone fort. It would seem to command the entire valley. Now it's a restaurant.

The southern legs of the figure eight, the Passo di Falzarego and the **Passo Pordoi,** make up part of the **Great Dolomite Road** which goes east from the **Brenner** road to Cortina. This is the most touristy part of the Dolomites and the oldest pavement. Still, it's so exciting as to be a must. An occasional tour bus may require every inch of the road to get around a hairpin. Remember, when tempted to duck past a bus, that the rear wheels will track inside of the front. In the Alps when the going gets tight, the descending vehicle is supposed to back up. Tourists are early risers, and are usually off the roads by 4 p.m. The roads and colors are good through the long summer evenings.

Each of the passes on the figure eight has tourist facilities. There are several cable cars to the peaks.

One of the hairpins on the east side of Passo Pordoi, part of the Great Dolomite Road. These bikes are heading to Arabba on the Figure Eight.

During World War I, the Austrians defended the top of the Passo di Valparola from the Italians with a massive stone fort, all in a never-never land of jagged peaks and boulders. The fort overlooks a long deep valley to the right. Winter snows are pretty deep here and that fort must have been pretty drafty (see Trip 48).

Pension La Fontana's parking lot is almost always full of bikes. Here it accommodates some tire kicking before breakfast.

At Arabba, the Falzarego joins the **Passo di Campolongo** heading north, and the **Passo Pordoi,** still the Great Dolomite Road, climbing west. Passo Pordoi has 33 numbered hairpins on the east side out of Arabba, and 27 down the west side to **Canazei.**

Before the west base of the Passo Pordoi at Canazei, the **Passo di Sella** starts heading north on the figure eight. All of the massifs are famous for mountain climbing, but the Sella is probably the best known. Usually there will be climbers hundreds of meters overhead and hikers with binoculars watching them from below.

The Sella comes down a bit on the north, only to intersect the **Passo di Gardena** heading east on the figure eight. The passes intersect at a road heading west to the Brenner through the **Val Gardena,** a valley very popular with German tourists, who call it Grodner Tal. The valley is loaded with Germanic hotels, and shops selling copper and leather goods.

About halfway up the west side of the Passo di Gardena is **Restaurant Gerard** with a view terrace. It also rents rooms. It's much nicer than the tourist traps atop the pass.

The Passo di Gardena's east end is downtown **Corvara,** where one fork in the Y intersection is the Passo di Campolongo climbing south to Arabba, ten kilometers away.

CHAPTER
14

Trip 49 Dolomites: Giau and Marmolada ★★

Distance *About 50 kilometers from Canazei to Pocol*

Terrain *Steep mountain roads with hairpins*

Highlights *Almost as fantastic as Trip 48, plus a narrow gorge, all with a lot less traffic. Includes: The Marmolada (Passo di Fedaia) (2,057 meters), and ★Passo di Giau (say JOW, rhymes with how) (2,233 meters)*

These passes are east-west connections south of the **Great Dolomite Road.** They're all Italian, from **Canazei** at the bottom of the **Pordoi** on the west, to **Pocol** on the east, just above **Cortina** on the **Falzarego.**

In the Sottaguda, the road takes up all the bottom of the gorge and the vertical walls block views of the sky.

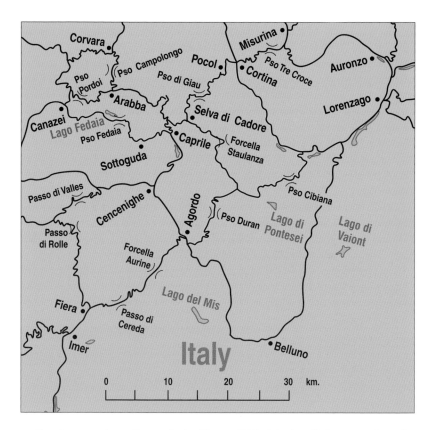

Starting east from Canazei, the **Passo di Fedaia** is off the normal tourist route. It climbs the flank of the **Marmolada,** the largest massif of the Dolomites and the site of some of the bloodiest fighting of World War I. There's a lake at the top of the **Fedaia** and a ristorante across the dam on the south side of the lake, with views of the massif.

At the tree line on the east side of the Fedaia, the old road descends through a narrow spectacular gorge, only one lane and one vehicle wide. Overhanging rocks obscure the sky. A new highway, built around the gorge, tunnels through the mountain and daylights onto a bridge that crosses the gorge at right angles, only to disappear back into a tunnel on the other side. The view from the bridge is good. The view in the tunnels isn't.

The gorge road is one way, from the bottom up. To get on it from the top, go through the tunnel, across the bridge (stopping to look over the edge) and down into the village, **Sottoguda.** It's a left turn, upstream on cobblestones back into the gorge. Coming up the pass to Sottoguda, go straight through town where the main road goes left. There are picnic tables along the road in the gorge and a small chapel from World War I. A very nice spot.

CHAPTER

14

The area is noted for hand wrought iron work. Some interesting, some weird creations are displayed on buildings in the valley.

Down east below the Sottoguda gorge is the village **Caprile.** There are two twisty roads from Caprile, back north to the figure eight loop. But go past them and through Caprile, and start climbing the wonders of **Passo di Giau,** following signs to **Selva di Cadore.** First comes a spectacular view area known as **Colle Santa Lucia** looking to Dolomite peaks and down over feathery forests and a blue lake. Just before Selva, the Passo di Giau road turns up. It's a motorcyclists dream: continuous curves on an alignment laid out in the 1980s. There are a couple of rifugios on Giau, including a handsome new one at the top, the **Cima Passo Giau.**

Going into Selva instead of turning up the Giau leads you to **Passo Forcella Staulanza** (1,773 meters) and either **Passo Duran** (1,601 meters) or **Passo di Cibiana** (1,530 meters). From either, main valley roads lead back to the figure eight. The east side of the Giau has some delightful picnic spots.

The Giau comes out on the Falzarego pass road just above Cortina at a small village called **Pocol.** Here is one of the most impressive World War I monuments and mausoleums in the Alps, and the best view of Cortina. Neither the monu-

The rifugio on Passo Giau is packed with wood carvings and stone details, and, on a pillar outside, an antique Falcone.

The top of Passo di Giau in the Dolomites has a new rifugio and gorgeous views with lots of examples from local wood carvers.

ment nor the view are visible from the road, and they are not well-marked. To find them, turn up a little driveway just below a big old hotel, usually closed. There's a little sign, SACRARIO. It's just a hundred meters up the drive to the monument entry gates. They may have an international DO NOT ENTER sign, but the keepers have usually let motorcyclists with respectful attitudes ride in. The monument itself is a church, with the stations of the cross set on each side of a stair cut through the mountain leading to it. The cut frames the monument against the Cortina valley.

The best view of Cortina is from a *Belvedere* (a terrace with a view) just a few meters past the gate to the monument.

CHAPTER
14

Trip 50　I Dare You; 17 Passes in One Day　★ ★

Distance　*About 400 kilometers*

Terrain　*Every kind of Dolomite pass road, all paved*

Highlights　*Each pass on this route is described elsewhere in shorter trips*

This is just a pass-bagging trip. No discussion of lunch or hotels or views. Probably there's nowhere but the **Dolomites** where seventeen passes can be ridden, bagged, in one long day. Most places, it's a major undertaking to cross seven passes in a day.

　　Here's the suggested route, starting at **Arabba** or **Corvara,** listing the passes in a sort of clockwise order, wasting as few kilometers as possible between one and the next. This circuit is all west of **Cortina.** If your day is long enough, you could bag more by adding passes east of Cortina.

The vertical massifs of the Dolomite range never fail to inspire. Dolomite pass roads play among feathery green forests, massive vertical peaks, and occasional flowering meadows.

1. Valparola
2. Falzarego
3. Giau
4. Staulanza
5. Duran
6. Aurine
7. Cereda
8. Rolle
9. Valle
10. San Pellegrino
11. Lavaze
12. Costalunga
13. Fedaia
14. Pordoi
15. Sella
16. Gardena
17. Campolongo

Trip 51 Southern Dolomites

Distance *About 130 kilometers from Arabba (add another 100 to San Baldo)*

Terrain *Paved mountain roads, some steep tight turns*

Highlights *Feathery forests, dramatic vertical mountains, little traffic, several rifugios. Includes: Passo Forcella Staulanza (1,773 meters), ★Passo Duran (1,601 meters), Passo Cibiana (1,530 meters), Passo di Valles (2,033 meters), Passo di San Pellegrino (1,918 meters), Passo di San Boldo (703 meters), Passo di Rolle (1,955 meters), Passo di Cereda (1,378 meters), Passo di Brocon (1,616 meters)*

A 15-kilometer jaunt south, down the valley south from **Caprile,** away from the figure eight, leads to **Cencenighe,** the gateway to **Passo di Valles** and **Passo di San Pellegrino.** Both go west.

Passo di Valles has a comfortable rifugio at the top with good lasagna. The western slope of Passo di Valles is velvety green. It looks like a park, and it is. Both passes descend deep into the **Valle di Fassa,** the west extension of the **Great Dolomite Road.**

Way down south is a pass of amazing audacity: Passo di San Boldo. Each end of each traverse is a hairpin in a tunnel! The tunnels are stacked five or six deep. Now they are controlled by traffic lights so that traffic enters them one-way at a time.

The westerly end of the Passo di Valles road is at a T intersection with the **Passo di Rolle** road. Head north at the T to go back to the Great Dolomite Road. Or head south, up and over Passo di Rolle to **Fiera,** where a northeast turn leads over **Passo di Cereda.** Passo di Cereda has two humps, the lower of which is called **Forcella Aurine.** From the north end of the Cereda, it's possible to head back to the figure eight through **Agordo** or to continue on over more passes. **Passo Duran** climbs up to 1,601 meters. From the north end of Duran, it's possible to head back toward the figure eight via the **Passo Forcella Staulanza,** or continue on in the direction of **Cortina** via the **Passo di Cibiana.** These passes offer Dolomite type views and usually have little traffic.

To explore farther or to head toward **Trento,** go south five kilometers from Fiera on the Passo di Rolle road to **Imer.** At Imer, take a road up and west to **Passo di Brocon,** where a rifugio awaits you at the top.

These passes mark the southern edge of the Dolomites. There are some good twisties farther south, and one more pass worth a detour because of the audacity of its construction. Called **Passo di San Boldo,** it crosses a ridge at only 706 meters, not high enough to note otherwise. It's about 15 kilometers southwest of **Belluno,** one of the major cities south of Cortina, and was the high water mark of

A view point near Selva di Cadore on the Passo Staulanza road affords spectacular vistas to the west of the road up Passo Fedaia toward the Marmolada, all highlighted here by sun and cloud shadow. The town immediately below is Caprile. Other roads to the right snake up the mountains toward the Passo Falzarego Pass.

This Triumph rider from New York met the "King of the Alps" atop Passo Falzarego. He found the pass using *Motorcycle Journeys Through the Alps & Corsica.*

the Austrian advance during World War I. The Austrians got down over the ridge in one place, but there was no supply road. So they had to build one. This road is carved out of the cliff face back and forth. But there was no room for a hairpin at the end of each traverse. So the road goes into the mountain in a tunnel, makes a hairpin, and comes out going the other direction. Then it does the same thing in reverse. The hairpin tunnels are stacked five or six deep, one on top of the other, at each end. The tunnels have recently been lighted and equipped with traffic signals.

Once, pulling into **Pocol** at the east end of **Passo di Giau,** a rider at the side of the road was studying a map. He was on a Munch, that massive, in-line, four-cylinder machine made in Germany before the Japanese made such a layout their own. "Hey, wait while I get a picture of you and the bike." "Sure, but if you wait a minute there will be a hundred Munchs." And there were.

CHAPTER
14

Trip 52   Adige Canyon

Distance *From Arabba via Wurz Joch, about 60 kilometers to Brixen; via Passo Nigra, about 60 kilometers to Bozen; via Passo di Lavaze and Passo Manghen, about 140 kilometers to Trento*

Terrain *Often narrow, occasionally challenging pass roads. Wurz Joch and Passo Manghen have practically no traffic*

Highlights *A sense of exploring on traffic-free routes to the Brennero Autostrada; ★ Wurz Joch (2,002 meters) and ★Passo Manghen (2,047 meters) have attractive rifugios. Includes: the Brenner Pass, the canyon of the Adige River, Passo di Costalunga (Karer Pass) (1,745 meters), Passo Nigra (Niger Pass) (1,688 meters), Passo di Lavaze (1,805 meters), Monte Bondone (1,537 meters), Passo di Pinei (Panider Sattel) (1,437 meters), Passo Redebus (1,449 meters)*

On the great Dolomite passes, even the bottoms of the passes are high. **Cortina** at the east end is over 1,200 meters, and **Canazei** at the west end is over 1400, so there's still a lot of mountain riding to get to the bottom of things. The great divide, the canyon of the **Adige River,** home to the Brennero Autostrada, is close to bottom at about 250 meters.

Much of the west end of the **Great Dolomite Road** has been realigned using tunnels. After a final descent through orchards and vineyards on a road shared with trucks and buses and bicycles and pedestrians, it finally gets down to the Adige River canyon and the autostrada at Ora.

Many alternate roads go up over mountain passes on the way to the Adige, and all of them finally find a tributary gorge to follow down. Better to take one of the up and over and down routes than the Great Dolomite Road.

The most beautiful and most fun motorcycle road between the Great Dolomites and the Adige Canyon is the **Wurz Joch,** known in Italian as Passo di Erbe. Find it downstream (north) from **Corvara,** about 15 kilometers north of **La Villa** and the figure eight. The sign points west to a village across the valley called **St. Martin,** but there should be a brown sign for Wurz Joch (Passo di Erbe). Above St. Martin, the pass road goes right around a private little castle. (There's another village called St. Martin down the valley north, near Brunico, Bruneck in German. It also has a castle, but it's the wrong St. Martin.)

The pass reaches the Brennero Autostrada in three humps. Wurz Joch is the highest. The road is good as far as the top of the Wurz Joch, where there's an attractive rifugio called **Utia de Borz.** The deck is a great place to contemplate a first or last view of the Dolomites. West from there, the road is one lane through woods and meadows. Hardly anybody there. When the road splits, follow signs to **St. Andra.** The other road gets to the Brennero Canyon via St. Peter (Trip 43).

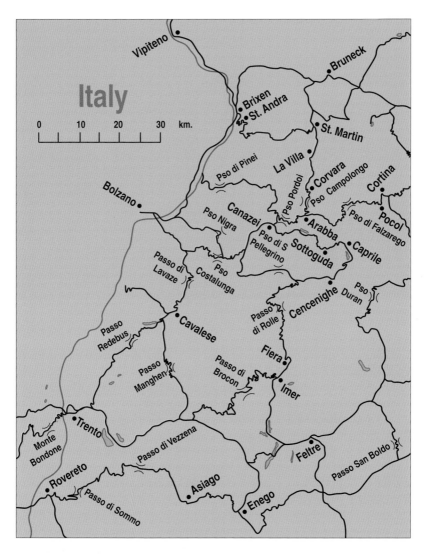

Before St. Andra are several attractive hotels. One with Dolomite views is the **Edith.** From St. Andra on into **Millan** and **Brixen** (Bressanone), the road sports two lanes.

Brixen is a handsome city with shaded streets, squares, motorcycle shops, and a famous restaurant called **Elefant.** Seems some eastern potentate of the Middle Ages was shipping a prize elephant to the German emperor across the Brenner Pass. The elephant expired in Brixen. The restaurant named after the unfortunate beast is attractive and has many dining rooms, all different and interesting, some with balconies. The menu is huge, eating there an adventure.

Every Dolomite Pass road has a rifugio at the top.

Going east toward the Dolomites from Brixen, the Wurz Joch is not marked. Follow signs to Millan, a neighboring village, and then to St. Andra. From St. Andra the one-lane road seemingly going downhill is the Wurz Joch road.

Another major access route into the Dolomites from the Brennero Autostrada is the **Val Gardena.** Unlike the Wurz Joch, the Val Gardena route is well marked from the autostrada. It leads through a popular resort area known to the Germanics as **St. Ulrich,** and to the Italians as Ortisei. The area is full of hotels. The Val Gardena road ties into the figure eight trip between the Passo di Sella and the Passo di Gardena. A variation is the **Passo di Pinei** (Panider Sattel) south from Ortisei in the Val Gardena.

About 11 kilometers west of Canazei is the turnoff to the north for the **Passo di Costalunga** road. Then, just past the top of the Costalunga, the **Passo Nigra** goes up again, north and west. Both continue down to the Adige Canyon at **Bozen** (Bolzano) on the Brennero Autostrada. The Costalunga (Karer in German) goes down by a small lake, the **Karer See,** that's famous for its special colors. It's easy to find the lake because of the tour buses. Bozen has all services expected of a major city, including traffic. It's home to Iveco trucks and buses (Trip 43.)

Finding the Costalunga and/or the Passo Nigra from the bottom at Bolzano requires careful attention. Both take off just north of the city from the old highway that parallels the Brennero Autostrada. There's no connection or marking from the autostrada. The signs are easy to miss among the traffic and commercial activity of the highway, even though the highway seems to be hugging the edge of high cliffs. It's worth the effort, though, because either of two roads will provide both instant relief from the congestion and some fun riding. The crowds will not be going this way.

Passo di Lavaze is a north-south mountain connection roughly parallel to and east of the Brenner Pass. It starts up and south from the Passo di Costalunga road at a country intersection downstream from the village of **Nova Levante** (labeled Welschnofen in German). Signs point to Nova Ponente (Deutschnofen). At the top of Passo di Lavaze, an unpaved pass called **Passo di Occlini** (Grimm Joch) goes westerly. Lavaze is anchored on the south by the town **Cavalese** on the Great Dolomite Road. (Cavalese is the town where an American jet accidentally cut a cable car wire). Just cross the Great Dolomite Road for further north-south mountain connections. Go down into the valley below Cavalese through a village called **Molina** where the road forks. Straight ahead skirts a lake to **Brusago** where brown signs point to **Passo di Redebus** then down to the main highway toward Trento.

But the best road from the fork at Molina follows the brown sign to **Passo Manghen** up a finger canyon. It's about 20 kilometers through forested hairpins to the top. Most experienced Dolomite hands don't know of Passo Manghen, even though it is great riding: one lane wide with two-way traffic. The top is just above the tree line. Near the top is a little rifugio, and on the south slopes there's a rustic but attractive rifugio called **Bar Trattoria Molga-Voltrighetta,** and farther south, one just above the road called **Ristorante Malga Baessa.** The south end of the Manghen is in a village called **Telve** where several routes lead to the main valley road and on west to **Trento** (Trent in German and English). Trento is a major city of historic note in the Adige Canyon and on the Brennero Autostrada. Coming the other way, from Trento, the Manghen is signed through several twists and turns off the main road, which is sort of a freeway, into the town Borgo, and then to Telve where a sharp uphill right turn starts you on the pass road.

Maps show **Passo Cinque Croci** just east of the Manghen. It's not open to the public. Just a bit farther east is the south end of **Passo Bracon** (Trip 51).

The main valley road to Trento goes west into a tight gorge with tunnels and then traverses down and around Trento without ever going into it, crossing the Brennero Autostrada and the Adige River and the railroad tracks. Finally, there are signs for **Riva del Garda** that seem to be pointing in the wrong direction, but work. (In order to make the Riva exit, you have to go around more than 360 degrees.) The signed route to Riva climbs a new road west out of the Adige Canyon. Go all the way west to Ponte Arche and then south for Riva.

Or, just a few kilometers up west of Trento, an exciting road into Riva turns sharply uphill, signed **Monte Bondone.** With too many hairpins to count, it climbs to over 1,500 meters, passes **Hotel Montana** (see hotel listings at the beginning of the chapter on Riva and Lago di Garda), and then swoops and sweeps down to Riva.

Trip 53 Monte Grappa

Distance *180 kilometers from San Boldo to the Brennero Autostrada at Rovereto, gateway to Lago di Garda*

Terrain *All kinds of rural road, some very remote, some rough, some twisted, and some banked like a race track*

Highlights *From the tunnels of San Boldo to a spumante center, to the top of Monte Grappa (1,775 meters), Passo di Vezzena (1,402 meters), Passo di Sommo (1,343 meters).*

Narrow **Passo Duran** (Trip 51) comes down in an Alpine Valley at **Agordo,** and downstream from Agordo is **Passo San Boldo.**

After the hairpin tunnels of Passo San Boldo, head southwesterly along pleasant rural roads to **Valdobbiadene,** a town famous for its spumante (champagne) which can be sipped in the town's pleasant plaza. Then cross westerly over the Piave river to the town, **Alano,** and follow signs for **Monte Grappa,** but maybe not as many signs as needed. The road becomes very narrow at points as it climbs into several valleys, some of which are lovely. Further up, it barely hangs on the edge of a cliff before becoming a sweeping smooth road to the sum-

Not a pass, but a mountain top, Monte Grappa has several fun roads to its peak. This one comes up from the east.

mit of Monte Grappa, where there are some military installations, and a parking lot offering views to the east and north. The road down to the south is fine, well defined and banked. Before getting into the traffic of Bassano, turn west to the main, mostly four lane valley highway and head north in the direction of Trento for about twenty kilometers, exiting up and over into Enego. This is the same road to Trento that's at the south end of Passo Manghen (Trip 52) and Passo di Bracon (Trip 51).

From Enego, the road to Asiago climbs steeply, through switchbacks and hairpins, then sweeps 30 kilometers through pleasant high valleys and towns to Asiago where a good quality road swoops and switchbacks down to an autostrada. But the mountain way is northwest over **Passo di Vezzena.** At Lavaronne, it connects with a road west over **Passo di Sommo** to Folgaria, then down past a fine castle, **Castel Pietra,** to the Brennero Autostrada near Rovereto.

Trip 54 Cortina

Distance *About 40 kilometers to Drei Zinnen; about 120 over Kreuzberg and back*

Terrain *Irregular sweeping mountain pass roads*

Highlights *Mind-boggling views from Drei Zinnen (2,320 meters) (toll); forests, vertical massifs, restaurants and hotels. The trip includes: Passo Tre Croce (1,805 meters), ★ Misurina and Drei Zinnen (Tre Cime di Lavaredo) (2,320 meters), Passo del Zovo (1,476 meters), Passo di Monte Croce (Kreuzberg Pass) (1,636 meters), Furkel Sattel (1,759 meters), Passo Cimabanche (1,529 meters)*

Like many European cities, **Cortina** has a one-way loop street system. Some of the core inside the loop is pedestrian zone. If you miss a stop or turn, the only solution is to go around again. Cortina's loop isn't round—there are some switchbacks and some hairpins—but by the third or fourth circuit, it becomes familiar. In the course of circling Cortina, you'll see brown signs pointing the way to the

This best of all views of Cortina is from the Passo Falzarego.

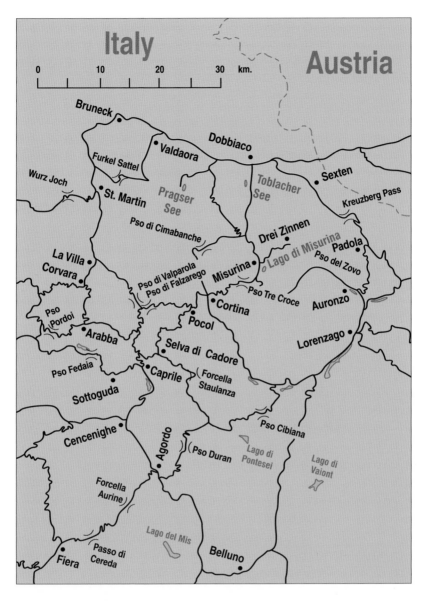

Passo di Falzarego and to **Passo Tre Croce.** Both start climbing right in the village, the Falzarego westerly, and the Tre Croce easterly.

The Tre Croce is pleasant enough. The prize is **Lake Misurina** just east of the pass. Its exquisite blue reflects the surrounding Dolomite massifs. There is a bit of entrepreneurial clutter. On the north side of Lake Misurina, still just minutes out of Cortina, there's a sunny view restaurant with tables on the lakeside, and a little road marked *Drei Zinnen* and/or *Tre Cime* takes off to the east. It's a dead-end, private toll road that climbs up several hundred meters in a seies of hairpins and sweepers that reveal dramatic views of Dolomite crags, the very best view of the Dolomites possible with wheels still on the ground. The cameras will be out. Traffic is encouraged to park below the rifugio at the top, but bikes should ride right on up. There's room to park.

Seven kilometers north of Misurina, it's possible to turn west over **Passo Cimabanche** back to Cortina. North, it's all downhill to **Dobbiaco** (Toblach) and the main roads into Austria, unless you'd like to check out another jewel lake set amidst towering Dolomite peaks, **Pragser Wildsee** (Lago di Braies in Italian). It's up a dead end road that can be found about seven kilometers west of Dobbiaco. Turn south, under the railroad tracks, and climb the west fork. At the end of the road, there's an old time hotel by the lake. (The east fork climbs higher to a rifugio. No lake.)

The roads east of Misurina are not Dolomite dramatic. At **Auronzo** it's possible to go back behind the big domed church and get out of the valley traffic on the **Passo del Zovo.** It heads north and connects with the **Kreuzberg Pass** in the direction of Austria.

The Kreuzberg Pass (Passo di Monte Croce in Italian) has nice hotels and good views of the Dolomites. **Hotel Kreuzberg Pass** has many facilities including an indoor pool. The turn off for the Kreuzberg from Austria is at **Sexten** (Sesto in Italian).

A one-way loop road on the north side of Lago di Misurina has the restaurant with the best views. The best seats are out over the lake, under the umbrellas.

Bikes usually fill the parking lot at the rifugio atop Drei Zinnen. The view is down the valley toward Auronzo and Lago di Santa Caterina.

An audacious piece of road that seems without purpose except that it exists can be found east of Auronzo and San Stefano heading south from Campolongo. It's a rough gravel trail up a canyon. Alas, about eight kilometers up, it turns to marvelously engineered asphalt so tightly lapping its hairpins that it looks like a piece of ribbon candy. Turn after tight turn scales the mountain, to end in more rock trail.

North of Corvara, a little-known pass called **Furkel Sattel** cuts across some pleasant mountains. Its chief interest is that it cuts out a bunch of congested valley traffic and makes a direct connection with **Staller Sattel,** one of the best ways into or out of Austria. From the road north of Corvara, five kilometers downstream from the turnoff to the Wurz Joch at St. Martin, is the village **Longega,** squeezed in the gorge. That's where the Furkel Sattel road heads up a finger valley. Then at St. Viglio, the pass road goes north. The road straight ahead through St. Viglio dead-ends, but the Furkel Sattel passes some minor ski resorts and some lovely vistas over Tiroler countryside, then comes out on the north at the village **Valdaora** (Olang in German) on the main road into Austria, and at the south end of the Staller Sattel (for another way to use the Furkel and Staller Sattels, see Trips 43, 55, and 64).

Trip 55 Austrian Connections ★

Distance *About 70 kilometers from Cortina to Austria at Staller Sattel; about 150 kilometers to Austria at Plocken Pass; about 175 to Austria at Nassfeld Pass*

Terrain *Exciting climbs by forests and lakes*

Highlights *Green lake, one-lane road on ★ Staller Sattel (2,052 meters); populated valley roads wind to Plocken and Nassfeld Pass (1,557 meters). Interesting switchbacks on Plocken Pass (1,362 meters), Sella Ciampigotto (1,790 meters), Forcella di Lavardet (1,542 meters), Sella di Razza (1,760 meters), Passo Zovello (963 meters), Passo della Mauria (1,298 meters), Passo del Pura (1,425 meters), Passo Carson di Lanza (1,552 meters), Forcella di Luis (1,010 meters), Sella de Cereschiatis (1,066 meters), Cima di Sappada (1,286 meters).*

North of **Cortina** and about ten kilometers east of **Brunico** (Bruneck) at **Valdaora** (Olang), the **Staller Sattel** takes off toward Austria. The intersection is right beside a lumber yard. The pass road winds through lovely Tiroler fields, past a glacier blue-green lake, and climbs to the pass in a fun-and-games, one-way road through the forest. The one-way part is controlled, so there's 15 minutes for up traffic and 15 for down, with 15 minutes to clear each way. So there's only 15 minutes an hour to start up or down.

About 75 kilometers east of Misurina, through moderately interesting countryside and the town of **Cima di Sappada,** the **Plocken Pass** makes a dramatic climb into Austria. The Plocken Pass (Passo di Monte Croce Carnico) isn't high, but the switchbacks are dramatic. It's a good gateway to the south end of the **Grossglockner** via the **Gailberg Sattel** (see Trip 64). Another 30 kilometers farther east, the **Nassfeld Pass** road climbs quickly into Austria from the autostrada at **Pontebba** (see Trip 71).

There's an interesting, occasionally rough little road parallel to the east-west road through Sappada, and just south of it, known as **Forcella di Lavardet.** There are two ways to it, starting in the main valley just downstream from **Auronzo.** (Auronzo has to be one of the longest villages in the Alps. It goes on and on.) The main route goes by the village **Larenzago,** made famous by the visits of Pope John Paul II. The turnoff is marked "Casera Razzo." (Casera is an Italian army installation). The road climbs ruggedly over a pass called **Sella Ciampigotto,** wends past the usually unoccupied military base at **Sella Razzo,** then goes over the **Forcella di Lavardet.** (At this point it meets the other connection.) It's good pavement with lots of markers on down east through forests to **Comeglians.** From there, a road east crosses a low pass (Passo Zovello, 963 meters) to Sutrio, where the Plocken Pass road heads north into Austria.

The other connection from the area of Auronzo is through **St. Stefano.** At Campolongo this connection heads south, up a rocky valley. Parts are not paved.

Then, wonder of wonders, it climbs the mountain side in a stacked series of perfectly matched and paved hairpins, looking something like that hard ribbon Christmas candy. Then it joins the Lavardet road.

The more traveled commercial route would go on east from Larenzago crossing **Passo di Mauria** in about 12 kilometers. On toward Tolmezzo this route passes a loop about 25 kilometers long over **Passo del Pura**. The loop road is north of the main road. A connection shown on some maps between the loop and the Forcella di Lavardet is closed.

Ready to climb the switchbacks of the Plocken Pass into Austria? (Or maybe you've just crossed the Plocken from Austria.) Here's a little exploring to do first. Just south of the Plocken, turn into Paluzza and climb over the **Forcella di Luis** to Paularo, and then head north on the little forest road over **Passo Carson di Lanza.** There's a rifugio atop Carson di Lanza. East of the rifugio there has been some problem with the road slipping down the mountain. If the road's closed, head back south from Paularo, and loop east of Tolmezzo to Moggio where a remote little road climbs north over **Sella di Cereschiatis,** to daylight at Pontebba right where the Carson de Lanza would have taken you, ready to turn up the **Nassfeld Pass** into Austria.

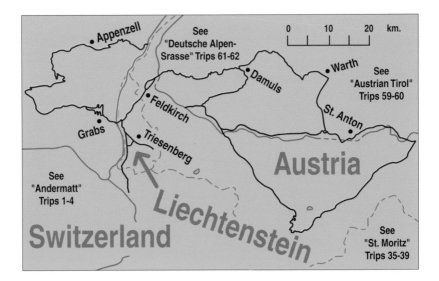

Liechtenstein

Liechtenstein is that little, rich country where the prince lives in the castle on the hill and every once in a while they have a skier in the Olympics. About 30 kilometers long and 15 wide, it's sort of in the Alps, using Swiss money, German language, but its own stamps. Switzerland is to the south and west; Austria is to the north and east. The Rhein, flowing north now, marks much of the boundary with Switzerland. This is downstream from the Vorderrhein and the Hinterrhein and the Via Mala and Chur (see Trips 35, 36, 37). Just across the Rhein is the Swiss Autobahn. You can get anywhere from Liechtenstein.

Vaduz, the capital, and several other villages in Liechtenstein are pleased to accommodate motorcyclists as well as sell stamps.

From the castle-topped village in the south called **Balzers,** an interesting road runs through the woods, over a little pass, and through a stone military gate into Switzerland and the cute Swiss village called Maienfeld, leading to Landquart and Wolfgang Pass (see Trip 37).

In the middle of the country, starting at Vaduz or the village of **Triesen,** a Liechtenstein mountain road climbs to the villages of **Triesenberg** and **Malbun.** Triesenberg hangs high on the mountainside and has gorgeous views of the valley of the Rhein and Schwagalp. Malbun, on through a tunnel from Triesenberg, is in a high ski bowl at about 1,600 meters.

The secret way up to Triesenberg and Malbun is the narrow, cliff-hanging, one-way (up only) road that starts at the prince's castle.

At Triesenberg a good hotel is the **Martha Buhler** (named after the skier). Farther up is **Rizlina Berg Gasthaus,** hung on the edge of the mountain. One of many hotels in Malbun is the **Montana. Hotel Landgasthof Schatzman** is on the main road in Triesen.

About that (FL)? Furst is a German word for prince. So the Principality of Liechtenstein becomes Furstentum Liechtenstein.

Across the Rhein, right on the main drag in **Buchs,** Switzerland, is a Honda dealer, **Stricker Motos,** that has been very helpful to foreign bikers.

Trip 56 Liechtenstein

Distance *About 60 kilometers explores the whole country*

Terrain *A few narrow, one-way roads, some sweeping climbs, a slippery tunnel*

Highlights *Good views of the Rhein Valley, castles, hotels, restaurants*

THE main road in Liechtenstein, almost all of it but two lanes wide, runs south in the **Rhein Valley** from **Feldkirch** in Austria to Switzerland. There is a border crossing check at Austria as it's in the European Union and Liechtenstein, along with Switzerland, is not. No guards or stops between Liechtenstein and Switzerland. The gas stations just inside Liechtenstein sell Swiss Autobahn vignettes, and Swiss police have been noted checking for them on the on-ramps just across the Rhein. It's best to mind the posted limits as well as the automatic limit of 50 kilometers per hour in villages. Fines are high and payable on the spot. (One story quotes a Liechtenstein policeman, "Your passport please." Pocketing the passport, he said, "That'll be 100 Francs. If you don't have it, go get it.") There is one brief spot where the posted speed limit is up to 80 kilometers per hour (about 48 mph).

In the north, Liechtenstein is mostly flat valley farm land. About 14 kilometers south of the Austrian border, just south of the village, **Schaan,** there's a sign

According to the sign, the old walls of Colmar built by Louis XIV contain a "WC," a toilet. The sign must be more recent than the walls. Presumably "WC" stands for "water closet," and just how this strictly English term became the international clue is hard to imagine.

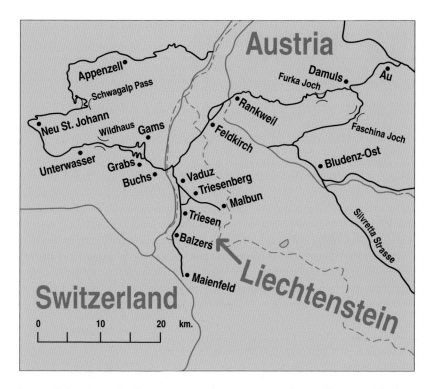

for the Prince's castle, Schloss, indicating a turn up and east. You can ride right by the front gate of the castle. Continuing on, the road becomes narrow, one-way, climbing up through forests to the village, **Triesenberg,** where it joins the main road from the valley. Hanging on the mountain with vistas westerly over the Rhein to Alps in Switzerland, the road climbs up to an abrupt ninety degree turn into a narrow tunnel through the mountain. The tunnel daylights on the east in a high Alpine valley. Then the road sweeps on up to about 1,600 meters at the village called **Malbun,** where the road ends amid a cluster of hotels and shops and ski lifts.

Coming down, watch the slick pavement in the tunnel and the sharp ninety degree right turn at it's west end. Straight ahead is an Armco barrier, and beyond the barrier is a long straight drop down.

Sweep back down through Triesenberg on down to the main valley road at Triesen. **Vaduz** (say fah DUTZ), the small capital village, is back north a few kilometers. **Balzers** with its castled peak, and Switzerland are south.

There is a stone arch gate at the Swiss border amid concrete hulks that were placed there to deter tanks, standing in a field.

Just westerly from all this a few kilometers is the Rhein River, the border with Switzerland, and immediately across the river is the Swiss Autobahn, with on-ramps located near each of the several river bridges.

CHAPTER
15

Trip 57 Santis and Schwagalp

Distance About 100 kilometers round trip from Liechtenstein

Terrain Gently climbing and sweeping mountain roads

Highlights Less-traveled Switzerland, Schwagalp Pass (1,278 meters), Wildhaus (1,090 meters)

A loop climbs through the lower Swiss Alps just across the Rhein from Liechtenstein into the remote little canton of **Appenzell.** Appenzell has been most famous recently for its method of voting in public meetings, from which voting, women have historically been excluded. Still, it's sort of romantically quaint, with buildings and people that look the way Swiss buildings and people should.

Across the Rhein from Liechtenstein, past the sizable Swiss town of **Buchs,** at the village of **Gams,** a road climbs west across the south side of **Santis** mountain. This road with little traffic crosses a minor pass of about 1,000 meters at **Wildhaus,** and comes in about 25 kilometers to the village **Neu St. Johann.**

Most motorcyclists stop for coffee or cappuccino at the rifugios atop each pass in the Alps.

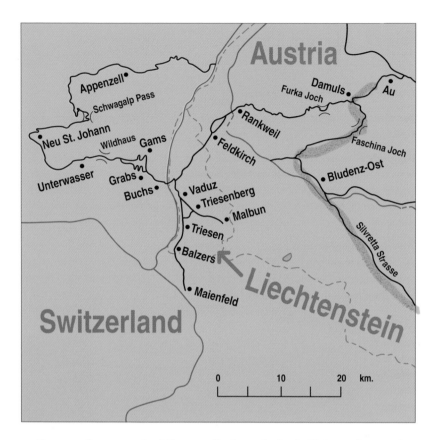

For more fun, go south of Gams to **Grabs** and take the little one lane road to Grabser Berg and on to Wildhaus. Then at Wildhaus, take the little road south to Schwendi, where there's the **Alpenrose Hotel.** The road wanders across the mountain, finally rejoining the main road at **Unterwasser,** right at the fine **Hotel Santis.**

From **Neu St. Johann,** a mountain road heads east toward Appenzell over **Schwagalp Pass.** This is no Furka nor Susten Pass, but a forest and meadow road, with some imposing granite peaks around. At the top of the pass, a turnoff leads to the base station of a cable car that goes up the mountain, Santis. For some reason, the parking lot and restaurant at the cable car is a *Tofftreffpunkt.* The road goes on down to Urnasch, then to the town of **Appenzell,** where a small road heads back over a mountain toward the Rhein Valley at Oberriet.

Trip 58 Western Austria

Distance *About 260 kilometers*

Terrain *Some sweeping, some twisting climbs and descents; narrow road on Furka Joch*

Highlights *Lovely farms, forests, glacier views at ★ Silvretta (2,036 meters), hotels, restaurants, ski resorts. Includes: Arlberg Pass (1,793 meters), Flexen Pass (1,773 meters), Hochtannberg Pass (1,679 meters), Faschina Joch (1,487 meters), Furka Joch (1,761 meters) (Vignettes, stickers, are required to drive on Austrian Autobahns. They can be purchased at most gas station and borders)*

Austria knows how to take care of tourists. Practically every corner has an attractive Gasthaus or hotel, with "Zimmer freis" in between. *Zimmer frei* means "room available," and is the Germanic equivalent of "bed and breakfast." Invariably, they're good and reasonably priced.

Austrian restaurants and hotels often fly this flag, *Motorradfahrer Willkommen,* "Motorcyclists Welcome." This one is at a hotel restaurant atop Silveretta Strasse, also known as Bieler Hohe.

The most western state of Austria, called **Vorarlberg,** and its capital, **Feldkirch,** are right at Liechtenstein, but separated by high Alps from the rest of the country. So it takes some pretty good pass roads to tie Austria together. Since most Alpine pass roads run north-south, these Austrian roads going mostly east-west can be entertaining as well as useful.

The main one is the **Arlberg Pass,** now with an Autobahn and a tunnel to take the trucks and buses off the good mountain road. It starts at **Feldkirch,** which is really on the north border of Liechtenstein. Might as well take the Autobahn from Feldkirch as far as **Bludenz-Ost.** (Don't confuse Bludenz on the Arlberg road with Bregenz, north of Feldkirch on the Boden See, site of popular summer music festivals.)

At Bludenz-Ost, one of the best roads in Austria heads south. Called the **Silvretta Strasse,** it roughly parallels the Arlberg, but takes a rollicking time getting there, so it has only enthusiasts on it. And, welcome to Austria, there's a toll. Austria has a lot of toll roads.

After a short run up a valley past sturdy Austrian farm houses and neatly manicured pastures, and 50 kilometer speed limits seriously enforced, the road has an exciting steep climb with switchbacks and hairpins and views of the same, up to a lake. This is a *Stau See,* a good German word meaning a lake created by a dam. Then there's more climb to a higher lake and the pass, **Bieler Hohe,** where there's a delightful restaurant terrace with views over the lake reflecting snowy peaks.

A refreshing non-alcoholic drink available nowhere but Austria and Bayern (Bavaria) is Spezi (spait zee). It's an orange flavored cola. A big one, a *grosse Spezi,* usually comes in a half-liter beer glass.

From the top, the pass road works down eastward through a valley, pleasant enough in the summer, but the site of deadly avalanches in recent winters. About six kilometers down, there's a side road that climbs up north to another Stau See with a restaurant. On down east, the valley road connects again with the Arlberg road. Just before the junction, there's a good view of a castle and an often photographed high bridge called **Trisannabrucke** that carries the railroad up the Arlberg.

Heading west, back up the Arlberg from the junction, the old road is a good climb that also avoids the toll tunnel under the pass. Watch for the beautiful Austrian farm houses showing considerable pride of ownership. With elaborate corner bay windows, deep arched doors, balconies, and wide, overhanging roofs, they are often decorated with pictures and maybe poems or historical names in Gothic script. Contemporary ones are of block construction with light beige stucco and dark brown trim. The gable end almost always faces the road. On a pole over the front gable end is a lantern-like bell tower. Some of the lanterns are pretty ornate.

The old road up the pass is okay because the traffic is taking the Autobahn tunnel. Along it are a bunch of saintly towns: St. Jakob, St. Anton, St. Christoph, all of them labeled *am Arlberg* to distinguish them from saintly towns of the same name scattered all over Austria.

Just west of its summit, the Arlberg intersects the **Flexen Pass.** The Flexen heads north in a series of fairly tight sweeps covered by wooden snow sheds hung on the mountain. Just over its top are the famous ski resorts of **Zurs** and **Lech,** in the valley of the Lech river (Lech Tal) and the Austrian state of Tirol. Both towns have noteworthy buildings decorated with pictures of saints and local heroes, or maybe the building's first owner. The **Hotel Post** in Lech is particularly nice. (Every town in the Alps has a Hotel Post.) Lech has attractive outdoor restaurant facilities. If tablecloths and umbrellas are out, the place is in operation.

Seven kilometers below Lech, at **Warth,** there's an intersection where the **Hochtannberg Pass** heads northwest. East is the Lech Tal and roads described in Trip 60. Just west of the intersection on the **Hochtannberg** road is **Hotel Warther Hof:** large, handsome, and well known to Edelweiss Tour folk. Its brochures show bikes and bikers.

It's about 23 kilometers westerly over the Hochtannberg to the village of **Au,** where the **Furka Joch** road heads back to **Rankweil** and **Feldkirch.** (This is Furka *Joch*. Furka *Pass* is at Andermatt, Switzerland, and Furkel Sattel is in the Dolomites.) Above Au, at a village called **Damuls,** a new road heads back to Feldkirch over the pass **Faschina Joch,** 1,487 meters. It's completely roofed with grass growing on top. From above, it looks like a long line of windows.

The **Furka Joch,** a remote, nobody-takes-it-on-purpose road, goes through Damuls.

Atop Kuhtai, this interestingly decorated restaurant advertises itself as a "Bikers Stop."

Damuls has a couple of nice hotels. One, **Hotel Adler,** in a crook of the Furka Joch road, has a good baker as well as a cook. The hotel dates from before Columbus, but has every modern convenience.

Above Damuls, the Furka has some one lane parts. Just east of the summit is a restaurant with a sweeping mountain view, **Jagerstuble,** advertising good "burger" food—not ham-burger food, as well as deer specialties.

Heading the other way, looking for the Furka Joch and Damuls roads from Fieldkirch, follow signs first to Rankweil. Here's the best, and almost secret way.

In downtown Feldkirch, just east of the tunnel that takes the main road around the old town is a plaza, platz, with motorcycle parking yet. On the edge of the platz, right where the cobblestoned street is marked for pedestrians only, there's a sign for **GOFIS.** It points up a steep cobbled road. Take it. In a minute you're high above Feldkirch, in fields crossing over everything, including the Autobahn, all down in tunnels below. Gofis is a village on the mountain. From it, more signs point to Rankweil, gateway to the Furka Joch.

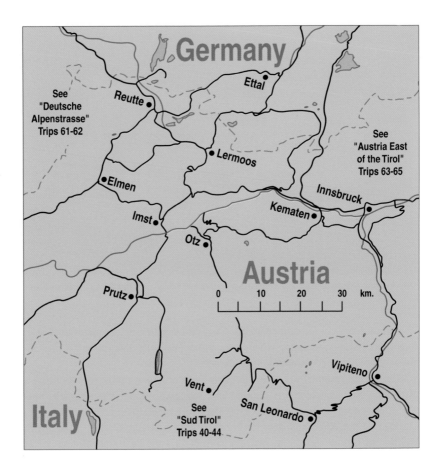

Austrian Tirol

Innsbruck is the historic capital of the Tirol, site of Olympics, and a good-sized city that's no fun to drive in or through. Strategically located where the Brenner Pass to Italy reaches the **Inn Tal** (valley), it's hard to miss. The Autobahn in the Inn Tal goes by Innsbruck hung on the edge of the mountains. It's free and it's the recommended route around Innsbruck. Innsbruck looks nice from the Autobahn. The Brenner Autobahn from Italy makes a T with the one in the Inn Tal at Innsbruck, but it's a toll road.

The Inn River comes down from St. Moritz in Switzerland (see Trips 35–39) and heads easterly through Innsbruck, where there is indeed a *brucke,* a bridge, and finally north to Germany where it flows into what we call the Danube (in German, it's Donau). The Autobahn follows the Inn around to Germany, so while Munchen lies straight north of Innsbruck, the Autobahn connection loops around to the east. The Autobahn remains the fastest way to get to Munchen.

To add to the general geographic confusion, the only Autobahn route from the Tirol in Austria to Salzburg and Wien (Vienna), both also in Austria, goes into and through Germany.

For tourist information about Innsbruck and the immediate area, contact the Tourist Office; A-6021 Innsbruck; Austria; T 051 259-850; F 051 259-8507.

Imst is a town about 70 kilometers west of Innsbruck in the Inn Tal, where several good pass roads come together. The area is packed with elaborate hotels, comfortable in every aspect, including price. A good hotel in Imst is **Hotel Linserhof.** It's several kilometers above Imst on the **Hahntenn Joch** road, well signed, but way back from the road. It has lovely views.

In the tiny village of **Berwang** has a large hotel with all kinds of services, the **Kaiserhof.**

A beautiful hotel with a spectacular view, the **Ferienschlossl,** hangs above the Inn Tal, about 35 kilometers west of Innsbruck at Haimingerberg, on the Haiming Joch road (Trip 59).

Or check the hotels listed in Trip 58 at Damuls and Warth, or the ones listed on Trip 59 along the Timmels Joch road.

Trip 59 Innsbruck Passes

Distance Via Brenner Pass, about 30 kilometers to Italy; via Timmels Joch, about 100 kilometers to Italy; via Reschen Pass, about 100 kilometers to Italy; about 100 kilometers via Piller Hohe up Kauner Tal

Terrain Brenner: low pass, major Autobahn; Timmels Joch: long, sweeping valley to high exotic pass; Reschen: long valley run, low pass; Kauner Tal: steep mountain climb

Highlights Brenner Pass (1,374 meters) quick route to Italy (toll), fantastic bridges; Timmels Joch (2,509 meters): nice valley villages, sweeping climb to high mountains (toll); Piller Hohe (1,558 meters), Kauner Tal (2,750 meters), Reschen Pass (1,504 meters) (no toll) leads to Passo dello Stelvio

It's a short, quick run, less than 50 kilometers, over the Brenner Pass from Innsbruck to the area of the Italian passes around Merano (see Trips 40–44) and the Dolomites (Trips 48–55). That's the Brenner's chief merit. But it's so low and so congested that it hardly deserves other comment.

There is a *Bundesstrasse,* a non-freeway, non-toll, federal road, across the Brenner alongside the Autobahn. It has usually been the choice for motorcyclists. From it, the gigantic structures of the Autobahn, including the famous **Europabrucke bridge,** look awesome. But the road goes through a picturesque town called **Matrei am Brenner** with one narrow street that has tried to outlaw motorcycles. Various courts are hearing appeals of the arbitrary decision. The only way around Matrei is the toll Autobahn. So far, motorcycles are legal.

Investing a little time, many motorcyclists avoid the Autobahn by using mountain roads south of Innsbruck: not spectacular, but not a freeway either. From Hall in Tirol, about 15 kilometers east of Innsbruck, the route crosses the mountain to Matrei on the Brenner. Exit at Hall, cross under the Autobahn, and climb up through Sistrans and on south to Matrei.

Approaching the Innsbruck area fromt the west, like from Kuhtai or Garmish, follow the signs to Axams, then to Mutters and on to the Brenner Autobahn. The same route can be used eastbound on the Autobahn. Just take the Zirl exit (Ausfahrt). Heading west from the Brenner, exit Innsbruck Sud and follow the signs for Mutters or Natters.

The Ice Man

In those glaciers, along the Italian border, is where the Similaun ice man was found. The family at Vent's Hotel Post has been seen on TV in reports about the find. (The story is that he was wearing leather pants and laced boots and carried a long knife and had tattoos, but they can't find his bike). ∎

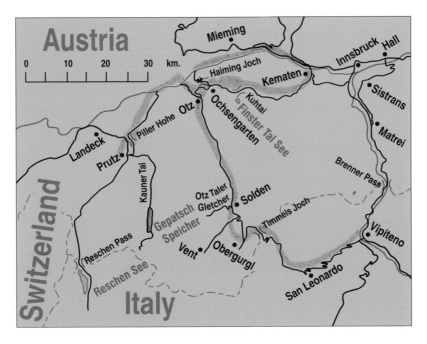

About 13 kilometers up **Stubai Tal,** a dead-end finger valley, west off the Autobahn at the famous **Europabrucke,** is the motorcycle friendly **Hotel Capella.**

If there's time, it's more fun to take the **Timmels Joch** rather than the Brenner Pass, or even the Reschen Pass. The Timmels Joch (its other end is described in Trip 40) parallels the Brenner starting about 45 kilometers west of Innsbruck, near **Kuhtai** and **Haiming** (Trip 60). It climbs south up the Otz Tal, through the town, **Otz,** where there's the large comfortable old time **Hotel Post** (of course). Farther up the Otz Tal, just upstream, south of Solden, there's a dead-end valley road to the west, **Rettenbach Tal,** the top of which claims to be one of the highest paved roads in the Alps. It's called **Otz Taler Gletscherstrasse,** and there is a toll. Then, a couple of kilometers further up the Otz Tal, at Zwieselstein, a finger valley called **Vent Tal** climbs up west. At the end is another **Hotel Post.** It's at almost 1,900 meters and sports a small indoor pool looking out at glaciers.

The **Reschen Pass** (see Trip 41) starts up out of the Inn Tal at **Landeck,** about 75 kilometers west of Innsbruck. It's mundane, lower, and a bit more of a detour than the Timmels Joch. A good way to get to the Reschen is to head south, up and out of the Inn Tal from Imst, short of Landeck, over a little-known pass, **Piller Hohe,** and come out on the Reschen Pass at **Fliess** or **Prutz.** Little Piller Hohe allows the rider to sail along the high mountain, occasionally looking down on the traffic in the Inn Tal. From Prutz a road up the dead end Kauner Tal valley leads to a *Stau See* and one of the highest roads in Austria. The upper part has a toll.

Trip 60 Obscure Tiroler Roads

Distance *About 250 kilometers*

Terrain *Some sweeping, some tight, narrow mountain roads*

Highlights *Famous castles, churches, little-used mountain roads, nice restaurants and hotels. Includes: Ammer Sattel (1,118 meters), Berwang (1,336 meters), ★Hahntenn Joch (1,894 meters), ★Halming Joch (1,685 meters), ★Kuhtai (2,017 meters), Seefeld in Tirol, Telfs, Holzleitner Sattel (1,126 meters), Fern Pass (1,209 meters)*

In **Ober Bayern** (southern Bavaria), the mountains and roads are exciting when compared to the Great Plains, but the real riding is readily available in the high Alps of the Austrian Tirol just across the border. This trip is easily accessible from Munchen as well as **Oberammergau** and **Garmisch,** and anywhere in the Tirol.

Starting from the town of **Ettal,** just outside Oberammergau and just north of Garmisch, escape the traffic and tourists by turning south over the **Ammer Sattel.** Ettal has a huge domed baroque monastery church right near the intersection. Apparently the monks make good brandy, and the handsome interior of the church has consumed some of the profits. The interior is spectacular in gilt and white with plenty of baroque cupids hanging around the pillars and over pictures, and with a celestial dome, all in the style of the mid-1700s. Some exterior traces of the original Gothic building (like the front doorway) are still visible. Worth a visit, and it's free. Park close, at the east end of the lot, in front of the shops.

The turn for the Ammer Sattel is marked with signs for the **Konigschloss Linderhof,** one of Mad King Ludwig's castles which is ten kilometers up the road. The German noun *Schloss* is almost always translated to the English word "castle." This can be misleading, because Schloss can also mean "palace." (No walls or battlements on a palace; a castle may have a moat and other fortifications.) This Konigschloss, royal castle, is Ludwig's small baroque jewel of a palace, with a jet fountain and an underground lake for Wagnerian opera, built in the late 19th century. It can't be seen from the road. Tours take a couple of hours.

Ludwig was king of Bayern in the days that Bismarck was uniting Germany under a German, rather than an Austrian Kaiser. Ludwig's sympathies were with the Austrians, which as it turned out, was unfortunate. Meantime, he built two other castles besides Linderhof to play in: **Neuschwanstein** is the turreted wonder on every travel poster, near Fussen and Reutte; and **Herrenchiem See,** on an island in a lake named Chiem See, between Munchen and Salzburg. Of course, he had inherited other castles and palaces. Neuschwanstein was the inspiration for Disney's Magic Kingdom castle. Herrenchiem See on the island is supposed

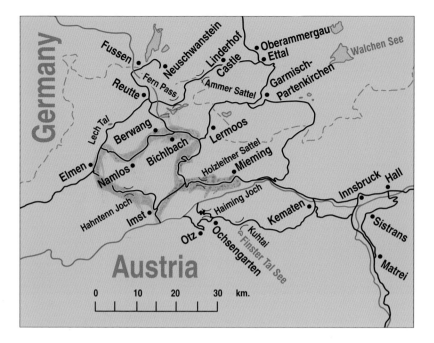

to look like the French Chateau of Versailles. It's necessary to take a ferry to Herrenchiem See.

Past Linderhof, the Ammer Sattel road goes through a forest and climbs to the low Sattel which happens to be the Austrian border. Into Austria a few kilometers, the road winds around an Alpine lake called **Plan See,** with a nice hotel at the end of the lake closest to the border and several serviceable restaurants. Then it makes a quick descent into **Reutte** (say Roy tuh), a bustling Tiroler town.

Reutte has a two-lane Autobahn around it which can seem confusing. Follow signs south toward **Lermoos** and **Fern Pass,** away from Germany (D), and exit in a couple of kilometers at **Bichlbach** and head for **Berwang** and **Namlos.** This is delightful rural Tirol. Some of the road is barely one lane, dancing around high Alpine meadows. Berwang has nice-looking hotels.

The road comes down in the **Lech Tal** (the valley mentioned in Trip 58). Five kilometers west up the Lech Tal at **Elmen** is the obscure turnoff for a great, usually ignored pass, the **Hahntenn Joch.** The narrow road crosses a little field and then starts climbing the rock face in a long steep traverse before turning into a high valley for some more twisting fun. There are no facilities at the top, which has a huge slope of sliding alluvial granite, but short of the top is a cute Gasthaus named **Zur Gemutlichkeit** in the town of Bschlabs. (How many other towns start with five consonants?) It faces an equally cute onion-domed church. Prices at Zur Gemutlichkeit are very reasonable.

The narrow road comes down through the woods, past the **Hotel Linserhof,** into **Imst,** another prosperous Tiroler town with a typical Austrian church.

CHAPTER

16

If you've time for one church, try this one at Rottenbuch, just meters off the main road from Oberammergau. It's a baroque riot featuring the birth of Mary. You can park at the door, and they have rest rooms.

Bavarian churches typically have onion domes on the tower. Austrian churches, like that at Imst, have a square tower with a clock face on each side, then an open belfry topped with four gables finished off with a tall pointed steeple.

Imst, like Reutte, has a two-lane bypass Autobahn around it, connecting with the major east-west Autobahn in the Inn Tal between the Arlberg and Innsbruck.

Head toward Innsbruck about ten kilometers to a small village named **Haiming.** Haiming is a marked Autobahn Ausfahrt (exit). Opposite the village, heading south up the mountainside, is the Haiming Joch road. It's hardly more than a driveway. The signing is to **Ochsengarten.** This narrow, one-lane road climbs past steep fields, with little haystacks and occasional Zimmer Frei signs, a Gasthaus and a delightful new hotel with a view of the whole valley: **Hotel Ferienschlossl.** Past the hotel, the road climbs into a high forest, and then comes down just a bit to the **Kuhtai** road at the intersection called Ochsengarten.

Kuhtai is a high pass, but for some reason it's never called a pass, just Kuhtai. It goes east-west, roughly parallel to the Arlberg-Innsbruck Autobahn down in the Inn Tal, but higher in the Alps. Even though it's close to such traveled ways and to Innsbruck, it never has traffic. At Ochsengarten, it seems hardly more prominent than the tiny Haiming Joch road.

West from Ochsengarten, the Kuhtai road makes a steep descent to **Otz,** on the **Timmels Joch** road. Kuhtai, the pass, is the other way, east and up over the tree line past a massive earth dam and its lake. There are a couple of ski hotels at the top. And a "Bike Stop," called **Kuhtaier Dorfstadl** on the north side of the road. You have to go in. The interior is a delight, and so is the staff. Nothing wrong with the outdoor view terrace, either.

Then a fairly modern road sweeps down east in a long valley called the **Sellrain Tal.** Some straights end in rather abrupt tight corners through villages, including Gries, with attractive **Hotel Antonie.** Then the road enters a tight gorge shared with a raging mountain torrent, exiting without further ado in the Inn Tal, at a village named **Kematen.** From there you can stay above the crowd following signs to Axams and the Brenner Pass, all just a couple of kilometers above Innsbruck.

Here, the secret is to go straight ahead through Kematen and under the Auto-bahn, and sweep up the mountain on the north side of the Inn Tal. This is the main *Bundesstrasse* (federal road) toward Garmisch in Germany. But up the mountainside a few kilometers, still in Austria, is the exit for **Seefeld.** Seefeld is famous for cross-country skiing. Guess that means it's flat on top. West of Seefeld, a delightful little road hung on the mountainside heads for the Tiroler town of Telfs. Straight on through Telfs toward **Holzleitner Sattel,** the road passes through **Mieming,** known to many motorcycle tour-takers as the home of Edelweiss Bike Travel.

The west side of the Holzleitner has wonderful, wide sweepers down to the picturesque village of **Nassereith.** But first, on the way down, pause to view the lush green Tiroler valley below. Often there's a vendor selling *heiss Wurst und Brot,* the Tiroler equivalent of a hot dog, only better. A good munch helps you contemplate the view. (Sometimes "heiss wurstl" gets translated, "hot sausage." In this instance, it's hot, cooked, not HOT HOT.)

North from Nassereith is the **Fern Pass,** a nice road, with too much traffic and too many anxious drivers, that fortunately isn't too long. There's a Gasthaus at each side of the top, both with elaborate painted scenes on the exterior walls. The southern one has historical pictures, including the arrival of American tanks near the end of World War II, with the building in flames.

Even though it's pretty low by Alpine standards, the Fern Pass is the closest mountain pass for many Germans, and always has a lot of tour bus traffic. To accommodate all the traffic, the north side has new tunnel work that leads quickly toward Lermoos and back to Germany at Garmisch, or on to Reutte.

Just across the German border from Reutte is **Fussen,** and Ludwig's castle **Neuschwanstein,** alongside the older castle, **Hohenschwangau.**

If there's time for one Bayrisch baroque church, choose the one at **Rottenbuch,** just a few kilometers north of Oberammergau. It's just off the main road through a low arch gate. Typically, baroque churches are very plain on the outside with no stained glass. But the inside of Rottenbuch is astonishing. Elaborate carving and plaster detail have run riot. It's delightfully flamboyant. The frescoes cast a rosy glow, much cozier than the famous Wies Kirche only ten kilometers away. Tours never go to Rottenbuch, probably because buses can't get through the village gate.

CHAPTER
16

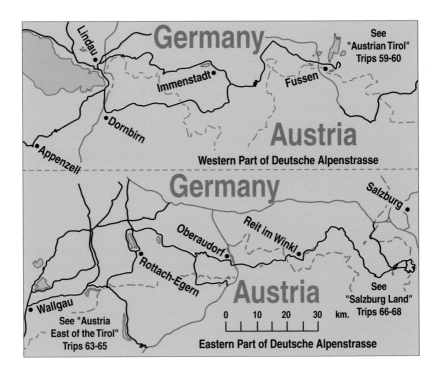

Germany

Lindau

See
"Austrian Tirol"
Trips 59-60

Immenstadt

Fussen

Dornbirn

Austria

Appenzell

Western Part of Deutsche Alpenstrasse

Germany

Salzburg

Oberaudorf

Reit im Winkl

Rottach-Egern

Wallgau

Austria

See
"Salzburg Land"
Trips 66-68

See "Austria
East of the Tirol"
Trips 63-65

0   10   20   30   km.

Eastern Part of Deutsche Alpenstrasse

Deutsche Alpenstrasse

The southern border of Germany, and of Bayern, is where the Alps begin. The big stuff is all south of Germany. In fact, the **Zugspitze,** the highest point in Germany, is on the Austrian border.

In fits and starts, Germany has been constructing a road along the border, called the **Deutsche Alpenstrasse.** Little of it bears comparison with the high Alps. But a few parts are interesting and are popular with German motorcyclists. The best part by far is a little loop, the **Rossfeldringstrasse** on the mountain above **Salzburg** and **Berchtesgaden.**

As a well-promoted vacation area, the Bayern region is full of hotels and restaurants. One less-trafficked village is **Lenggries,** northeast of the town of Garmisch-Partenkirchen, and just a few kilometers from Austria. From Lenggries, a hardly used one-lane road goes west along the Alp foothills past sturdy Bayrisch farmhouses, the kind with the barn attached to the house. It's signed to Jachenau, and on to **Wallgau** (see below) and Garmisch.

South of Lenggries is the low **Achen Pass** leading directly to the Inn Tal in Austria and across to the **Ziller Tal** and **Gerlos Pass.**

A large, multi-storied, full-service hotel in Lenggries is the **Brauneck.** Nearby, a smaller Gasthof is the **Lenggrieser Hof.**

Closer to Munchen is the **Waldgasthof Buchenhain.** It's in the woods, as its name implies, all by itself. Very Bayerisch in style, it has a beer garden out front. And it has its own train station, so that it's only a few minutes from the city by train, and right on the highway heading for the Alps.

Be wary of train tracks. They may create a hump in the highway that can surprise the unwary rider if there's not a train on them.

Trip 61 Deutsche Alpenstrasse West

Distance *About 110 kilometers from Lindau to Fussen*

Terrain *Gently sweeping asphalt, one tight climb*

Highlights *Bucolic countryside, some traffic, photogenic towns, Oberjoch Pass (1,180 meters), Riederberg Pass (1,430 meters)*

Lindau is a picturesque island town in **Boden See,** the very large lake called Lake Constance in English, which is really part of the Rhein River, downstream from all those good passes in Switzerland (see Trips 35, 36) and just west of

Mad King Ludwig's fantasy castle, Neuschwanstein, crowns a mountain knob across from his childhood home, the yellow castle called Hohenschwangau. The castles are just outside of Fussen in Germany and Reutte in Austrian Tirol.

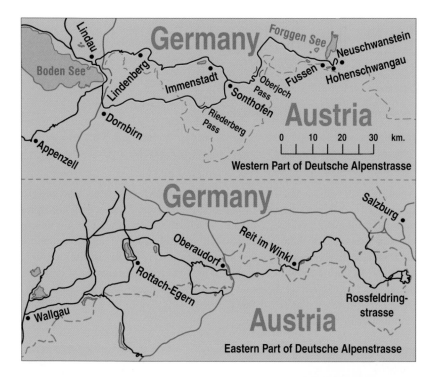

Western Part of Deutsche Alpenstrasse

Eastern Part of Deutsche Alpenstrasse

Bayern. There's a causeway onto Lindau for trains and vehicles. The trains come in frontward, and exit backward, or vice versa. Other vehicles have to park and turn around to leave. The town is all foot traffic. There is marked motorcycle parking.

East from Lindau, the Deutsche Alpenstrasse makes a pleasant sweeping run along the Austrian border. Green meadows and farms. No big mountains.

At **Immenstadt** a dead-end valley cuts south into the Alps and toward Austria. A part of it, called **Klein Walser Tal,** actually is in Austria, but you can't get to the rest of Austria from it.

(A parallel and more interesting route starts just south in Austria by Dornbirn, climbs up a valley called **Balderschwang** into Germany, where it crosses over **Riederberg Pass,** then down toward Sonthofen, and the Klein Walser Tal at a village called Fischen. Riederberg is sort of gnarly.)

Heading east, the road climbs up the only really good twisties, the **Oberjoch Pass,** only to run into the Austrian border at 1,180 meters elevation. Straight ahead, another small pass, **Gaichtberg** (1,093 meters), leads down to Lech Tal and Reutte in Austria (see Trip 60).

Meanwhile, the Deutsche Alpenstrasse detours north in Germany to **Fussen,** site of Ludwig's Neuschwanstein castle, where it sort of ends, to resume farther east beyond Garmisch-Partenkirchen.

CHAPTER

17

Trip 62 Deutsche Alpenstrasse East

Distance *About 200 kilometers*

Terrain *Some rough narrow, some sweeping*

Highlights *Cute villages (like Wallgau), popular biking roads like Kesselberg (858 meters), Sudelfeld (1,097 meters), Ursprung Pass (849 meters), and ★ Rossfeldringstrasse (1,536 meters)*

About 12 kilometers east of **Garmisch-Partenkirchen** on the road toward Innsbruck, a fork goes north to some interesting riding and a delightful picture-perfect Bayrisch village, **Wallgau.** It's close to all the tourists in Garmisch, but hardly touched by them. Several buildings are elaborately painted, including the **Post Hotel.** The inside of the hotel is as interesting as the outside, and so is the food. In the morning, locals have *weiss Wurst,* a sausage made of white meats. Try *Grill Teller,* on the menu at most Bayrisch and Austrian restaurants. *Grill Teller* means a plate of grilled meats, usually five or six kinds, garnished with interesting vegetables.

Kesselberg is one of the motorcycle favorites not too far south of Munich. The round sign indicates that motorcycles are forbidden (in this direction). This prohibition is modified by the little white sign under it reading "Saturdays and Sundays and holidays." This is further modified by the next sign which reads that mopeds are always permitted. So, it's okay for bikes on weekdays that aren't holidays and it's okay in the other direction (north bound) any day.

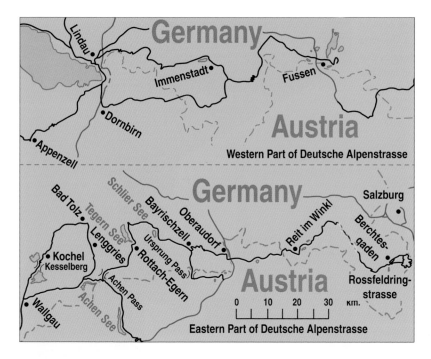

Before heading on east, a German rider would suggest going north from Wallgau a few kilometers around a lake, **Walchen See,** famous for windsurfing, to climb a little mountain called **Kesselberg.** The tight sweepers of Kesselberg attract motorcyclists from all of Bayern. So many, in fact, that the road has been closed to southbound motorcycles on weekends and holidays. There's a rest area turnout on the inside of a long sweeper that's a *Tofftreffpunkt.* The village of **Kochel,** at the north base of Kesselberg, has attractive country hotels.

Back to the Deutsche Alpenstrasse. From the north edge of Wallgau, a tiny, rough, one-lane toll road heads east along the border toward Achen Pass (941 meters). Before it gets to the pass, it becomes a sweeping modern highway.

Once again, straight ahead leads into Austria, a wonderful way to get to the Inn Tal below Innsbruck and the Ziller Tal without any traffic. (Into Austria, the Achen Pass road skirts an Alpine lake with many hotels, then makes a sweeping descent into the Inn Tal. A hairpin on the descent, called the **Kanzel curve,** has a restaurant with a magnificent view of the Inn Tal and the Ziller Tal).

From the **Achen Pass,** the Deutsche Alpenstrasse goes north again toward a lake, **Tegern See,** which has too much traffic. The old, one lane section east from Rottach-Egern has been closed to motor vehicles, so it's necessary to detour north around **Schlier See.** (Schlier See is known in history as the site of the "Night of the Long Knives," when, in the mid-thirties, Hitler turned on the brownshirts after they helped him rise to power, and had them killed.)

In some parts of the Alps, churches have steeples that sort of look like witch's hats. This one is at Gsteig (Trip 10).

East from Schlier See toward **Bayrischzell,** the Alpenstrasse again becomes a modern road—for a while. And from Bayrischzell, another road heads south into Austria and the Inn Tal over another little pass, **Ursprung** (849 meters). Ursprung has two parallel legs descending to **Kufstein** in the Inn Tal. The southern one is the most fun.

But the best is yet to come: **Sudelfeld.**

East from Bayrischzell, the road climbs and sweeps in a fashion so delightful that it attracts motorcyclists by the hundreds. On weekends, every corner and the little restaurant at the top is full of motorcyclists watching friends sweep back and forth. So much sweeping, in fact, that the local authorities got the road closed to motorcycles. Court cases got it opened again, but with a speed limit.

Funny thing. The great sweeping road just *ends,* or almost does, at a little, narrow toll tunnel that leads down into the Inn Tal. It's possible to turn off east just before the tunnel and head down another narrow, winding road called **Tatzelwurm,** past a Gasthaus of the same name with a pleasant terrace. Tatzelwurm gets down to the Inn Tal town of **Oberaudorf** on the German side of the Austrian border. Another end of the Deutsche Alpenstrasse.

From Oberaudorf, the best bet is to head straight on east into Austria, over the Inn River (which is the border). About 25 kilometers into Austria, cross back into Germany at **Reit im Winkl,** a village with many cute buildings decorated in Bavarian style. Here the Deutsche Alpenstrasse takes off again in good sweeping style toward **Berchtesgaden.** (South of Reit im Winkl, a wide, smooth Austrian road winds easily through mountains to Lofer and the roads of Trip 65.) Berchtesgaden is touristy.

On the mountain above Berchtesgaden is the best part of the whole Deutsche Alpenstrasse, the **Rossfeldringstrasse.** This trip (about 25 km) is high dancing along the Austrian border, with gorgeous views across Salzburg and its valley to the high Tannengebirge mountains in Austria and in the other direction, over Berchtesgaden. There are several restaurants on the ring road. To get up on the ring from Berchtesgaden, follow the signs to Obersalzberg, a steep climb in the direction of Hitler's Eagles Nest. The Rossfeldringstrasse turns off, and then there's a toll booth! In fact, there are two toll booths, one at each end of the toll part of the ring road (see Trip 66).

From the ring road there's a well-kept secret way down into Austria with easy access to the Austrian Autobahn. It's pretty and fun and hardly ever used by anyone. Just below the northerly toll booth, a small road heads north. That's it. It has no significant marking, but it goes to a tiny border crossing, and then down to the Austrian mountain town, **Durrnberg,** site of the famous **Salzburg salt mines,** then on down to come out in the valley of the **Salzach River** at the Austrian village of **Hallein.** It's much easier to get to the Rossfeldringstrasse on this road from **Hallein,** just south of Salzburg, than from Germany through Berchtesgaden. From Hallein, Austria, look for the new bridge looping over the main street and up the mountainside just north of the old town. The new bridge is the road (see Trip 66).

Hordes of tourists visit the salt mines at Durrnberg, but they come up a little cable car from Hallein, not the road.

See
"Austrian Tirol"
Trips 59-60

Germany

Salzburg

See
"Deutsche
Alpenstrasse"
Trips 61-62

Golling

Rottach-Egern

Lofer

HochKonig

Austria

Zell am See

See
"Salzburg Land"
Trips 66-68

Konigsleiten

0   10   20   30   km.

Fusch

Badgastein

Heiligenblut

Italy

Lienz

Valdaora

See
"The Dolomites"
Trips 48-55

Cortina

Austria East of the Tirol

Central Austria south of Salzburg is the very narrow waist of the country, just over 100 kilometers across, from Berchtesgaden in Germany to Italy. Innsbruck, Tirol, and Vorarlberg are in the west, and Wien (Vienna) is to the east. Since the narrow waist area is all high mountains with many good north-south pass roads, there's a lot of good riding.

The narrow old road above Mayrhofen up to Schlegeis hugs the cliffs under overhanging rocks.

There are millions of Germans on one side and millions of Italians on the other side of Austria's narrow waist, all busy going back and forth across little Austria, such a short distance across that they need not stop even for a WC, let alone gas. Except that prudent Austria has concluded that most of this north-south traffic should pay a toll. A couple of the roads are actually private enterprise endeavors.

Austrian private enterprise has also provided a plethora of tourist accommodations. In the first two trips described here, there's a Gasthaus on practically every corner, with Zimmer Freis in between. Most hotels are attractive Austrian mountain style, with huge roofs, balconies garlanded with flower boxes, and interesting illustrations painted on exterior walls. They almost guarantee good food, attentive service, and spotless, attractive accommodations. Many have elaborate carved wood and wrought iron detailing. There are so many establishments, all so inviting, that any traveler with an economic bent must wonder how they can possibly produce a return on what has to be a very large investment. To an American mind they just don't make economic sense, but they surely are nice.

Most of the hotels spend as much on cooking as on decoration. Area sweet specialties besides *Apfel Strudel* include *Toffel Strudel* (more of a custard base), both with vanilla sauce or the more standard whipped cream. *Kaiser Schmarrn* is a crepe-like concoction smothered in fruit. Practically every menu will have a *Grill Teller,* or mixed grill platter. Sometimes it's good to ask for recommendations. Find out what is just out of the oven, or is specially prepared.

The **Hotel Glocknerhof** is spectacularly set in the high mountain village of **Heiligenblut** on the south side of the **Grossglockner.** It hangs on the mountain edge at the entrance to the village with views of the very Austrian village church (tall steeple) and craggy mountains across the green *Moll Tal* (valley) below. Even the indoor swimming pool has sweeping mountain views. The interior is spacious and charming modern mountain design.

Four hotels in central Austria advertise themselves as **MoHo**, Motorrad Hotels in the Alps. They specialize in serving motorcyclists. Each is different. They are completely adequate and moderately priced. You can be sure that some part of the family running each is a motorcycle enthusiast, and that all involved will speak motorcycle.

Landhaus Jausern is high in a dead-end valley just north of **Zell am See** and south of Salzburg. From the main road into Saalbach, turn south. It's behind and above a larger hotel.

Hotel Iselsbergerhof is on the low pass road of the same name south of the Grossglockner and just north of Lienz.

One of the MoHo's, **Hotel Solaria,** is a good choice for trips in the next chapter, Salzburg Land, where it's listed. Another, **Hotel Capella,** is south of Innsbruck, so it's listed with Trip 59.

Sometimes an early snow dusts the Grossglockner. This view, toward Hoch Tor, is from Edelweiss Spitze.

CHAPTER
18

Trip 63 Achen Pass and the Ziller Tal

Distance *About 170 kilometers from Germany via Zillertaler Hohenstrasse, Schlegeis, Gerlos Pass, to Grossglockner*

Terrain *Good sweepers, narrow erratic road on Zillertaler Hohenstrasse, old Gerlos*

Highlights *Lovely farms and villages, fun roads with some traffic spots, good hotels and cafes. Includes: Achen Pass (941 meters), Zillertaler Hohenstrasse, Schlegeis (1,784 meters), Gerlos Pass (1,507 meters), Konigsleiten, Pass Thurn (1,273 meters)*

The **Achen Pass** (see Trip 62, Deutsche Alpenstrasse) sweeps magnificently down into the Inn Tal, and it's possible to proceed across the autobahn and right up the **Ziller Tal,** a valley with every imaginable shade of green. The Ziller Tal is decorated with a narrow gauge railroad, sometimes sporting a chuffing steam-powered train. At **Zell am Ziller,** the **Gerlos Pass** road leaves the Ziller Tal and starts climbing a finger valley to the east.

But before that, at **Ried,** the **Zillertaler Hohenstrasse** climbs the mountainside to the west, where it hangs and dances in a one-lane game in and out of the tree line, offering dazzling views of the yellow-green, blue-green, and just-green quilt below and the Gerlos Pass road snaking up opposite. It finally comes back down in the Ziller Tal at Ramsberg. There's a toll.

Atop the Zillertaler Hohenstrasse is the **Almgasthof Zirmstadl** of interesting log construction and sporting a terrace with a fine view.

Head farther south up the Ziller Tal past **Mayrhofen** and **Finkenberg.** Just above Finkenberg, traffic is directed to a new road and tunnel going farther up the valley. The old road, to the right, is the correct choice. It snakes through a gorge with overhanging cliffs. Snuggled against the cliffs is the **Gasthaus Jodburg.** Another hotel is **Sporthotel Stock.**

Farther up, a toll road with a one-way-at-a-time traffic light leads into the high **Schlegeis.** Near the end of the road, a gravel drive leads up above a lake to the **Dominikushutte,** a restaurant with a view of Italian mountain peaks. It's a good turnaround spot.

Back down at Zell am Ziller, the Gerlos climbs east through a tourist town of the same name, **Gerlos.** Near the top there's a toll gate onto a new swooping alignment that supposedly offers views of the **Krimmler waterfall.** The views are from quite a distance. Turn north and take the old road instead. It bounces and weaves and heaves in great sport down the mountain. Part is narrow. Some bridges are wooden.

Near the top of the Gerlos, just about where the toll road splits off, is an opportunity to climb a bit higher to a ski village called **Konigsleiten,** with a couple of good hotels like **Hotel Gasthof Ursprung.**

From the Gerlos pass, it's straight ahead east to **Zell am See** and the **Grossglockner,** skirting the high Tauern mountain spine of Austria to the south, and the Kitzbuhel Alps to the north. At **Mittersill,** little **Pass Thurn** joins from the north, and the big **Felbertauern** toll tunnel road joins from the south, coming out from under the **Hohe Tauern** mountains. The Felbertauern tunnel is the main north-south, all-weather connection across the waist of Austria, parallel to the Grossglockner.

Trip 64 Passes From Italy

Distance *From Italy to Grossglockner, via Staller Sattel, about 65 kilometers; via Plocken Pass, about 50 kilometers; via Nassfeld Pass, about 60 kilometers*

Terrain *Via Staller Sattel, good sweepers; via Plocken Pass, pleasant road; via Nassfeld Pass, pleasant road*

Highlights *Via ★ Staller Sattel (2,052 meters), pretty country, hotels in east Tirol; via Plocken Pass (1,362 meters), quick connection over Gailberg Sattel (982) to Grossglockner; via Nassfeld Pass (1,557 meters), good escape from Italian autostrada; ★ Kartischer Sattel (1,526 meters)*

Staller Sattel is the fun one-way-at-a-time pass into Austria from the **Dolomites** in Italy (see Trip 55). It comes down into Austria from the one-way part, past the **Tandlerstub'n** hotel restaurant in St. Jakob, joining the Felbertauern road south of the tunnel, and goes on into the major city of the Ost (east) Tirol, **Lienz.** (The Ost Tirol is the part that voted to rejoin Austria in the 1920s after it had been awarded to Italy at Versailles. It is separated from the rest of the Austrian Tirol by the Sud Tirol, still part of Italy.)

From Lienz, a fine sweeper climbs the **Iselsberg Pass** (site of one of the motorcycle hotels) toward Heiligenblut and the Grossglockner. The Iselsberg provides the last (or first) glimpses of the Dolomites.

Tandlerstub'n

About 14 kilometers into Austria, just below the village of **St. Jakob** (one of those villages where the road jogs around an old house), there's a beautiful hotel restaurant right beside the road called **Tandlerstub'n.** It's a great place to try Schweinshax'n, a Bavarian and Austrian specialty. The best translation is "hog knuckles," and that falls far short of describing the succulent slices of pork here. The "joint" will be dramatically served on a huge platter with all kinds of trimmings including Semmelknodel, a kind of dumpling. ∎

Another route from Lienz is to head back toward Italy about 28 kilometers on the main highway, almost to Sillian in order to catch the dancing **Kartischer Sattel** road. From its well-marked intersection, the sattel has been improved through several curves and hairpins. Once across the sattel, into Karnten Land, it becomes a tortuous dance down to **Kotschach-Mauthen** where it meets the **Plocken Pass** and the **Gailberg Sattel** roads right by one of the MoHos, the **Gailtaler Hof.**

East of the Dolomites and east of Cortina, two seldom-used passes (**Plocken and Nassfeld**) cross from Italy into Austria (they aren't

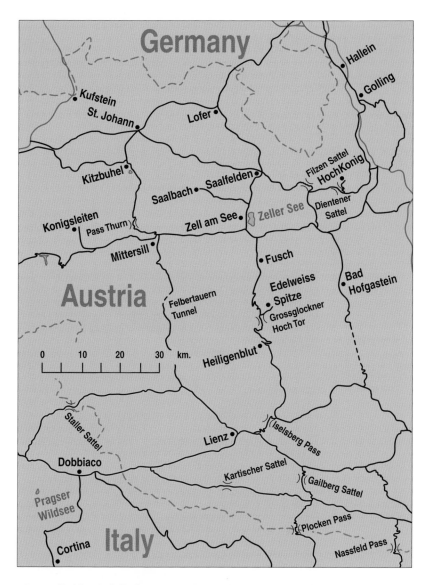

often called by their Italian names, Passo di Monte Croce Carnico and Passo di Pramollo) (see Trip 55).

The Plocken especially has an exciting climb up out of Italy in layered switchbacks through forests. The Nassfeld is just ten kilometers off the auto-strada/Autobahn between Venezia and Wien. It's a wonderful way to escape the diesel trucks and buses of the autostrada. Both passes enter a seldom-traversed Austrian valley of pleasant interest. From it, the Gailberg Sattel connects directly to Lienz in the East Tirol, Iselsberg, and the Grossglockner.

Trip 65 Grossglockner ★★

Distance   *About 200 kilometers over Grossglockner (toll) to Salzburg*

Terrain   *Every kind of mountain road: tight, sweeping, narrow hairpins over a major pass and a couple of lesser ones*

Highlights   *Exhilarating riding and scenery. Includes: ★Grossglockner Hoch Tor (2,575 meters), Edelweiss Spitze (2,577 meters), ★Grossglockner Fuscher Tor (2,428 meters), Filzen Sattel (1,291 meters), Dientener Sattel (1,357 meters)*

The **Grossglockner Hochalpenstrasse,** Grossglockner for short, is one of the major play roads of the Alps. In crossing the highest spine of the Austrian Alps, it combines every test of driving skill: hairpins, sweepers, jig-jags, cobblestones,

Only seven more cobblestone hairpins lead from the car park at the Grossglockner's Fusher Tor to the pinnacle at Edelweiss Spitz.

steep descents, narrow ledges, sometimes ice and snow and hanging clouds of fog, along with spectacular views and plenty of restaurants. It's only a half-day's drive from Munchen and the big cities of northern Italy, and even less from Salzburg, so it is a testing spot for the latest machines and visiting drivers. And it's private enterprise.

Yes, it's a private toll road. And fairly expensive. Typically, the Austrians in cute costumes at the toll booths will take any kind of money. Once through the toll booths, it's possible to play back and forth and up and down to the heart's content, even stay at one of the several hotels. If a return trip is anticipated from outside the toll booths, it's possible to arrange a slightly reduced price in advance. Environmentalists are raising some Cain about limiting access to the Grossglockner Hochalpenstrasse—too many tourists tramping about looking for Edelweiss—but private enterprise and the profit motive have kept it open so far.

CHAPTER

18

(Sorry, Austrians don't know the popular song, "Edelweiss," from *The Sound of Music*.)

The south half of the Grossglockner is in the state of **Karnten,** which we English speakers call Carinthia. The north part of the Grossglocker is in **Salzburg** Land.

The approach from the north is up the **Fuscher Tal,** a lush green valley, from Zell am See and Bruck, past the village of **Fusch.** Then the climb.

There are two short tunnels and two humps across the top. The north hump is called **Fuscher Tor** (Fusch Gate) and the other **Hoch** (high) **Tor,** with a high Alpine valley between the two, where the road often cuts through deep snow banks.

Near the Fuscher Tor, what looks like a restaurant parking lot leads to the snaking little road up to the highest point, **Edelweiss Spitze.** The road's worth the trip. The view from the restaurant at the top is reward enough. The restaurant, **Edelweiss Hutte,** is down over the edge from the parking lot. Sometimes it's possible to ride down to it. Above, all around are high peaks, and below, bits of ribbon roads. To the south, the ribbon, not really a ribbon but a string, works across the Alpine meadows. Until August it's just a slit in deep snow banks that disappears into a tunnel. To the north, the road seems to weave to the mountain's edge and then disappear into the Fuscher Tal.

Time for hot chocolate.

About halfway down the south side, well below the Hoch Tor, a road leads about nine kilometers around the mountain to a huge parking garage called **Franz Josefs Hohe.** There's a view of the Grossglockner itself, the big mountain that's supposed to look like a big bell, and a cable car ride down onto the ice of the **Pasterze Glacier.** Bikes can usually find a nook or cranny or a piece of sidewalk to park on outside the huge garage. Some of the road to the garage and back is in concrete snow sheds.

Just outside the southern toll booths is the high village of **Heiligenblut** (Holy Blood), whose name sounds better untranslated. Besides the **Glocknerhof,** there are several other hotels and Gasthaus possibilities. There's often an evening brass band concert in the little town square, backed by a fountain made of huge mountain crystals. The little church at Heiligenblut is a good example of the original Austrian Gothic that has not been baroqued. The memorials in it illustrate the horrible costs of 20th century wars to families of the village.

South from Heiligenblut, down the **Moll Tal,** is the **Iselsberg Pass** (site of one of the MoHos) up and over toward Lienz and the Dolomites of Italy, the passes of Trip 55. North of the Grossglockner, and north of Zell am See about five kilometers, is the turnoff to **Saalbach,** site of another MoHo. A few kilometers farther north is **Saalfelden** and the pleasant Austrian roads to **Reit im Winkl** on the Deutsche Alpenstrasse.

A new tunnel through the adjacent mountain eases the traffic around Zell am See. But a better route is to head around the east side of the See (Zell's on the west), then continue on country lanes through Gerling to **Maria Alm.**

258

Franz Josef Bernard is the town manager of Heiligenblut on the Grossglockner, and he has his own copy of *Motorcycle Journeys Through the Alps.* **He sent the author a sign from the top of the Grossglockner, marked 2,428 meters.**

The main road north from Zell am See goes to **Saalfelden,** then heads east to Maria Alm, a pleasant village pleasantly bypassed by the new road up the **Filzen Sattel.** Beyond Maria Alm, the Sattel road climbs steeply and irregularly. Parts have been improved, but the old sections are the most fun. All of this is just south of Berchtesgaden and the Rossfeldringstrasse in Germany.

The road dips, then climbs the **Dientener Sattel.** Over the sattel an interesting road climbs up toward the German border. Signed for Hochkonig, it deadends at a hotel called **Arturhaus.**

The countryside is rural, remote and tourist free all the way across the Sattels and down a twisting gorge to **Bischofshofen.** The road bypasses most of Bischofshofen, connecting straight across the Salzach River to the Tauern Autobahn high on the mountain opposite. The Autobahn connects Salzburg with southern Austria and Italy. It's free except for a toll tunnel through the highest part of the Tauern mountains.

Take the Autobahn about ten kilometers south to the Lammer Tal exit, and follow the Tal north on the Salzburger Dolomitenstrasse along a raging mountain stream through Annaberg to Abtenau, sweeping down to the Salzach at **Golling.** Might as well take the Autobahn to Salzburg.

CHAPTER
18

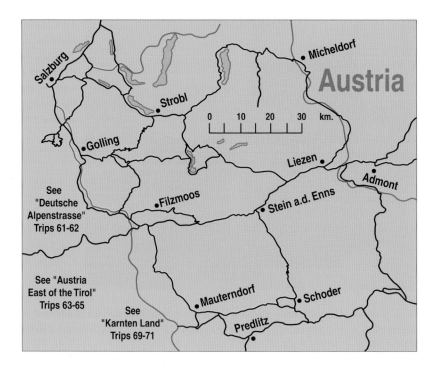

Salzburg Land

Salzburg is the name of a state, Salzburg Land, as well as of the city.

Bookshelves are full of stuff about the romance of Salzburg, the city, what with Mozart and the *Sound of Music*. But are there many about the entertaining roads around it?

And there's an easy-to-get-to hotel, **Gasthof Brauwirt,** out on the fringe of congestion that's motorcycle friendly. (And it got its beer license several hundred years ago.) Find it by going a couple of kilometers north from the Salzburg Nord Autobahn Ausfahrt (Salzburg North exit). The hotel is off the road on the west side.

One of the MoHos, **Hotel Solaria,** is in Salzburg Land atop **Radstadter Tauern Pass.** Balconies have views of snowy slopes. The turn is marked by a brightly painted old motorcycle for a sign. The hotel has recently been completely renovated.

Four hotels in Austria advertise themselves as MoHo, Motorcycle Hotels. Hotel Solaria, high atop the Obertauern Pass, and set back from the main road, is easy for a biker to find.

Trip 66 Post Alm

Distance *165 kilometers*

Terrain *Narrow mountain roads and pretty country*

Highlights *Salzkammergut lakes, Post Alm (about 1,500 meters) (toll), Gaisberg (1,287 meters) bucolic mountains and views*

From Sazburg, take the Autobahn in the direction of Wien, east, for about 25 kilometers, exiting at **Mond See.** This is the **Salzkammergut,** land of lakes and mountains. South along some lakes, and over a low pass brings you to **St. Gilgen** on **St. Wolfgang See.** Mozart's mother lived here. The main road east from St. Gilgen follows the south shore of the lake as far as **Strobl,** where a mini-interchange has a sign pointing south to **Post Alm.** It's a little road that climbs through the forest with some switchbacks. No tourists. There's a toll.

Hardly anyone bothers to see this lovely view near Salzburg as the Post Alm road sweeps down through lush green valleys toward Abtenau.

CHAPTER

19

262

Near the top, the through road turns sharply left, signed for **ABTENAU.** Straight ahead goes to a parking lot for hikers. Climbing up over another hump, **Gasthof Alpenrose** can be spotted on the mountainside with a little drive leading up to it.

After wandering down into a lovely valley, the Post Alm road gets to a tee-intersection. Turning east is a real adventure. It seems like driving through farm driveways. But it connects with the main road back through Abtenau and down to **Golling.**

North of Golling, at **Hallein,** detour up the Durrnberg road to the **Rossfeldringstrasse,** if you haven't done it (Trip 62). It affords great views of Salzburg, Golling, and the mountains of this trip.

From Hallein, a road heads northeast, behind Salzburg, coming out east of the city right at the **Salzburgring,** the famous G.P. race track. Back toward Salzburg five miles, a road climbs **Gaisberg** mountain. From it, Salzburg is all spread out below.

Trip 67 Filzmoos and Tauern Passes ★

Distance *130 kilometers, plus a turn on the Autobahn*

Terrain *Back and forth on the Tauern mountains, some small roads, steep climbs and switchbacks*

Highlights *Filzmoos (1,056 meters), Ramsau (1,135 meters), Solker Tauern Pass (1,788 meters), Radstadter Tauern Pass (1,739 meters), Seetaler Sattel (1,246 meters)*

Hotel Solaria, one of the MoHos listed at the head of the chapter, Salzburg Land, is atop the **Radstadter Tauern Pass** on this trip.

Two rivers run roughly parallel, from west to east, south of Salzburg, the **Enns** and the **Mur** with the Tauern mountains in between. This route crosses the Tauern mountains from one valley to the next, and then back. Trip 69, Turracher and Nockalm, adjoins this trip on the south.

South of Salzburg, on the Tauern Autobahn, exit at the Eben Ausfahrt, just past the Gasthofgut, and head east up the mountain road to **Filzmoos,** an attractive mountain village with lots of hotels and restaurants. East of Filzmoos, toward **Ramsau,** the road becomes much less traveled. Keep east and the road eventually comes down in the valley of the Enns River, the Enns Tal. There'll be signs to **Stein a.d. Enns,** across on the south side of the river. That's the gateway to **Solker Pass,** a non-commercial north-south crossing of the Tauern mountains. It's a good road, decorated by many signs, each the silhouette of a motorcycle with the words "slowly" in many languages, including English. But it's a great climb. On the north side, short of the top, is a gravel driveway leading to a

Solk Pass crosses through a park, and motorcyclists are advised to keep the throttle under control. Between the two black motorcycles is the word "Please." Then "Drive slowly and quietly here, or else:" and a motorcycles forbidden sign.

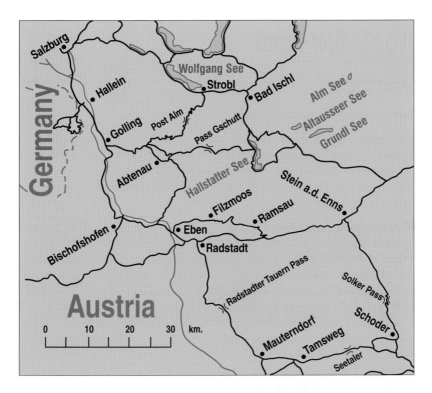

very comfortable restaurant, the **Erzherzog Johann Hutte.** At the top of the pass is a big sign in German addressed to "Dear Motorcycle Riders" and saying in effect that if you don't watch your playful speed on this road, maybe, and then there's the symbol of "motorcycles forbidden." It's a good ride anyway. The south side is through mostly unoccupied forests.

From **Schoder** at the south base of the Solker, head west on very lightly traveled roads high above the Mur Tal, playing along the south edges of the Tauern mountains through **Krakaudorf,** over **Seetaler Sattel,** and on west to **Tamsweg,** a fair sized town, and on to **Mauterndorf.** At 1,122 meters, with a photo-worthy castle, Mauterndorf is the gateway back north over the Radstadter Tauern Pass to Salzburg. The pass road climbs through high meadowlands, then rather steeply to the top of the pass at the village, **Obertauern,** site of the MoHo Solaria. (Look for the motorcycle beside the road.)

A short way down the north side of the pass there's a small monument which recognizes the work of Russian prisoners who built the road during World War I. (Austria was pretty successful in its eastern front battles with Russia in that war. Of course, the Russian revolution started. Meanwhile, the serfs built this road for us to enjoy.) Below the monument, the road enters a narrow gorge and twists beside a rushing stream before daylighting in some rolling hills with quaint farmhouses leading to the town Radstadt and the Autobahn back to Salzburg.

Trip 68   Near Vienna

Distance *About 300 kilometers from Salzburg to Aflenz-Kurort*

Terrain *Gently sweeping over low passes*

Highlights *Popular, scenic lakes and lower mountains, occasional narrow roads, popular motorcycle cafe at Kalte Kuchl. Includes: Pass Gschutt (969 meters), Potschen Hohe (992 meters), Aflenzer Seeberg (1,253 meters), Rottenmanner Hohentauern (1,278 meters), Lahn Sattel (1,015 meters), Kalte Kuchl, Gaberl Sattel (1,547 meters)*

Motorradhotel Hubertushof is almost at the eastern terminus of this trip, just south of **Mariazell,** just north of **Bruck an der Mur,** and not too far west of **Wien,** at **Aflenz-Kurort.** The owner is a dealer for several brands of bikes. Kurort roughly translates as spa, or cure, village. So Aflenz-Kurort is an attractive village nestled in alpine foothills, bypassed by main highways, with public baths and pools. It's hardly ever seen an American.

East of the Solker Pass, almost to Wien, are lovely lakes and low mountains that have captured the hearts of romanticists. Names like Salzkammergut, St. Wolfgang See, **Bad Ischl** (a favorite of Kaiser Franz Joseph up to World War I), **Gesause,** Mariazell, and Raxalpe are all famous. Some roads are nice. Some, not so nice. Nothing is exotic. Nothing like the Dolomites, Andermatt, or the Grossglockner. Some of the valleys are rather tedious and industrial.

South of Salzburg on the Autobahn, past Hallein where the road climbs up to the Rossfeldringstrasse, at the Golling Ausfahrt, a wonderfully pleasant sweeping road heads up and east through a fine mountain village, **Abtenau,** and on across low **Pass Gschutt,** to a popular mountain lake, **Hallstatter See.** Almost

Almost to Wein, the most easterly passes of the Alps attract motorcyclists from the city. The Gasthaus at Kalte Kuchl is right where a couple of good roads intersect.

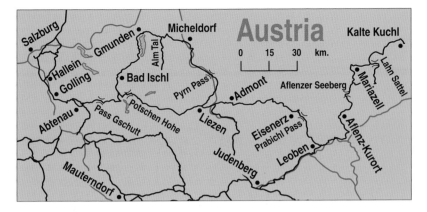

the whole thing is new, sweeping, smooth asphalt. North around the Halstatter See leads to another lowly pass, **Potschen Hohe** and to **Bad Aussee.** South around Halstatter See is a smaller road that takes a tunnel around a village, then makes a steep rough climb to Bad Aussee.

Bad Ischl and **St. Wolfgang See** are north of this route on the main road east from Salzburg. North of Bad Ischl are some nice roads climbing small passes between lovely lakes. There's one between Bad Ischl and **Attersee,** and one between Attersee and **Gmunden,** and one between Gmunden and **Micheldorf.** Midway on the latter is **Scharnstein.** South from Scharnstein, an interesting dead-end road up the **Alm Tal** leads to a tight, twisting climb through the woods on a one-lane paved road to a high restaurant-hotel called the **Hochberghaus.** The road up is called the **Bergstrasse Farrenau.**

The main road south from Micheldorf climbs over the low **Pyhrn Pass** (954 meters) to the **Gesause** region at **Admont.** A quick climb over a little path straight south from Admont connects in 16 kilometers to **Trieben** and the **Rottenmanner Hohentauern** pass road, and immediately south of that through **Judenburg** is the **Gaberl Sattel** toward **Graz.** The **Osterreichring race track** is just northeast of Judenburg.

Meanwhile, the Gesause road, east from Admont, is rather uneventful, although famous. It runs east toward the **Prabichl Pass** at **Eisenerz.** The countryside looks like it has been strip mined, and Eisenerz looks like a "company town" in Wales or West Virginia. **Steyr,** home of **Puch,** is downstream from Eisenerz, and the **Prabichl,** the source of its iron ore.

The Alps have their last fling about 90 kilometers short of Wien. The area is easily reached from the **Motorradhotel Hubertushof** at **Aflenz-Kurort,** listed above. The *Tofftreffpunkt,* for riders of Wien and eastern Austria, who know where the nearby good roads are, is an intersection with a Gasthof called **Kalte Kuchl.** Despite its name ("cold kitchen"), it has good hot food, and the terraces are full of bikers on weekends. The two passes of note, **Lahn Sattel** and **Aflenzer Seeberg,** are between Aflenz-Kurort and Kalte Kuchl.

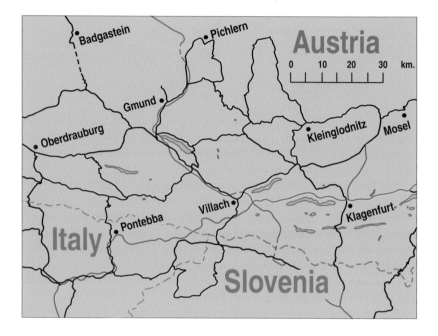

Karnten Land

Austria's southern state **Karnten,** that we call Carinthia, borders both Italy and **Slovenia.** Slovenia is that northern part of former Yugoslavia that ajoins Italy. Karnten is a land of mountains and lakes, which some have called warmer than the rest of Austria. Routes of Trip 67 are to the north, and routes of Trip 55 are southwest of it.

Two possible hotels illustrate the area's variety.

One is in **Villach,** a medium size town in the valley of the **Drau River** that flows out of the Dolomites of Italy and across southern Austria into Slovenia.

Almost next door to the cathedral, **the Dom,** in Villach, is the **Hotel Post.** Another Hotel Post on Hauptplatz. The Hauptplatz is a walking zone, so it's necessary to ride in to the hotel's courtyard from the back.

A road west right out of the middle of Villach climbs in a couple of kilometers to almost 1,000 meters at **Bad Bleiberg.**

About 30 kilometers north of Villach is the mountain village **Bad Kleinkirchheim** with several hotels capitalizing on the mountains and the water. One is the **Hotel Pulverer.** It's pretty fancy with many pools inside and out, water slides, huge jacuzzi baths, very good food, heated bathroom floors, towel racks, and terry robes.

Hotels abound in the Alps, capitalizing on and marketing to motorcyclists. This is the Hotel Drei Konige and Post in Andermatt, where 200 years ago Goethe stayed.

Trip 69 Turracher and Nockalm ★

Distance *200 Kilometers*

Terrain *Seldom traveled mountain roads and passes, some narrow*

Highlights *Flattnitz (1,400 meters), Turracher Hohe (1,783 meters), Nockalmstrasse (toll) with Eisen Tal Hohe (2,042 meters) and Heiligenbach (1,920 meters), Dr. Josef Mehrl Hutte (1,700 meters), Katchberg Pass (1,641 meters), Hochrindl (1,561 meters), Porsche Museum*

The **Mur River** and the **Drau River** are roughly parallel, flowing from west to east. This route weaves back and forth several times across the mountain that separates them.

The south part of Trip 67 was across the Mur north of this trip.

Northeast of **Villach,** and east of **Bad Kleinkirchheim** is a village called **Ebene Reichenau.** Right by the church, a little road starts to climb east over **Hochrindl.** At a fork, the unpaved road is the pass. (The paved road goes quite a ways before it deadends). The unpaved road climbs several kilometers to Hochrindl where the asphalt begins again and forks. Either fork offers a nice ride down east to the village, **Kleinglodnitz,** where the **Flatnitz** road begins its climb north. Almost at the top of Flatnitz there's a fork, with the westerly branch being the pass. It wends down to the Mur River. You know when you get there because there's a railroad track beside the Mur. Cross the tracks and only six kilometers west is **Predlitz** where the **Turracher Hohe** road heads back south across the mountain. The climb is sweeping and fun to the top where there are several restaurants and hotels. Some have found the toilets in one, the **Schlosshotel Seewirt,** to be amusing. The descent on the south side is very steep, a 23% grade, so if it's cold on top, you can warm up fast.

As soon as the road flattens out there's an intersection with the **Nockalmstrasse,** marked by a cute waterwheel. (And you're just two kilometers north of Ebene Reichenau.) Make the sharp turn, back northwesterly across the mountain again. Like on the Grossglockner, there's a toll on the Nockalm, and like on the Grossglockner, there are restaurants and small hotels and you can play back and forth before exiting. In fact, the same company owns both roads. There are two high points on the road, which finally makes it down to the valley of the **Kremsbach,** at a village called **Innerkrems.** The other Krems is downstream. But don't go that way. Turn easterly, upstream on a road that doesn't look very promising. But it crosses the next mountain at a place identified only as **Dr. Josef Mehrl Hutte,** and comes down in the Mur side of the mountain in a tee-intersection. Head west through **Pichlern** and in six kilometers join the main highway crossing back south over the **Katchberg Pass.** The Katchberg is rather steep on both sides. And all of a sudden there is traffic, because the Katchberg

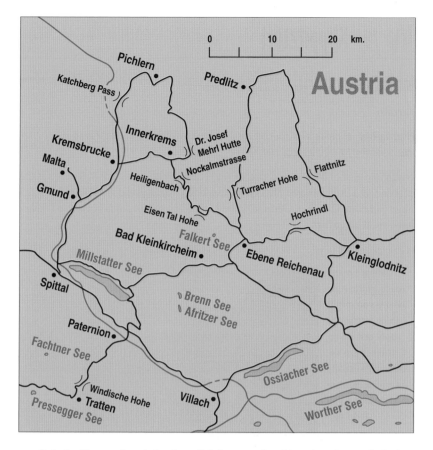

parallels the Tauern Autobahn from Salzburg, and at this point, the autobahn has a toll. The Katchberg doesn't.

South of the Katchberg, you'll be amazed at the towering concrete structures far overhead, carrying the Autobahn down the narrow valley without scarring the mountains, leaving farms and villages underneath it. There is an Autobahn connection just at the base of the Katchberg, and there's no toll to go on south. The entrance to the Autobahn is called **Rennweg** . . . raceway. On either road, up on the Autobahn or down below on the regular road, head south to **Gmund,** site of the famous **Porsche Museum.** It's necessary to loop into and around the village of Gmund to get to the museum. Many collector cars are on display.

Behind Gmund, a dead end road climbs the **Malta Tal** about 35 kilometers to 1,931 meters. There's a toll, and a hotel restaurant and a Stausee at the top.

Villach, the Drau, and Bad Kleinkirchheim are farther down south.

Trip 70 Klippitztorl

Distance *240 Kilometers, some Autobahn*

Terrain *Fun riding on narrow roads over moderately high forested mountains*

Highlights *Explore non-tourist, rural Austria: Klippitztorl (1,644 meters), Weinebene (1,688 meters), Hebalpe (1,360 meters), Soboth (1,349 meters)*

North and east of Villach and east of Bad Kleinkirchheim is **Althofen.** It's at the east end of a little valley called **Gurk** that has a little town called Gurk that has a huge cathedral (Dom, in German) called Gurk. All this is north of Karnten's capital city, **Klagenfurt.**

There are many roads in the Alps where you might think you're the only one riding them. Even so, there will usually be a restaurant or hotel awaiting you (Trip 46).

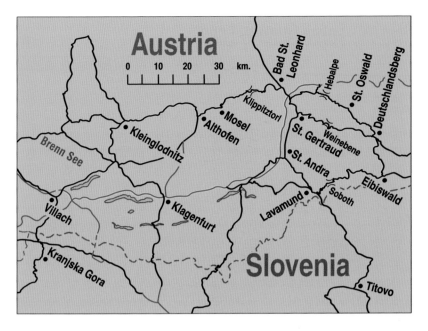

Anyway, east of Althofen about seven kilometers is the village **Mosel,** and just north of Mosel, the pass called **Klippitztorl** starts it's climbs east over the mountains. It wends to 1,644 meters and it must be good because trucks and trailers are forbidden. Not much of anybody there, but there is a restaurant hut near the top that may be surprised to see you.

On down east in the next valley, head south about 13 kilometers crossing under the Autobahn to **St. Gertraud,** where another nobody's-on-it road crosses the next mountain range on a pass called **Weinebene.** In about 35 kilometers, it comes down near a pretty good sized town, **Deutschlandsberg.**

Then you have a choice. Turn south about 15 kilometers to **Eibiswald,** then back west, skimming the Slovenian border, but staying in Austria on a motorcycle favorite called **Soboth.** Soboth is not usually listed as a pass, but it sweeps and swoops with occasional hairpins for 36 kilometers to 1,349 meters on open, smooth asphalt with wide vistas. It's a road guaranteed to please any rider. Near the summit there's a view park often filled with bikes, and a refreshment stand with a WC down under. From the westerly base of Soboth at **Lavamund,** it's a short ride north to the autobahn that connects Graz and Wien to the northeast, with Karnten to the southwest. Take it.

Or, in **Deutschlandsberg** there are signs for St. Oswald and the pass, Hebalpe, in a northwesterly direction. The route is very pleasant, crossing over the mountains to the autobahn.

Trip 71 Three Country Loop ★

Distance *200 kilometers*

Terrain *Modestly high passes, narrow roads*

Highlights *Loop across Wurzen Pass (1,073 meters) into Slovenia, through Triglavski Narodni, Slovenia's National Park, Vrsic Pass (1,611 meters) World War I fort and monument, Passo de Predil (1,150 meters) into Italy, Passo Sella Nevea (1,190 meters), Nassfeld Pass (1,557 meters) into Austria, Windische Hohe (1,110 meters) Kreuzberg Sattel (1,077 meters), Gailberg Sattel (982 meters)*

Villach is just north of where **Slovenia** (formerly part of Yugoslavia) borders Italy. This loop south from Villach explores that three country corner.

Wurzen Pass into Slovenia is signed, straight up and south from Villach. It's only 15 kilometers from downtown to the border at the top of the pass.

Insurance for vehicles registered in Europe should be valid in Slovenia, which many consider the most stable of the new republics. Check the green card to be sure SLO, Slovenia, is not crossed out. It probably is crossed out on most vehicles not registered in Europe. If it is crossed out, it will be necessary to buy Slovenian insurance at the border. It's not a bargain. It might be handy to get Slovenian money, too. Remember there will be both Austrian and Slovenian border checks. Slovenia does have moderately priced gasoline at modern stations with handicapped facilities.

Just down off the pass into Slovenia a few kilometers, there's a junction. Jog easterly a couple of kilometers and turn south by **Kranjska Gora** to climb southerly up the **Vrsic Pass.** The hairpins climbing the pass are cobblestone, and at one of them is a place to park because there's a very Russian looking church in the woods. It is Russian. It was built by Russian prisoners during World War I while they were working on the road. This is the National Park, **Triglavski Narodni,** that occupies a large part of northwestern Slovenia.

There's a modest restaurant at the top of the pass, and a good road down in a southwesterly direction with more than thirty numbered hairpins. At the junction at the bottom, head northerly, back up the **Passo de Predil.** In World War I, this area was all in Austria and the Predil was the border with the Italian enemy. So near the top of the pass is a stone fort much like those in the Dolomites. It's sited to command the valley approaches. There are metal rungs in the cliff opposite the fort, apparently installed like a ladder to some higher observation point. It looks pretty exposed. Nearby, in an arcing curve of the road, is an elaborate monument honoring an Austrian nobleman who apparently came to grief in the area. His name was von Hermann.

Across the border, it's only a couple of kilometers down to an intersection. The road southeast is a pleasant and forgotten pass, the **Passo Sella Nevea,**

through the **Julian Alps,** with a rifugio named **Julia.** West of the rifugio, the pass snakes down through hairpins and tunnels, then wanders west through relatively unoccupied mountains, finally meeting the main autostrada connecting this part of Italy with Austria. Take the regular road beside the autostrada north only eight kilometers to **Pontebba** (Trip 55). Cross the ponte (bridge) leaving the autostrada to head east. Go straight north. Actually, not very straight, very twistily. It's only 13 kilometers up to the Austrian border and the **Nassfeld Pass** (Passo di Promollo in Italian). It's just 12 kilometers down the pass. Head east seven kilometers to **Hermagor.**

Or get to Hermagor the long way, by heading west to **Kotschach,** north over the **Gailberg Sattel,** and east from **Oberdrauberg** to **Greifenburg,** then up the **Kreuzberg Sattel** to Hermagor. Just about 100 kilometers extra.

From Hermagor, head easterly to **Tratten,** and climb north over the **Windische Hohe,** down to the valley of the **Drau** and Villach.

To get to **Bad Kleinkirchheim** from the north end of the **Windische Hohe** road, cross under the Autobahn to Paternion and then cross the river Drau and turn north.

Corsica

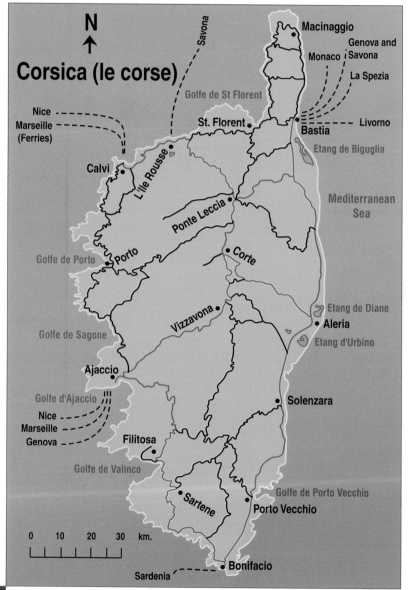

Corsica (le corse)

N
↑

Savona

Macinaggio

Genova and Savona
Monaco
La Spezia

Golfe de St Florent

Nice
Marseille
(Ferries)

St. Florent

Bastia

Livorno

Etang de Biguglia

Calvi

L'île Rousse

Mediterranean Sea

Ponte Leccia

Golfe de Porto

Porto

Corte

Vizzavona

Etang de Diane

Aleria

Golfe de Sagone

Etang d'Urbino

Ajaccio

Golfe d'Ajaccio

Nice
Marseille
Genova

Filitosa

Solenzara

Golfe de Valinco

Sartene

Golfe de Porto Vecchio

Porto Vecchio

0   10   20   30   km.

Sardenia

Bonifacio

Corsica

Corsica should be on every motorcyclist's must-do list.

Little more than 150 kilometers, north to south, and 80 kilometers wide, it's packed with high rugged mountains—even some skiing—and gorges and canyons and passes with enough tight, twisty roads to exhaust the most ardent enthusiast. It takes a week of all-day riding to cover the roads.

And it's breathtakingly gorgeous. Exotic rock formations in all colors, rushing streams and waterfalls, pine forests, chestnut forests, deserts, and cliffs down to private little beaches.

Because most Americans might have difficulty finding Corsica on the map (and because most Corsicans have never seen an American) here's a bit about it.

It's an island in the Mediterranean south of **Genova,** west of **Livorno** (and Pisa), and north of **Sardinia** (Sardegna in Italian). For 200 years it's been French. For a thousand before that it was Italian, under Genova or Pisa, with a bit of Spain thrown in. To Italians it was Corsica. That's what we call it. Germans use "k"s, Korsika. But in French, it's Corse, or le Corse. There's Italian food and French food. But the money, the stamps, the phone, and the police are all French. Le Corse is a department of metropolitan France. And there's the rub. Some locals would rather not be.

The difference need not affect motorcyclists. Surely not the thousands of bikers that fill most every ferry to and from the island. The ferries to Corsica often look like those to the Isle of Man during TT time, packed with every kind of motorcycle imaginable. There's play room for all.

You don't have to worry too much about high brow culture on Corsica. Some prehistoric types—like 20,000 years ago—carved figures on the southwest coast. The Romans tried unsuccessfully to farm the few level parts on the east coast. Since then various city states and kings fought with scant success to control the island. There were lots of places to hide in those mountains and canyons that we love today.

Several coastal towns, notably **Calvi** on the northwest coast and **Bonifacio** on the south tip, remain walled fortresses left over from the battles of the Middle Ages. Then there's the fortress of independent Corsica in the middle of the mountains at **Corte.**

The proud symbol of Corsica is a black head with a white headband. (Sardinia's symbol is a black head with a blindfold.) The island has two administrative departments: the southwestern part is **Corse du Sud** (southern Corsica), while the northeastern part is **Haute Corse** (high Corsica). The license plate of all vehicles registered on Corsica has a final digit "2," with an "A" or "B" after it.

There are only a couple of kilometers of more or less straight road, just south of **Bastia** on the northeast coast. The main road across the island and mountains from Bastia to **Ajaccio** on the opposite coast swoops and sweeps in daringly inviting asphalt—and the locals dare—to 1,163 meters at the **Col de Vizzavona.** Most other roads are so gnarly and/or so precipitous as to require constant attention while providing exciting riding pleasures. They climb through such wild landscapes that it seems you're exploring some strange planet, not a small European island. Ride in the mountains all day. Sleep by the seashore.

Tourist offices: Offices de Tourisme; 1 Place Foch; F-21076 Ajaccio; T 495 21 4087.

Offices de Tourisme de la Haute; Corse; F-20200 Bastia; T 495 31 0204.

Through the Gorges de la Restonica is one of the high mountain roads on the little Mediterranean island of Corsica. Corsica has more roads than a good rider can cover in a week, including passes through mountains like this.

The Corsica ferries always have a lot of motorcycle traffic. Somehow, the word is out among European motorcyclists that Corsica is a great place to ride.

How to Get There

Fly. Sail. Bikers will probably ferry to Corsica from the continent. There are multiple ways.

Three companies do most of the ferrying. One French. Two Italian.

The French one, **S.N.C.M. Ferryterranee,** sails from French ports like Marseille and Nice and Toulon. (You want to know what those letters stand for? Societe Nationale Maritime Corse Mediterranee.)

Corsica Ferries, an Italian company, sails from Nice and Toulon in France, and from Savona and Livorno in Italy. Both of these two lines have introduced fast boats, capable of about 40 knots that make the crossing from France or Savona in three or four hours. The fast boats have special facilities for securing motorcycles. Trouble is, they can't operate in heavy seas, so the crossings are subject to cancellation. The shortest crossing by standard ferry is from Livorno, the port near Pisa, a long way south of the Alps. Savona and Nice are the ports of embarcation closest to the Alps.

Navarma (Moby Lines) sails from Livorno.

An Italian company, **Happy Lines** runs boats from the Italian Riviera at La Spezia during summer months.

The standard ferries are large ships carrying several decks of trucks and busses and cars towing boats and trailers and lots of motorcycles. They're equipped with restaurants and lounges and maybe movies and pools. Overnight ferries have cabins with a private bath available for much less than most hotel rooms—a good choice. Ferries run on multiple schedules serving multiple ports on Corsica. Not all ports are served every day.

Bastia on the northeast coast of Corsica is the closest to Italy. **Calvi** on the northwest coast is the closest to France. **Ajaccio,** the only city on Corsica, is on the southwest coast.

Ferries ply regularly between **Bonifacio** on the south tip and Sardinia, about an hour boat ride, but a world away.

Savona is but a half day's ride from most any place in the Alps. Its port, called **Porto Vado,** has nice terminal facilities and the most sailings. Play in the Alps all morning, then cut to the coast. Terminals are signed from the autostrada.

Recommended is the overnight ferry from Savona. Just get there in time for the evening sailing. The crew secures the bike along the bulkhead of one of the garage decks. Head up to your cabin, clean up, have a nice dinner, and sleep in a cosy bunk. Get off the ferry in the morning for a great riding day on Corsica.

Ferry companies take credit cards and the Italian ones speak English.

Addresses, e-mail listings, FAX, and phone numbers for them are in the Hotel Addendum under Corsica.

Where to Stay

Like western Austria, Corsica is packed with hotels in exotic spots.

Take **Porto,** for instance, on the west coast. It's a tiny village that's a must see and stay, wedged in a crevice between towering pink mountains with surf crashing on pink rocks and good hotels and restaurants and three roads in (and out). Each of the three roads in (and out) rates three stars from Michelin. That's their top rating, and they're right. Mind, it's the roads that get the stars, not some building or other wonder. Each of the three roads is an exhilarating adventure.

At **Hotel Les Flots Bleus** (the blue waves) each room has a deck facing across water to mountains and the tumble-down watch tower built by the Genovese hundreds of years ago.

On the rocks beyond the watch tower is **Hotel Belvedere.** In complete contrast is the **Grand Hotel du Monte d'Oro.** It's in the forest, all by itself at about 1,000 meters elevation just off the main trans-island highway at the **Col de Vizzavona.** There's nothing grand about the hotel except its name. It faces the peak it's named after. And they do have snow. There's an old part to the hotel and a newer part. Neither would rate high on the amenities scale, but the lounge has a huge fireplace and lots of overstuffed chairs. Meals are family style. It's fun.

Twenty-five kilometers west and across a pass from Bastia is **St. Florent,** one of the few Corsican villages with a French name. It has a yacht basin, waterfront restaurants, and several hotels. One is the **Hotel Dolce Notte** (sweet night) directly on the beach (a bit rocky) on the edge of the village. The hotel has no restaurant, but serves breakfast on your patio, directly on the water.

It takes a lot of stones piled on stones to hold up the typical Corsican road.

Porto Vecchio is on the southeast coast, with a medieval town on the hill and newer stuff around its yacht basin. There's the **Hotel Shegara.**

Hotel Solemare is down at the southern point of Corsica at Bonifacio. The hotel faces the massive ancient walled city across the fjord-like harbor.

A few kilometers north of Porto Vecchio is a small village named **Favona.** Right on its curving white sand beach is **Hotel U Dragulinu.** The Mediterranean is crystal clear and the lounges on the sand have umbrellas and soft pads. Dinner and breakfast diners can look out on the waves. Maybe the first course for dinner will be wonderful mussels.

Most hotel operators will insist that bikes be parked in a locked garage at night. A good idea.

The first Corsica trip, below, starts as if you had just arrived on Corsica. The trips following are from the base communities listed above.

CHAPTER
21

Trip 72 Col de Vergio to Porto ★★

Distance *190 kilometers*

Terrain *Mountain roads, some very narrow*

Highlights *Delightful villages, some asleep; a couple of medieval relics; pine and chestnut forests, exotic gorges;* ★*Col de Vergio (1,477 meters)*

Leave **Bastia** or **Calvi** following the signs for **St. Florent.** It's only 25 kilometers and a pass (Col de Teghime, D81) away from Bastia. Just a little farther from Calvi. From Bastia, the road climbs aggressively and tight even while still in town. Toward St. Florent it passes through vineyards. If you're coming from an overnight ferry, St. Florent is a great place for breakfast. Right on the little main square is a *patisserie* serving fresh croissants and breakfast. There's a short one-way loop from the square into the old city and back by the yacht harbor lined with restaurants.

Take the tiny road going south from the little square (not the main one west of town). Very rural. In about five kilometers it passes a 12th century church, still a cathedral, called **Nebbio.** Nobody's there, but it's worth a look. It's a perfectly preserved Romanesque style building built by the best artisans Pisa could send.

Past Nebbio, climb on up the mountain road through open countryside to **Oletta** and on to **Murato.** Murato sits upon the crest of the island with views to the Mediterranean on the east and west. And there is a little black and white stone church (they couldn't decide whether to make it black and white stripes, or

The little Village, Porto, hugs the beach at the base of huge red rocks. Atop the rocks, right, is a square Genovese watch tower from the middle ages. The whole area is so spectacular that it's been declared a United Nations Preserve.

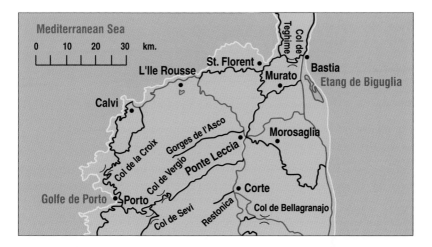

black and white checkerboard) built about the same time as the cathedral below, and a delightful contrast in craftsmanship. (It helps to remember that Pisa was building its cathedral and leaning tower about the same time in black and white, and seems to have been more ambitious, although Murato's tower doesn't lean quite enough to be famous.)

The road south from Murato (D5) to **Ponte Leccia** has just been paved—one narrow lane with a center stripe. Wide pavement buffs may want to backtrack a couple of kilometers and take the wild ride down the **Defile de Lancone** to the east coast, and then follow the signs south and west in the direction of Corte and Ajaccio.

Before either, but after climbing into the mountains, just nine kilometers south of Ponte Leccia (there is a bridge) leave the main highway and head west to **Porto** (D84). First comes the awesome **Scala de Santa Regina,** a gorge with the road barely hung on the edge. Then pine forests and the **Col de Vergio** with a monument figure of a beardless Christ. Heading down west the forest turns to chestnut, the **Forest d'Aitone.** Pigs like chestnuts. There may be some.

Below the forest, the road enters the **Gorges de Spelunca,** majestic walls and formations in pink. Somehow, the road has to get to the bottom of the gorge.

On the way down is a little village, **Evisa,** with a hotel restaurant called **Scopa Rossa.** There are several pull-out view sites.

At the bottom and mouth of the gorge is Porto. Everything is still pink, except the eucalyptus trees.

Some American bikers came upon some German bikers climbing the Col de Vergio. All but one of the Germans took the bait and played across the pass, stopping at a pull-out view spot. Finally, the holdout rode up and immediately fell over. Rushing to assist, the Americans noted the rider's leg alarmingly crumpled under the bike. "Not to worry," said the German, in English, "it isn't mine." It was a prosthesis.

CHAPTER
21

Trip 73 Calvi

Distance *160 kilometers (it'll take all day)*

Terrain *Very, very tight, twisting roads. No highway speed possible*

Highlights *Wild mountains and coast to Calvi, a medieval walled city with busy waterfront cafes and promenades*

Take the coast road north from **Porto** (D81), climbing the cliffs with views down over the village and gulf. The whole gulf is a **Unesco designated preserve.** There will be stops for pictures. However exciting the views north of the **Col de la Croix,** the pavement is patched and rough. Some may prefer to turn around and check the views going the opposite direction. **Calvi** is a busy town with a medieval citadel and waterfront cafes. Returning from Calvi, a bit better time can be maintained by taking the faster inland road south.

The Corniche road north of Porto hugs the massive red cliffs high over the Mediterranean.

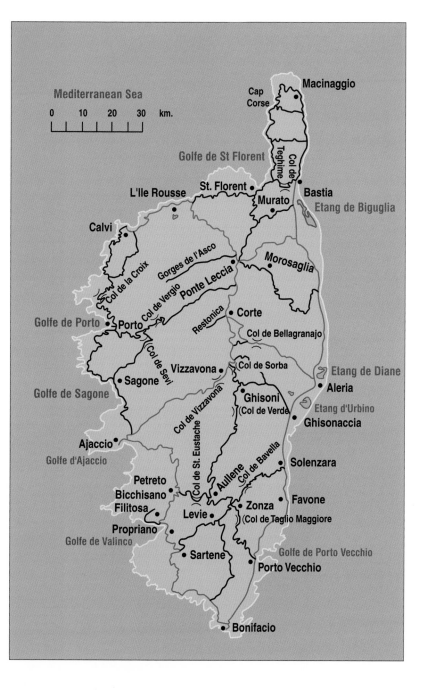

Mediterranean Sea

0   10   20   30   km.

Macinaggio

Cap
Corse

Golfe de St Florent

Col de Teghime

St. Florent

L'Ile Rousse

Murato

Bastia

Etang de Biguglia

Calvi

Morosaglia

Gorges de l'Asco

Col de la Croix

Col de Vergio

Ponte Leccia

Golfe de Porto

Porto

Col de Sevi

Restonica

Corte

Col de Bellagranajo

Etang de Diane

Vizzavona

Col de Sorba

Sagone

Col de Vizzavona

Ghisoni

Aleria

Golfe de Sagone

Col de Verde

Etang d'Urbino

Ghisonaccia

Col de St. Eustache

Col de Bavella

Solenzara

Ajaccio

Aullene

Golfe d'Ajaccio

Petreto

Favone

Bicchisano

Zonza

Filitosa

Levie

Col de Taglio Maggiore

Propriano

Golfe de Valinco

Golfe de Porto Vecchio

Sartene

Porto Vecchio

Bonifacio

Trip 74 Les Calanche

Distance *100 kilometers*

Terrain *Some tight, narrow road, but mostly more open two lane*

Highlights *More exotic pink rock formations and rocky coastline; beautiful beaches and forested mountain pass; Col de Sevi (1,094 meters)*

Follow the **Les Calanche** road (D81) south from **Porto.** The formations and the road will require some stopping and picture taking. Unbelievable. On through **Cargese** and down to the coast at **Sagone** which has a wonderful broad white sand beach. At the south end of the beach is a tiny hotel restaurant, **La Marine,** with a sublime location.

Head northwest on the inland road from Sagone (D70), climbing over the **Col de Sevi,** and connecting with the **Gorges de Spelunca** road back down to Porto.

A rider crosses a stone bridge and a small waterfall along the Les Calancehe road south of Porto.

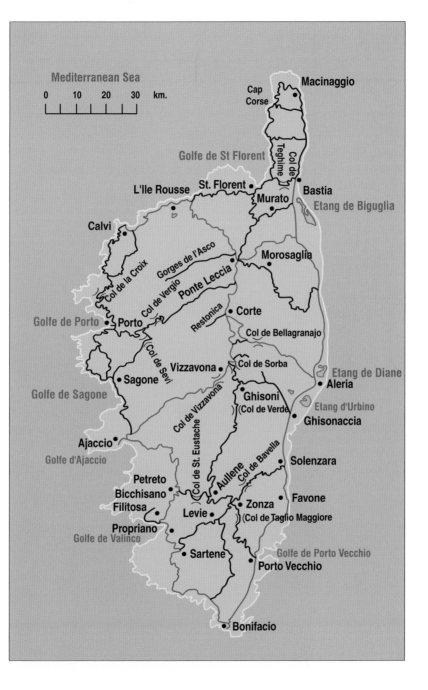

Mediterranean Sea

0   10   20   30   km.

Cap Corse

Macinaggio

Golfe de St Florent

Col de Teghime

L'Ile Rousse

St. Florent

Murato

Bastia

Etang de Biguglia

Calvi

Col de la Croix

Gorges de l'Asco

Morosaglia

Col de Vergio

Ponte Leccia

Golfe de Porto

Porto

Restonica

Corte

Col de Bellagranajo

Col de Sevi

Vizzavona

Col de Sorba

Etang de Diane

Sagone

Col de Vizzavona

Ghisoni

Aleria

Golfe de Sagone

(Col de Verde)

Etang d'Urbino

Ghisonaccia

Ajaccio

Col de St. Eustache

Aullene

Col de Bavella

Solenzara

Golfe d'Ajaccio

Petreto

Bicchisano

Zonza

Favone

Filitosa

Levie

(Col de Taglio Maggiore)

Propriano

Golfe de Valinco

Sartene

Golfe de Porto Vecchio

Porto Vecchio

Bonifacio

CHAPTER

21

Trip 75 Bonifacio

Distance *220 kilometers*

Terrain *Fairly open, smooth, two lane coastal roads, then some tight mountain stuff*

Highlights *The walled city of Bonifacio, fjord-like harbor, clifftop view of Sardinia, yacht-filled waterfront at Propriano, prehistoric carvings at Filitosa, mountain roads and villages, Col de St. Eustache (995 meters)*

Don't be tempted by the parking lots as you ride into **Bonifacio.** Go by them and drive right on up the steep road and in through the arched gate in the massive

Elaborate stone retaining walls hold up the road below Col de St. Eustache.

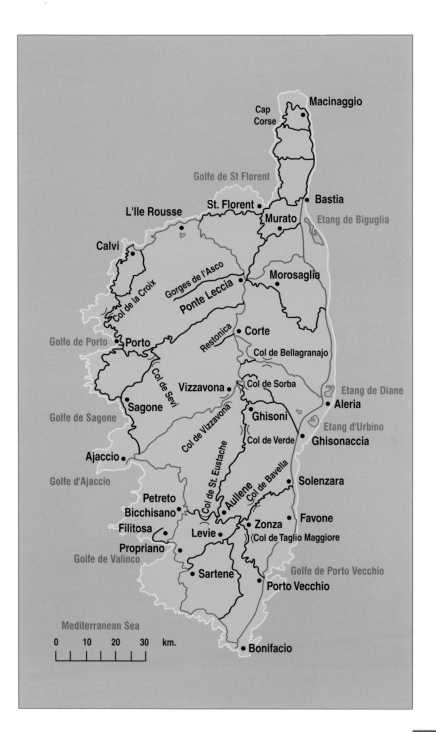

Macinaggio

Cap
Corse

Golfe de St Florent

St. Florent • Bastia

L'Ile Rousse • Murato • Etang de Biguglia

Calvi

Gorges de l'Asco • Morosaglia

Col de la Croix
Ponte Leccia

Golfe de Porto • Porto

Restonica • Corte

Col de Bellagranajo

Col de Sevi • Vizzavona • Col de Sorba

Sagone • Etang de Diane

Golfe de Sagone • Aleria

Col de Vizzavona • Ghisoni • Etang d'Urbino

Col de Verde • Ghisonaccia

Ajaccio

Golfe d'Ajaccio • Col de Bavella • Solenzara

Col de St. Eustache

Petreto • Aullene • Favone

Bicchisano • Zonza

Filitosa • Levie • Col de Taglio Maggiore

Propriano

Golfe de Valinco • Golfe de Porto Vecchio

Sartene • Porto Vecchio

Mediterranean Sea

0   10   20   30   km.

Bonifacio

Crossing Corsica between Propriano and Zonza over the Col de St. Eustache allows views of the island's central mountains and valleys.

The mighty walls of Bonifacio tower over its little yacht harbor lined with restaurants. Ride up into the citadel and back down to the port where bikes can usually find free parking. (Parking for a fee is available along the road into town).

The other side of Bonifacio rests high on these cliffs facing Sardinia across the "Bouches de Bonifacio."

walls of the Bonifacio citadel. On through the village and out atop the cliff (past the cemetary) it's possible to see crashing waves far below and Sardinia in the distance. Note the tiny stairway up the massive cliff that was supposed to give besieged defenders access to the sea.

Emerging from the citadel, take the road down by the very narrow harbor sheltered by cliffs. It usually sports an international collection of yachts. The little road along the harbor is lined with restaurants and souvenir shops and the ferry to Sardinia. Usually there's a place to park a bike or two.

It's open sweeping road north along the west coast (N196) for about 16 kilometers to a turn, easterly, marked for the airport (D859). Go 11 kilometers, on past the airport, to a turn north (D59). There begins a really fun, deserted road twisting over moutains, through a tunnel, for 40 kilometers to **Levie.** At Levie turn west (D268) to **Propriano,** a town with an active yacht harbor. On the north side of the harbor is the shoreline road toward **Filitosa,** the site of prehistoric carvings.

From Propriano, twist north on the main road (N196) to **Petreto-Bicchisano,** where another fun, twisting road (D420) climbs over several passes including the **Col de St. Eustache.** Parts of the road are modern, swooping and smooth. Parts aren't. Pass through Allene and Quenza to **Zonza** where there's sort of an x-shaped intersection. Follow the sign for **Porto Vecchio** (D368) around a lake through the forests of l'Ospedale, over the Col de Taglia Maggiore with views of the east coast, then sweep on down to Porto Vecchio.

Trip 76 Vizzavona and Restonica

Distance *About 150 kilometers one way from Ajaccio*

Terrain *Some very tight, twisty roads*

Highlights *Climb through forests alongside rushing mountain streams to a high mountain bowl at 1,300 meters;* ★*Col de Vizzavona (1,163 meters)*

From the south, cross the **Col de Vizzavona** (N193), a well-maintained sweeping highway, through forests and past the **Grand Hotel du Monte d'Oro** as far north as **Corte,** the historic capital of independent Corsica, noted for its citadel on a high rock outcropping. The highway loops east around Corte. Several roundabouts provide access to the town and the **Gorges de la Restonica** road (D623). Most of Restonica is a narrow, one-lane wide, rough road. It deadends at a peak-rimmed mountain bowl.

From Corte back to Vizzavona, try going a few kilometers down the main road southeast (through a grove of cork trees) and then climb back over the **Col de Bellagranajo.**

The little road between Murato and Ponte Leccia has recently been paved to a full ten feet, with a center line (Trip 72).

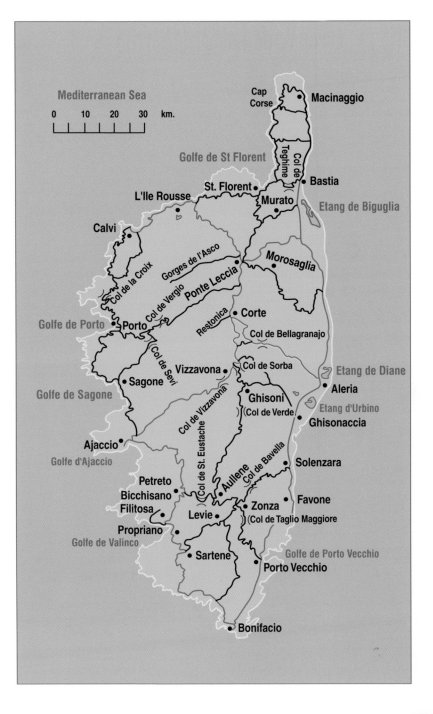

Mediterranean Sea

0   10   20   30   km.

Cap Corse

Macinaggio

Golfe de St Florent

Col de Teghime

St. Florent

Bastia

L'Ile Rousse

Murato

Etang de Biguglia

Calvi

Morosaglia

Col de la Croix

Gorges de l'Asco

Col de Vergio

Ponte Leccia

Restonica

Corte

Golfe de Porto

Porto

Col de Bellagranajo

Col de Sevi

Vizzavona

Col de Sorba

Etang de Diane

Sagone

Col de Vizzavona

Ghisoni

Aleria

Golfe de Sagone

Col de Verde

Etang d'Urbino

Ghisonaccia

Ajaccio

Col de St. Eustache

Col de Bavella

Solenzara

Golfe d'Ajaccio

Petreto

Bicchisano

Aullene

Favone

Filitosa

Zonza

Levie

Col de Taglio Maggiore

Propriano

Golfe de Valinco

Sartene

Golfe de Porto Vecchio

Porto Vecchio

Bonifacio

Trip 77   Col de Verde and Col de Bavella   ★

Distance *225 kilometers (a long day)*

Terrain *Mostly rough paved, narrow, tight mountain roads*

Highlights *Wandering mountain roads with remote villages and a couple of good passes, especially the Col de Verde (1,289 meters) and the ★Col de Bavella (1,218 meters), Col de Sorba (1,311 meters)*

From **Vizzavona,** ride north (N193) about 12 kilometers and then turn east (D69) over the **Col de Sorba,** through lovely forests to the mountain village of **Ghisoni.** Ghisoni has a few commercial establishments, and each will be pleased to see customers. The road works (that's the right term) its way on south through woods and past small waterfalls over the **Col de Verde,** finally reaching **Aullene,** a mountain crossroad village with restaurants and services (see Trip 75). On east from Aullene (D420), cross a canyon to **Zonza** where all of a sudden, and inexplicably, there's a fine sweeping highway northerly up the **Col de Bavella** (D268). The top of the col, in a pine forest, has several rustic restaurants and views across miles of island peaks and the sea. The road down the northeast

From the pine forest atop Col de Bavella there are sweeping views of mountains and sea.

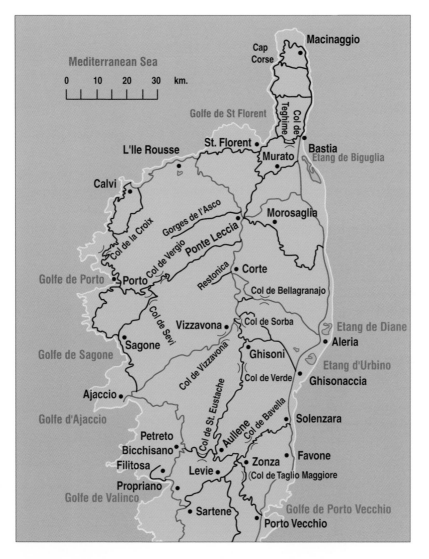

Mediterranean Sea

0   10   20   30   km.

Macinaggio

Cap Corse

Golfe de St Florent

Col de Teghime

St. Florent

L'Ile Rousse

Murato

Bastia

Etang de Biguglia

Calvi

Gorges de l'Asco

Morosaglia

Col de la Croix

Col de Vergio

Ponte Leccia

Golfe de Porto

Porto

Restonica

Corte

Col de Bellagranajo

Col de Sevi

Vizzavona

Col de Sorba

Etang de Diane

Aleria

Sagone

Golfe de Sagone

Col de Vizzavona

Ghisoni

Etang d'Urbino

Col de Verde

Ghisonaccia

Ajaccio

Col de St. Eustache

Golfe d'Ajaccio

Col de Bavella

Solenzara

Aullene

Petreto

Bicchisano

Zonza

Favone

Filitosa

Levie

(Col de Taglio Maggiore

Propriano

Golfe de Valinco

Sartene

Golfe de Porto Vecchio

Porto Vecchio

side of the col to the coast is being rebuilt. It had been notoriously rough, narrow, and potholed. It traverses wild forests with views of Dolomite-like peaks, bridges, trout streams, and passes spots popular for stream-side bathing, before reaching the east coast at **Solenzara.** (Favone with the beachfront Hotel U Dragulinu is 12 kilometers south.) From there, follow the coast road (N198) north 17 kilometers to **Ghisonaccia.** Then turn inland (D344), westerly through the exotic gorges called the **Defile de l'Inzecca** and **Stretta** to Ghisoni, the Col de Sorba and Vizzavona.

Trip 78 St. Florent

Distance *180 kilometers*

Terrain *Mountains and desert and forest*

Highlights *Ski bowl at 1,450 meters, desert that looks like southern California (but just a few kilometers of it) with more twisty mountain roads*

The main road southwest from St. Florent (D81) crosses the **Desert des Agriates** that seems like the desert mountains of southern California, except that

The roads around Cap Corse, the north finger of Corsica, have much in common with Highway One in California. But Cap Corse and its roads are much more rugged.

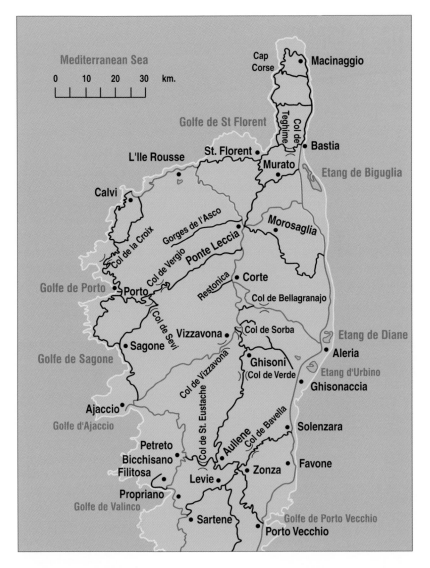

there's that sea out there. The road is sort of tortured for about 25 kilometers. Then it joins the main road (N1197) heading inland (southeasterly). Make time, maybe speed, toward **Ponte Leccia,** just before which there's a small road that follows the **Gorges de l'Asco** southwesterly into a high mountain bowl (D147). It's about 30 kilometers one way to the bowl where there is a bar restaurant.

Back at Ponte Leccia, cross the main Bastia-Ajaccio highway and head southeasterly up the small mountain road to **Morosaglia** (D71), climbing over some minor cols and finally wending down to the main road on the east coast. Then it's probably best to head north to Bastia and across to St. Florent.

Trip 79 Cap Corse

Distance *170 kilometers*

Terrain *Tight, twisting roads along rugged coast*

Highlights *Similar to California Highway One north of San Francisco, except more precipitous*

Cap Corse is the name usually given to the whole mountainous finger that projects about 50 kilometers north from **Bastia** and **St. Florent.** There's nothing flat on the finger. One road (D80) circles it following the coastal cliffs as best it can. Sometimes there are little clusters of houses along the road. Sometimes they are far below on the beach with minimal trails down to them. Start out on the road north from St. Florent. The only recommended detour down to the water is at the north end. A windy loop road goes right down to the water at the northernmost point of Corsica with a cluster of buildings known as **Barcaggio.**

This is as far north as you can get on Corsica, on the point called Cap Corse. Over the horizon (beyond that island) are Italy and France.

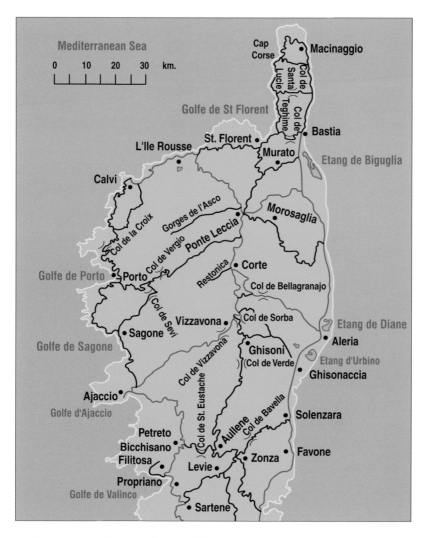

Then the main loop road around Cap Corse actually gets down to the beach on the east coast at **Macinaggio** which happens to have a nice row of waterfront restaurants.

There are two transpeninsular roads that climb across the mountains from coast to coast. They're roughly parallel. So it's possible to take one, and come back on the other. The more northerly one (D36) is just four kilometers south of Macinaggio at **Marine de Meria.** The second (D180) climbs back over the **Col de Santa Lucie** and gets back to the east coast at **Marine de Luri.**

Then follow south along the east coast, which is a pleasantly sweeping highway, to Bastia, and home to St. Florent.

Appendices

Looking down on the stacked hairpins on the Swiss side of the Splugen Pass almost always calls for a photo moment.

Hotels

Hotel addresses here use the alphabetic country code before the postal code: A for Austria, F for France, I for Italy, CH for Switzerland, FL for Liechtenstein, and D for Germany. The telephone and fax numeric country codes are: Austria 43; France 33; Italy 39; Switzerland 41; Liechtenstein 41; Germany 49. Calling within any country use a zero before the area code just as you would use a one (1) in the USA.

ANDERMATT

Note, the country code for Switzerland is 41 and the area code for Andermatt is also 41. Calling from abroad, you dial 41 twice. If you're calling from within Switzerland, dial one 41 with a zero (0) before it.

Tourist Office; T 41 887 1454; F 41 887 0185; www.andermatt.ch; e-mail info@andermatt.ch

Hotel Monopol-Metropol; CH-6490 Andermatt; T 41 887 1575; F 41 887 1923; www.forum.ch/monopol-andermatt.htm; e-mail hotel-monopol@bluewin.ch

There are always motorcycles coming off of the Oberalp Pass. Or heading up it from its intersection with the main street through Andermatt. Right at that corner is Hotel Monopol-Metropol.

Hotel 3 Konige & Post; CH-6490 Andermatt; T 41 887 0001; F 41 887 1666

Sport Hotel Sonne; CH-6490 Andermatt; T 41 887 1226; F 41 887 0626

Alpenhotel Schlussel; CH-6490 Andermatt; T 41 888 7088; F 41 888 7089; e-mail hotelschluessel@hotmail.com

Hotel Steingletscher; CH-3863 Gadmen/Meiringen; T 33 975 1222; F 33 975 1422

Hotel Olivone and Post; CH-6718 Olivone (Ticino); T 91 872 1366; F 91 872 1687

Hotel Posthaus CH-Urigen; 6465 Urigen; T 41 879 1153

Hotel Rhodannenberg; CH-8750 Klon Tal (Glarus); T 55 650 1600; F 55 650 1601

THE BERNER OBERLAND

Strand Hotel; CH-3807 Iseltwald; T 33 845 1313; F 33 845 1315

Hotel Blumlisalp; CH-3803 Beatenberg; T 33 841 4111; F33 841 4144

Hotel Goldey; CH-3800 Interlaken; T 33 822 4445; F 33 823 2345

City Hotel; Am Markplatz; CH-3800 Interlaken; T 33 822 1022; F 33 823 1018 e-mail city-hotel@bluewin.ch

Hotel Krebs; Bahnhofstrasse 4; CH-3800 Interlaken; T 33 822 7161; F 33 823 2465; www.krebshotel.ch; e-mail hotelkrebs@bluewin.ch

Strand Hotel Seeblick; CH-3705 Faulen See; T 33 854 2321; F 33 854 2348

Hotel Schutzen; 3822 Lauterbrunnen; T 33 855 2032; F 33 855 2950

Hotel Jungfrau; 3822 Lauterbrunnen; 33 855 3434; F 33 855 2523

Motel Restaurant Brunig; 6082 Brunig; T 33 971 1133

Sternen Hotel am See; CH-6375 Beckenried; T 41 620 6161; F 41 620 6925

LEYSIN/VILLARS

Hotel Mont Riant; CH 1854 Leysin Feydey; T 24 494 2701; F 24 494 2704

Hotel Colina; CH-1854 Leysin; T 24 493 3111; F 24 493 3199

Eurotel; CH-1884 Villars; T 24 495 31313; F 24 495 3953

E and G Hotels; Case Postale 160; CH-1884 Villars; T 24 495 1111; F 24 495 7514; e-mail e&g@rooms.ch; www.rooms.ch

MONT BLANC REGION

La Mainaz; Route Nationale 5 La Faucille; F 01170 Gex; T 45 041 3110; F 45 041 3177

La Porte d'Octodure; CH-1920 Martigny Croix; T 27 722 7121; F 27 722 2173

Aux Mille Etoiles; CH-1923 Les Marecottes; T 27 761 1665; F 27 761 1600

Hotel Miramonti; I-11012 Cogne; T 01 65 74 030; F 01 65 74 9378; www.romantikhotels.com/rhcogne; e-mail miramonti@galactica.it

Relais du Foyer; I-11024 Chatillon; T 0166 511251; F 0166 513598; e-mail relais.foyer@cervinia.alpcom.it

LAC D'ANNECY

Hotel Valle d'Aosta; I-11100 Aosta; T 01 655 1845; F 01 65 233 6660
Le Cottage; F-74290 Talloires; T 45 060 7110
Hotel le Lac; F-74290 Talloires; T 45 060 7108; F 45 060 7299
Hotel la Charpenterie; F-74290 Talloires; T 45 060 7047; F 45 060 7907
Hotel Beau Site; F-74290 Talloires; T 450 607104; F 450 607922
Hotel Sapins; F-74220 la Clusaz; T 450 024012; F 450 024324
Alp Hotel; F-74220 la Clusaz; T 450 024006; F 450 026016; e-mail
info@clusaz.com
Hotel Bergerie; F-75480 Bonneval-sur-Arc; T 479 059497; F 479 059324
Hotel Alpazur; F-73480 Lanslebourg-Mont-Cenis; T 479 059369; F 479 058655

GRENOBLE HIGHS

Hotel Ibis; F-38610 Gieres; T 476 440044; F 476 510358
Hotel Hermitage; F-38410 Uriage; T 476 899321; F 476 899530
Chateau du Passieres; F-38930 Chichilianne; T 476 344548; F 476 344625
Hotel Chalet; F-38650 Gresse-en-Vercors; T 476 343208; F 476 343106

THE GRAY ALPS

Chateau Renard; F-05350 St Veran Haute Alpes; T 049 245 8543; F 049 245
8420
Hotel Les Barnieres; F-05600 Guillestre; T 492 450507; F 492 452874
Hotel le Catinat Fleuri; F 05600 Guillestre; T 492 450762; F 492 452888
Relais du Galibier; F-73450 Valloire; T 479 590045; F 479 833189;
www.relais-galibier.com; e-mail info@relais-galibier.com

SOME HIGH STUFF

Azteca; F-04400 Barcelonnette; T 492 814636; F 492 814392
Alp Hotel; F-04400 la Sauze; T 492 810504; F 492 814584; e-mail
alphotel@club-internet.fr
Le Soleil des Neiges; F-04400 la Sauze; T 492 810501; F 492 814800
Prieure de Molanes; F-04400 Pra Loup; T 492 841143; F 492 840188
Hotel Le Chalet Suisse; F-06470 Peone; T 493 025009; F 493 026192
Tonic Hotel; F-04000 Digne les Bains; T 492 322031; F 492 324454 e-mail
tonic.hotel.digne04@wanadoo.fr

EN PROVENCE

Mas de Vence; F-06140 Vence; T 493 580616; F 493 240421; e-mail
mas@azurline.com
Les Florets; F-84190 Gigondas; T 490 658601; F 490 658380
Tonic Hotel; see "Some High Stuff" above

SOUTH OF ANDERMATT

LAGO MAGGIORE

Beau Rivage; Viale Verbano 31, or Box 43; CH-6600 Locarno Muralto; T 91 743 1355; F 91 743 9409

Hotel Carmine; Via Sempione 10; CH-6602 Locarno-Muralto; T 91 743 6033; F 91 743 8433; e-mail carmine@rooms.ch

Hotel Consolina; CH-6575 San Nazzaro; T 91 794 2335; F 91 794 1472; e-mail consolina@rooms.ch

EAST OF ANDERMATT

ST. MORITZ

Hauser; CH-7500 St. Moritz-Dorf; T 81 833 4402; F 81 833 1029

Hotel Crystal; CH-7500 St. Moritz-Dorf; T 81 836 2626; F 81 836 2627

Hotel Le Prese; CH-7746 Le Prese; T 81 844 0333; F 81 844 0835

Post Hotel Engiadina; CH-7524 Zuoz; T 81 854 1021; F 81 854 3303

Hotel Allegra, CH-7504 Pontresina; T 81 888 7088; F 81 888 7089; e-mail info@allegrahotel.ch

Hotel Vittoria; Via Dogana 12; I-23020 Monte Spluga; T 03 435 4250; F 03 433 6197

Hotel Stilfser Joch (Passo dello Stelvio); I-39020 Stelvio; T 0342 903162; F 0342 903664

Hotel Stelvio; CH-7536 Santa Maria; T 81 858 5358; F 81 858 5039

Hotel Garberhof; I-39024 Mals; 0473 831 399; F 0473 831 950; e-mail info@garberhof.com

SUD TIROL

Hotel Augusta; via Otto Huber 2; I-39012 Merano; T 0473 222324; F 0473 220029

Kurhotel Palace; via Cavour 2; I-39012 Merano; T 0473 271000; F 0473 271181

Hotel Stroblhof; I-39015 St Leonhard; T 047 365 6128; F 047 365 6468

Hotel Kabis; I-39040 Vilnoss; T 047 284 0126; F 047 284 0395

Dolomitenblick; I-39054 Klobenstein; T 047 135 6367; F 047 135 6503

Gasthof Plorr; I-39050 Oberinn 45 am Ritten; T 0471 602118

Albergo la Mela d'Oro; I-38010 Sanzeno; T 04 633 4384

Hotel Belvedere; I-38018 Molveno; T 04 6158 6933; F 04 6158 6044

RIVA AND LAGO DI GARDA

Hotel Bellevista; I-38066 Riva del Garda; Piazza C. Battisti 4; T 0464 554271; F 0464 555754

Hotel Sole; I-38066 Riva del Garda; Piazza 3 Novembre 35; T 046 455 2686; F 046 455 2811

Hotel Centrale; I-38066 Riva del Garda; T 046 455 2344; F 046 455 2138

Hotel San Giovanni; T and F 046 454 0101

Grand Hotel Riva; Piazza Garibaldi 10; I-38066 Riva del Garda; T 0464 521800; F 0464 552293; www.garda.com; e-mail ghr@anthesi.com

Hotel Panorama; I-3860 Pregasina; T 0464 520344; F 0464 556963

Hotel Paradiso; I-25010 Tremosine (Pieve); T & F 0365 953 012; www.terazzadelbrivido.it; e-mail info@terrazzodelbrivido.it

Hotel Montana; I-38040 Monte Bondone; T 046 194 8200; F 046 194 8177

THE DOLOMITES

Hotel de la Poste; Cortina d'Ampezzo; T 0436 4271; F 0436 868435; www.hotels.cortina.it/delaposte; e-mail posta@hotels.cortina.it

Hotel Evaldo; I-32020 Livinallongo (Arabba); T 0436 79109; F 0436 7935; www.hotelevaldo.com; e-mail hotel.evaldo@rolmail.net

Hotel Olympia; I-32020 Arabba; T 0436 79135; F 0436 79354; www.ski3.com; e-mail olympia@arabba.com

Hotel Posta Zirm; I-39033 Corvara; T 0471 836175; F 0471 836580; e-mail postzirm@altabadia.it

Pension La Fontana; I-39033 Corvara; T 0471 836000; F 0471 936707; e-mail pension.la.fontana@rolmail.net

Hotel Col Alto; I-39033 Corvara; T 0471 836009; F 0471 836066; www.colalto.it; e-mail hotel.colalto@rolmail.net

Restaurant Gerard; I-39048 Selva Gardena; T 047 179 5274; F 047 179 4508; e-mail gerard@val-gardena.com

Hotel Edith; I-39040 Palmschoss; T 0472 52 13 07; F 0472 52 12 11; www.hotel-edith.it; e-mail hotel.edith@rolmail.net

Hotel Kreuzberg Pass; I-39030 Sexten Hochpuster Tal; T 047 47 0328; F 047 47 0383

Tandlerstub'n; A-9963 St. Jakob; T 4873 5365

LIECHTENSTEIN

Nurnberger's Hotel Martha Buhler; FL-9497 Triesenberg; T 75 237 3777; F 75 237 4770

Rizlina Berg Gasthaus; FL-9497 Triesenberg Liechtenstein; T 75 262 0224

Montana; FL-9497 Malbun Liechtenstein; T 75 263 7333; F 75 264 2272

Hotel Landgasthof Schatzmann; FL-9495 Triesen; 75 399 1212; F 75 399 1210

Tourist Office; FL-9490 Vaduz; T 75 232-1443; F 75 392-1618.

Alpenrose Hotel; CH-9658 Wildhaus; T 71 998 5252; F 71 998 5253

Hotel Santis; CH-9657 Unterwasser; T 71 999 2811; F 71 999 5021

Hotel Warther Hof; A-6767 Warth; T 5583 3504; F 5583 4200; www.vol.at/wartherhof; e-mail wartherhof@warth.at

Hotel Adler; A-6884 Damuls Bregenzerwald; T 55 10 2200; F 55 102 2010

AUSTRIAN TIROL

Hotel Linserhof; Teilweise 1, A-6460 Imst; T 54 12664 1516; F 54 12664 15133

Kaiserhof; A-6622 Berwang; T 5674 8285

Hotel Capella; A-6167 Neustift; T 5226 2515; F 5226 25155; e-mailcappella@netway.at

Hotel Post; A-6433 Oetz; T 52 52 6303; F 52 52 2176

Hotel Post; A-6458 Vent; T 5254 8119; F 5254 81194; e-mail info@vent-hotel-post.com

Zur Gemutlichkeit; A-6644 Bschlabs; 31 Lech Tal Tirol; T 56 35 259; F 56 35 521

Hotel Ferienschlossl; A-6425 Haimingerberg Tirol; T 5266 87178; F 5266 871787; e-mail ferienschloessl.hotel@telecom.at

Hotel Antonie; A-6182 Gries in Sellrain; T 5236 203271; F 5236 20349

DEUTSCHE ALPENSTRASSE

Brauneck; D-8172 Lenggries; T 80 42 2021

Lenggrieser Hof; D-8172 Lenggries; T 80 42 8774

Waldgasthof Buchenhain; D-82065 Baierbrunn/Isar Tal; T 89 793 0124; F 89 793 8701

AUSTRIA EAST OF THE TIROL

Hotel Glocknerhof; A-9844 Heiligenblut; T 4824 2244; F 4824 224466; e-mail glocknerhof@heiligenblut.at

Landhaus Jausern; A-5753 Saalbach; T 6541 7341; F 6541 734110; e-mail landhaus@jausern.com

Hotel Iselsbergerhof; A-9991 Iselsberg; T 4852 64112; F 4852 641124; e-mail iselsbergerhof@netway.at

Gasthaus Jodburg; A-6292 Finkenberg; T 052 851 8110

Sporthotel Stock; A-6292 Finkenberg; T 5285 6775; F 5285 6775421; e-mail sporth.stock@netway.at

Hotel Gasthof Ursprung; A-5742 Konigsleiten Wald Pinzgau; T 65 648 253 8271; F 65 648 2538

Gailtaler Hof; A-9640 Kotschach-Mauthen; T 4715 318; F 4715 3185

SALZBURG LAND

Gasthof Brauwirt; Lengfelden 21; A-5101 Bergheim; T 6624 52163; F 6624 5216353; e-mail braeuwirt@net4you.co.at

Hotel Solaria; A-5562 Obertauern; T 6456 7250; F 6456 7549; e-mail info@hotel-solaria.at

Motorradhotel Hubertushof: 45 A-8623 Aflenz Kurort; T 38 61 3131

Hochberghaus; A-4645 Grunau im Alm Tal Salzkammergut; T 76 16 8477

KARNTEN LAND

Hotel Post Hauptplatz; 26 A-9500 Villach; T 42 422 61010; F 42 422 610 1420; w.w.w.romantik-hotel.com; e-mail romantik-hotel@magnet.at

Hotel Pulverer; A-9546 Bad kleinkirchheim; T 4240 744; F 4240 793; www.pulverer.at; e-mail hotel@pulverer.at

Schlosshotel Seewirt; A-8864 Turracherhohe; T 4275 8234; F 4275 8234 215; www.schlosshotel-seewirt.com;
e-mail info@schlosshotel-seewirt.com

CORSICA

Ferries

Corsica Ferries: (I) T 019 215511; F 019 2155300; www.corsicaferries.com
on Corsica (F) Bastia; T 495 32 9595; F 495 321471
in Nice (F) T 492 004376; F 492 004377
in Munchen (D) T 89 389 991
in Zurich (CH) T 1 364 1600
S.N.C.M./Ferryterranee: (F) T 836 679500; F 491 563586; www.sncm.fr
in Nice (F) T 493 136699; F 493 136689
in Paris (F) T 139 447206; F 139 447210
on Corsica (F) Bastia; T 495 545599; F 495 546669
Navarma/Moby Lines: (I) T 0565 918101
on Corsica (F) T 495 348494
Happy Lines: (I) 018 756 4530
on Corsica (F) 495 552552

Hotels on Corsica

Les Flots Bleus; F-20150 Porto; T 495 261126; F 495 261264
Hotel Belvedere; F-20150 Porto; T 495 161201; F 495 261197; www.hotel-le-Belvedere.com
Grand Hotel du Monte d'Oro; F-20219 Vizzavona; T 495 472106; F 495 472205
Hotel Dolce Notte; F-20217 St Florent (Corse); T 495 37 0665; F 495 37 1070
Hotel Shegara; F-20137 Porto Vecchio (Corse); T 495 70 0431; F 495 70 2338
Hotel Solemare; F-20169 Bonifacio (Corse); T 495 73 0106; F 495 73 1257
Hotel U Dragulinu; F-20144 Favona; T 495 73 2030; F 495 73 2206
Scopa Rossa; F-20126 Evisa; T 495 262022
La Marine; F-20118 Sagone; T 495 28 0003; F 495 28 0398

After you ride the best motorcycle roads in the world, you'll understand why many motorcyclists come back again and again.

Alps Pass Bagging List

How many of the 271 on this list can you bag?

To help you keep track of the passes you've bagged, here's a list based on their height in meters, in "descending" order, along with the country and trip in this book where you can find them. (Most are in the index, in alphabetical order along with all the other good places in the Alps.)

All the passes of the high Alps are on this list. That is, the ones that are roads. Some passes with names are little more than foot trails. They aren't on this list. A couple here have short unpaved sections, all noted in the text, but all can be enjoyed on road bikes. Highest is always best, just because it exists. The best rides are starred. Opinions as to elevations may vary. A meter here, a meter there, might change the rankings listed here. But the elevations seem to be from reliable sources.

The intention is to list every significant paved Alpine pass. There are a lot of passes at about 1,000 meters or less that aren't significant. Major passes on Corsica are included in order of their height, but they're numbered separately.

1. ★★ 2,862 la Bonette (F) Trip 23 & 25
2. ★★ 2,769 Col de l'Iseran (F) Trip 17
3. ★★ 2,758 Passo dello Stelvio (Stilfser Joch) (I) Trip 38
4. ★★ 2,744 Col Agnel (del Agnello) (F-I) Trip 23
5. ★ 2,678 Col du Restefond (F) Trip 23 & 25
6. ★★ 2,645 Col du Galibier (F) Trip 22
7. ★★ 2,621 Passo di Gavia (I) Trip 39   *BLOCKED TRIP2*
8. ★ 2,575 Grossglockner Hoch Tor (A) Trip 65
9. ★★ 2,509 Timmels Joch (I-A) Trips 40 & 43
10. 2,501 Umbrail Pass (I-CH) Trip 38
11. ★ 2,478 Nufenen Pass (CH) Trip 2
12. ★ 2,469 Col du Grand St. Bernard (CH-I) Trip 13
13. ★ 2,431 Furka Pass (CH) Trips 1 & 2
14. ★ 2,428 Grossglockner Fuscher Tor (A) Trip 65
15. ★ 2,383 Fluela Pass (CH) Trip 37
16. ★★ 2,361 Col d'Izoard (F) Trip 22
17. ★★ 2,351 Col de Lombarde (I-F) Trips 23
18. ★ 2,328 Bernina Pass (CH) Trip 38
19. ★ 2,327 Col de la Cayolle (F) Trips 24 & 25
20. 2,320 Drei Zinnen (Tre Cime di Lavaredo) (I) Trip 54 (not a pass)
21. 2,315 Forcola di Livigno (I) Trip 39
22. ★★ 2,312 Albula Pass (CH) Trip 37
23. 2,291 Passo di Foscagno (I) Trip 39

24. ★ 2,284 Julier Pass (CH) Trip 36
25. ★ 2,284 Col di Sampeyre (I) Trip 23
26. ★ 2,244 Passo di Sella (I) Trips 48 & 50
27. ★ 2,240 Col d'Allos (F) Trip 24 & 26
28. ★ 2,239 Passo Pordoi (I) Trips 48 & 50
29. ★ 2,233 Passo di Giau (I) Trips 49 & 50
30. ★ 2,224 Susten Pass (CH) Trip 1
31. ★ 2,214 Penser Joch (Passo di Pennes) (I) Trip 42
32. 2,210 Passo d'Eira (I) Trip 39
33. ★ 2,192 Passo di Valparola (I) Trips 48 & 50
34. ★ 2,188 Col du Petit St. Bernard (I-F) Trip 13
35. ★ 2,165 Grimsel Pass (CH) Trip 1
36. 2,174 Col de Finestre (I) Trip 22
37. 2,149 Ofen Pass (CH) Trip 38
38. ★ 2,121 Passo di Gardena (Grodner Joch) (I) Trips 48 & 50
39. ★★ 2,113 Splugen Pass (Spluga) (CH-I) Trip 36
40. 2,111 Col de Vars (F) Trip 19
41. 2,108 St. Gotthard (San Gottardo) (CH) Trips 2, 3 & 30
42. ★ 2,105 Passo di Falzarego (I) Trips 48 & 50
43. ★ 2,094 Jaufen Pass (Passo di Monte Giovo) (I) Trip 42
44. ★ 2,087 Col de Champs (F) Trip 24
45. 2,083 Col du Mt. Cenis (F-I) Trip 22
46. 2,068 Col de la Croix de Fer (F) Trip 17
47. 2,065 Passo del San Bernardino (CH) Trip 31
48. 2,058 Col du Lautaret (F) Trip 22
49. 2,057 Passo di Fedaia (Marmolada) (I) Trips 49 & 50
50. ★ 2,052 Staller Sattel (I-A) Trips 55 & 64
51. ★ 2,047 Passo Manghen (I) Trip 52
52. 2,044 Oberalp Pass (CH) Trips 3 & 35
53. 2,042 Eisen Tal Hohe (Nockalmstrasse) (A) Trip 69
54. ★ 2,036 Bieler Hohe (Silvretta Strasse) (A) Trip 58
55. 2,,033 Sestriere (I) Trip 22
56. 2,033 Passo di Valles (I) Trips 50 & 51
57. ★ 2,017 Kuhtai (A) Trip 60
58. ★ 2,006 Brueil (I) Trip 14 (not a pass)
59. ★ 2,006 Simplon Pass (Sempione) (CH) Trips 12 & 32
60. ★ 2,002 Wurz Joch (Passo di Erbe) (I) Trips 43 & 52
61. 1,996 Col de Larche (Maddelena) (I-F) Trip 23
62. ★ 1,992 Passo di San Marco (I) Trip 46
63. 1,989 Col de Sarenne (F) Trip 20
64. ★ 1,984 Col de la Madeleine (F) Trips 17 & 18
65. ★ 1,971 Colle San Carlo (I) Trip 13
66. 1,955 Passo di Rolle (I) Trips 50 & 51

67. 1,951 Col du Glandon (F) Trips 17 & 18
68. 1,948 Klausen Pass (CH) Trip 4
69. ★★ 1,943 Passo di Croce Domini (I) Trip 46
70. ★★ 1,922 Cormet de Roselend (F) Trip 13
71. 1,920 Heiligenbach (Nockalmstrasse) (A) Trip 69
72. 1,918 Passo di San Pellegrino (I) Trips 50 & 51
73. 1,914 Lukmanier Pass (Lucomagno) (CH) Trip 3
74. 1,909 Mount Ventoux (F) Trip 29 (not a pass)
75. ★ 1,896 Passo di Mortirolo (I) Trip 39
76. ★ 1,894 Hahntenn Joch (A) Trip 60
77. ★★ 1,894 Passo di Tremalzo (I) Trip 45
78. 1,883 Passo Tonale (I) Trip 47
79. 1,875 Passo di Campolongo (I) Trip 48 & 50
80. 1,860 l'Alpe d'Huez (F) Trip 20 (not a pass)
81. 1,850 Col de Montgenevre (F-I) Trip 22
82. ★ 1,828 Passo di Vivione (I) Trip 46
83. 1,815 Maloja Pass (CH) Trip 36
84. 1,805 Passo Tre Croce (I) Trip 54
85. 1,805 Passo di Lavaze (I) Trips 50 & 52
86. 1,793 Arlberg Pass (A) Trip 58
87. 1,790 Sella Ciampigotto (I) Trip 55
88. 1,788 Solker Tauern Pass (A) Trip 67
89. 1,783 Turracher Hohe (A) Trip 69
90. ★ 1,778 Col de la Croix (CH) Trip 10
91. 1,775 Monte Grappa (I) Trip 53 (not a pass)
92. 1,775 Arosa (CH) Trip 37 (not a pass)
93. 1,773 Flexen Pass (A) Trip 58
94. 1,773 Passo Forcella Staulanza (I) Trips 49, 50, & 51
95. 1,761 Furka Joch (A) Trip 58
96. 1,760 Col de Joux Verte (F) Trip 15
97. 1,760 Sella di Razza (I) Trip 55
98. 1,759 Furkel Sattel (I) Trips 43 & 54
99. 1,745 Passo di Costalunga (Karer) (I) Trips 50 & 52
100. 1,739 Radstadter Tauern Pass (A) Trip 67
101. ★ 1,712 Col du Joux Plane (F) Trip 15
102. ★ 1,703 Col du Pre (F) Trip 13
103. 1,700 Dr. Josef Mehrl Hutte (A) Trip 69
104. 1,699 Cret de Chatillon (F) Trip 19
105. 1,688 Passo Nigra (Niger Pass) (I) Trip 52
106. ★ 1,685 Haiming Joch (Silzer Sattel) (A) Trip 60
107. 1,682 Passo Campo Carlo Magno (I) Trip 47
108. 1,679 Hochtannberg Pass (A) Trip 58
109. 1,678 Col de la Couillole (F) Trip 25

110. 1,668 Col Valberg (F) Trip 25
111. 1,668 Weinebene (A) Trip 70
112. 1,664 Col du Noyer (F) Trip 21
113. 1,656 Col du Lein (CH) Trip 13
114. 1,650 Chamrousse (F) Trip 20
115. 1,644 Klippitztorl (A) Trip 70
116. ★ 1,643 Glaubenberg Pass (CH) Trip 6
117. 1,641 Katchberg Pass (A) Trip 69
118. ★ 1,640 Col di Joux (I) Trip 14
119. 1,636 Passo di Monte Croce (Kreuzberg) (I) Trip 54
120. 1,633 Col des Saisies (F) Trip 13
121. 1,631 Wolfgang Pass (CH) Trip 37
122. 1,616 Passo di Brocon (I) Trip 51
123. 1,613 Col de la Colombiere (F) Trip 15
124. ★ 1,611 Glaubenbuelen Pass (CH) Trip 6
125. 1,611 Vrsic Pass (SLO) Trip 71
126. 1,608 Gurnigel Pass (CH) Trip 7
127. 1,604 Col de Turini (F) Trip 27
128. ★ 1,601 Passo Duran (I) Trips 50 & 51
129. 1,599 Malbun (FL) Trip 56 (not a pass)
130. 1,578 Col du Telegraphe (F) Trip 22
131. 1,561 Hochrindl (A) Trip 69
132. 1,558 Piller Hohe (A) Trip 59
133. 1,557 Nassfeld Pass (I-A) Trips 55 & 71
134. 1,552 Passo Carson di Lanza (I) Trip 55
135. ★ 1,550 Pragel Pass (CH) Trip 4
136. 1,547 Gaberl Sattel (A) Trip 68
137. 1,547 Lenzerheide (CH) Trip 37
138. 1,546 Col du Pillon (CH) Trip 10
139. 1,542 Forcella di Lavardet (I) Trip 55
140. 1,537 Monte Bondone (I) Trip 52
141. ★ 1,536 Rossfeldringstrasse (D) Trip 62
142. 1,531 Grand Colombier (F) Trip 16
143. 1,530 Passo di Cibiana (I) Trips 49 & 51
144. 1,529 Passo Cimabanche (I) Trip 54
145. 1,526 Col de la Forclaz (CH) Trip 13
146. ★ 1,526 Kartischer Sattel (A) Trip 64
147. 1,518 Gampen Joch (Palade) (I) Trips 42 & 44
148. 1,509 Jaun Pass (CH) Trip 9
149. 1,507 Gerlos Pass (A) Trip 63
150. 1,504 Reschen Pass (Passo Resia) (A-I) Trips 41 & 59
151. 1,502 Col du Chasseral (CH) Trip 11
152. 1,500 Post Alm (A) Trip 66

153. 1,500 Col St. Martin (F) Trip 27
154. 1,491 Mattarone (I) Trip 34
155. 1,487 Faschina Joch (A) Trip 58
156. 1,486 Col des Aravis (F) Trip 15
157. 1,486 Champex (CH) Trip 13
C-1. ★ 1,477 Col de Vergio (F) Trip 72
158. 1,476 Passo del Zovo (I) Trip 54
159. 1,467 Col de la Croix Fry (F) Trip 15
160. 1,461 Col des Montets (F) Trip 13
161. ★ 1,458 Acherli Pass (CH) Trip 6
162. ★ 1,457 Col de Menee (F) Trip 21
163. 1,449 Passo Redebus (I) Trip 52
164. 1,447 Col de Marchairuz (CH) Trip 11
165. 1,445 Col des Mosses (CH) Trip 10
166. 1,441 Col du Festre (F) Trip 21
167. 1,437 Panider Sattel (Passo di Pinei) (I) Trip 52
168. 1,434 Col du Coq (F) Trip 19
169. 1,431 Col de la St. Michel (F) Trip 26
170. 1,430 Reiderberg Pass (D) Trip 61
171. 1,425 Passo del Pura (I) Trip 55
172. 1,411 Col des Planches (CH) Trip 13
173. 1,406 Ibergeregg (CH) Trip 4
174. 1,402 Passo di Vezzena (I) Trip 53
175. 1,400 Flattnitz (A) Trip 69
176. 1,400 Reiderberg Pass (D) Trip 61
177. 1,395 Passo Alpi di Neggia (CH) Trip 34
178. 1,378 Passo di Cereda (I) Trips 50 & 51
179. 1,374 Brenner Pass (A-I) Trip 59
180. 1,371 Col d'Ornon (F) Trip 18
181. 1,369 Pas de Morgins (CH-F) Trip 15
182. 1,363 Mendel Pass (Passo di Mendola) (I) Trip 42
183. 1,362 Plocken Pass (I-A) Trips 55 & 64
184. 1,360 Hebalpe (A) Trip 70
185. 1,357 Dientener Sattel (A) Trip 65
186. 1,349 Soboth (A) Trip 70
187. 1,346 Col de Maure (F) Trip 26
188. 1,343 Passo di Sommo (I) Trip 53
189. 1,336 Berwang (Namlos) (A) Trip 60
190. 1,333 Col St. Jean (F) Trip 26
191. 1,320 Col de la Faucille (F) Trip 16
192. ★ 1,318 Col de Grimone (F) Trip 21
C-2. 1,311 Col de Sorba (F) Trip 77
193. 1,304 Madonna di Colletto (I) Trip 23

194. 1,301 Col de Pontis (F) Trip 26
195. 1,298 Passo della Mauria (I) Trip 55
196. 1,294 Passo di Presolana (I) Trip 46
197. ★ 1,293 Col de l'Aiguillon (CH) Trip 11
198. 1,291 Filzen Sattel (A) Trip 65
C-3. 1,289 Col de Verde (F) Trip 77
199. 1,286 Cima di Sappada (I) Trip 55
200. 1,283 Vue des Alpes (CH) Trip 11
201. 1,279 Weissenstein (CH) Trip 11
202. 1,279 Saanenmoser (CH) Trip 9
203. 1,278 Schwagalp (CH) Trip 57
204. 1,278 Rottenmanner Hohentauern (A) Trip 68
205. 1,273 Pass Thurn (A) Trip 63
206. 1,262 Col Luitel (F) Trip 20
207. 1,257 Col di Zambla (I) Trip 46
208. 1,253 Aflenzer Seeberg (A) Trip 68
209. 1,246 Seetaler Sattel (A) Trip 67
210. 1,237 Col du Corbier (F) Trip 15
211. 1,232 Prabichl Pass (A) Trip 68
212. 1,229 Col de la Givrine (CH) Trip 16
213. 1,227 Col du Mont Crosin (CH) Trip 11
C-4. ★ 1,218 Col de Bavella (F) Trip 77
214. 1,212 Col de l'Homme Mort (F) Trip 29
215. 1,209 Fern Pass (A) Trip 60
216. 1,204 Iselsberg (A) Trip 65
217. 1,201 Cirque de Vaumale (F) Trip 28
218. 1,190 Sattelegg (CH) Trip 4
219. 1,190 Passo Sella Nevea (I) Trip 71
220. 1,180 Oberjoch (D-A) Trip 61
221. 1,180 Col du Mollendruz (CH) Trip 11
222. 1,176 Passo dell'Aprica (I) Trips 39 & 47
223. 1,174 Col de Plainpalais (F) Trip 19
224. 1,167 Schallenberg (CH) Trip 6
C-5. ★ 1,163 Col de Vizzavona (F) Trip 76
225. 1,163 Col des Gets (F) Trip 15
226. 1,152 Col des Etroits (CH) Trip 11
227. 1,150 Col de la Forclaz (F) Trip 17
228. 1,150 Passo de Predil (I-SLO) Trip 71
229. 1,139 Col du Cucheron (F) Trip 19
230. 1,135 Ramsau (A) Trip 67
231. 1,134 Col du Granier (F) Trip 19
232. 1,126 Holzleitner Sattel (A) Trip 60
233. 1,120 Col de Toutes Aures (F) Trip 26

234. 1,118 Ammer Sattel (A-D) Trip 60
235. 1,110 Col Lebraut (F) Trip 26
236. 1,110 Windische Hohe (A) Trip 71
237. 1,097 Sudelfeld (D) Trip 62
C-6. 1,094 Col de Sevi (F) Trip 74
238. 1,093 Gaichtberg Pass (A) Trip 61
239. 1,090 Wildhaus (CH) Trip 57
240. 1,077 Kreuzberg Sattel (A) Trip 71
241. 1,073 Wurzen Pass (A-SLO) Trip 71
242. 1,068 Col de Macuegne (F) Trip 28
243. 1,,066 Sella di Cereschiatis (I) Trip 55
244. 1,060 Col de Richemond (F) Trip 16
245. 1,060 Col de Clavel (F) Trip 28
246. 1,056 Filzmoos (A) Trip 67
247. 1,054 Col de Luens (F) Trip 28
248. 1,032 Col d'Ayen (F) Trip 28
249. 1,015 Lahn Sattel (A) Trip 68
250. 1,010 Forcella di Luis (I) Trip 55
251. 1,008 Brunig Pass (CH) Trip 6
252. 1,002 Col de Braus Trip 27
C-6. 995 Col de St. Eustache (F) Trip 75
253. 992 Potschen Hohe (A) Trip 68
254. 982 Gailberg Sattel (A) Trips 64 & 71
255. 969 Pass Gschutt (A) Trip 68
256. 963 Passo Zovello (I) Trip 55
257. 963 Col de Vence (F) Trip 28
258. 954 Pyhrn Pass (A) Trip 68
259. 950 Etzel (CH) Trip 4
260. 941 Achen Pass (A-D) Trip 63
261. 940 Passo Durone (I) Trip 47
262. 902 Col de Tamie (F) Trip 17
263. 858 Kesselberg (D) Trip 62
264. 849 Ursprung Pass (D-A) Trip 62
265. 703 Passo di San Boldo (I) Trips 51 & 53

If you're in the Dolomites, the view from the Drei Zinnen Road is unbeatable.

Special Little Roads

In the Alps are many special little roads that might have been put there just for motorcyclists to play on. It has taken me many enjoyable years to discover them; this book is my tribute to the joy they have given me. For your convenience, they are arranged according to the regions they occupy. But some of these roads are so exceptional, their potential for enjoyment so great, that they deserve to be singled out and given special consideration by any motorcyclist.

All the roads I'll mention here are described elsewhere in the book, in their appropriate geographical context. Most of them don't go anywhere in particular, certainly nowhere of commercial importance. They are not necessarily high or awesome, although some are both. Most of them have stretches that are only one lane wide. They are all paved. Some of them are short and some long. Some remain obscure even though they're close to major tourist areas or routes.

From the Susten Pass road, bikes head up the military road to the base of Steingletscher. Traverses of the Susten Pass in the distance lead to its summit, up right (Trip 1).

Special Little Roads in Switzerland

1. Pragel Pass between the towns of Glarus and Schwyz (part of Andermatt Trip 4).

2. Glaubenbuelen Pass between the towns of Schupfheim and Giswil (part of The Berner Oberland Trip 6).

3. Glaubenberg Pass between the towns of Entlebuch and Sarnen (also part of The Berner Oberland Trip 6).

Special Little Roads in France

1. Cormet de Roselend and Col du Pre between the towns of Bourg St. Maurice and Beaufort (part of Trip 13, Mont Blanc region).

2. Col de Joux Plane between the towns of Morzine and Samoens (part of Trip 15, Lac d'Annecy region).

3. Col Agnel between Guillestre in France and Sampeyre in Italy (part of Trip 23, The Gray Alps).

Near the top of the Susten Pass, on the west side at Steingletscher, a military road leads up to the base of the glacier.

Special Little Roads in Italy

1. Colle San Carlo between the towns of Morgex and La Thuile (part of Trip 13, Mont Blanc region).

2. Passo di Croce Domini between the towns of Bagolino and Breno (part of Trip 46, Riva and Lago di Garda).

3. Passo di Vivione between the towns of Forno Allione and Shilpario (part of Trip 46, Riva and Lago di Garda).

4. Wurz Joch (Passo di Erbe) between the towns of St. Martin and Bressanone (Brixen) (part of Trip 43, Sud Tirol, and Trip 52, The Dolomites).

5. Passo Manghen between the towns of Cavalese and Borgo (part of Trip 51, The Dolomites).

6. Col di Sampeyre between Sampeyre and Donero (part of Trip 23, The Southern Alps).

7. Passo Duran between Villa and Agordo (part of Trip 51, Southern Dolomites).

Special Little Roads in Austria

1. Furka Joch between the towns of Rankweil and Damuls (part of Trip 58, Liechtenstein, Santis, and the Arlberg).

2. Hahntenn Joch between the towns of Imst and Elmen (part of Trip 60, Austrian Tirol).

3. Haiming Joch between the village of Haiming and Ochsengarten (part of Trip 60, Austrian Tirol).

4. Zillertaler Hohenstrasse between the towns of Ried and Ramsberg (part of Trip 63, Austria East of the Tirol).

If You Have Only a Little Time

It's better to ride a little in the Alps than not at all. So if you just have a few days, which country, which roads, should you aim for? Where will you have the most fun and see the most in just a few days? A week?

First Andermatt, Switzerland. It's covered right at the beginning of this book. The mountains are spectacular, the roads exciting, facilities plentiful, and there's no big city traffic to worry about. You can get to the area quickly by Autobahn, and then leave the Autobahn and traffic behind. There are several full days of riding around Andermatt.

Second, the Dolomites in northern Italy. They're covered in the section of the same name. Like those around Andermatt, the mountains are special and the roads are right up in them. Facilities are plentiful, and there is no big city traffic. You can get there quickly from the Brennero Autostrada. Several more full days of riding.

Just remember the warning in the front of this book. Alpinitis is contagious.

Here's why the Stelvio attracts riders from all over the world. It's the road.

Other European Goals

Are all the great roads in the Alps? Aren't there any others?

Of course. But truly, all suffer in comparison to the Alps. Try the roads anywhere else, as many have. They may seem pretty good. Sometimes the scenery is almost as good. Then come back to the Alps. There's no getting around it. The roads of the Alps are the best. Nothing compares. Except Corsica.

Other areas tested, in no particular order:

Norway

A real challenge. There is a lot of it, about 2,400 kilometers from Oslo to the North Cape. And there's almost nobody there. Cruise posters illustrate how lovely the fjords are. They don't show how tedious and occasional the roads are. There is a lot of water. But facilities are few, modest, and very expensive. One-lane roads with trucks and buses going both ways cling to the edges of the fjords. An overlay of skid marks is a constant reminder of what may be around endless blind corners. From the fjords, the roads climb up into a tundra-like crossing to the next fjord. And Norway is a long haul from the core of Europe.

It's possible to cut some of the travel time to and from Norway by using ferries from Newcastle in the north of England or from the Netherlands, to Bergen; or from Kiel, in north Germany to Oslo. All of the ferry connections take about 18 hours. However, it's also possible to fast ferry in 2-1/2 hours from Hirtshals, Denmark, to Kristiansand, on Norway's south coast, where Beach's Motorcycle Adventures (see their listing in **An Organized Tour?**) offers motorcycle tours or independent bike rentals throughout Norway. For about the price of a night in a modest hotel (less than any hotel in Norway), it's possible to get a tiny cabin on the ferry and eliminate a bunch of flat road time to boot. It is heady to ride all night in daylight. There can be a bit of a high about 1 a.m.

Pyrenees

Every once in a while, the high mountains that separate Spain and France look almost Alpine. A few of the passes are Alpine in height, and some of the snow bowls could double for those in the Alps. What's missing is the culture and the road network. The tiny independent country of Andorra has adequate facilities, and some, up above its main valley road, are very pleasant. As a tax-free country, it is jammed with tourists loading their cars with everything imaginable (including new motorcycles), and with trucks hauling the stuff in so the tourists can buy

Unlike most race courses, it's almost possible to get lost on the 14 kilometers of the Nurburgring.

it and haul it out. Americans are unknown in Andorra. The Spanish side is no longer cheap.

Sardinia (Sardegna)

Visible from the south of Corsica, Sardinia is not nearly as rugged, and doesn't make the cut.

★ Isle of Man

Since the first years of the 20th century, the first week of June has been motorcycle week on the Isle of Man. The adjective for it is Manx, for cats and for

Nortons. The island is in the Irish Sea, west of England, north of Wales, and east of Ireland. The collection of enthusiasts from all over the world is a joy to be part of. The major TT races are the first weekend of June, with practice during the prior week. Practice can be as much fun as the racing. The course is all public roads about the island, totaling about 30 miles. It's open to the public except during practice hours and during races. The course is open to all on the first Sunday in June. It's come to be known as Mad Sunday, as too many amateurs overestimate their skills. The atmosphere is motorcycle-friendly.

Accommodations are working-class British, as is the food. The island has some nice roads to explore besides the course. Access is by ferry from Heysham on the Lancashire coast of England, north of Liverpool, with a weekly run from Dublin. Both take about five hours. Reservations for the ferry are essential, and can be obtained from the Isle of Man Steam Packet Company in Douglas, T 1624 661661; F 1624 645697; e-mail: res@steam-packet.com. Accommodation information is available from the Isle of Man Tourist Board, T 01624 686766; or at their web site: www.isle-of-man.com. They do indeed speak English there, but they drive on the left, even on the TT course.

Nurburgring

The historic and famous Nurburgring is often available to riders. It's much longer than most tracks, the north ring being about 14 kilometers, and it sweeps and wiggles through the low Eifel Mountains up near the border of Belgium, about 40 kilometers west of Koblenz. (It's easy for the English speaker to confuse the Nurburgring up north with the Bayrisch city, Nurnberg, where the war crimes trials were held after World War II.)

Many Americans have participated in the driving school held over a period of several days each summer on the Nurburgring by the BMW Clubs of Europe. Contact Werner Briel in Mulheim am der Ruhr; T 020 335 8020; F 020 337-6372; e-mail: SchultenHL@t-online.de. The school concentrates on learning the multitudinous curves of the Ring. A reasonable beginning competence is presumed. It's a good place to make European contacts.

If you can't bring your own bike, borrow or rent one. But you simply must experience the Dolomites.

So, How About a Bike?

There are several ways to have a bike in the Alps. Each depends on two factors: time and money. Usually, a little of one will save a bit of the other.

    borrow or rent
    buy
    ship it from home
    keep a bike there

Borrow or Rent One

It surely would be nice to have a friend in Europe to borrow a bike from. Lacking that, you can rent one.

Bikes are available for rent from many sources. Most of the tour operators who are known in the United States rent bikes to riders who attend their tours. However, several tour operators will also rent motorcycles to riders who are not on tour with them.

BMW rents (and sells and services) from its Niederlassungs (that's an Anglicised plural of Niederlassungen), its company-owned subsidiaries located in several major cities, including Munchen. The BMW "factory," the museum and office tower are near the Olympic Center on Peutel Ring in Munchen. BMW Niederlassung Munchen is north of that on Frankfurter Ring. (Both are easily accessible by U-Bahn, subway.) T 89 35 35 180; F 89 35 35 1499. The Niederlassungs have several rental plans and several kinds of bikes available. They accept credit cards.

Several rental sources advertise in America.

Bosenberg Motorcycle Excursions in Bad Kreuznach, Germany; T 067 16-7580; F 067 16-7153; e-mail: bosenberg@compuserve.com.

Knopf Motorcycle Touring in Heidelberg, Germany; T and F 62 217-8213; e-mail:knopftours@aol.com Knopf will meet arrivals at the Frankfurt airport.

Motor Center Thun, Switzerland; T 33 439-5959; F 33 439-5950; web site: www.moto-center.ch.

Moto Touring, Milano, Italy; T 02 2720 1556; F 02 2720 1140; e-mail: info@mototouring.com; web site: www.mototouring.com.

Court Fisher of BMW Motorcycle Owners of America makes a continuous and experienced study of the motorcycle scene in Europe. Details about shipping, renting, insuring, and buying are constantly changing and he reports the shifts almost monthly in the *BMW Owners News*. He is most congenial about sharing his hard-learned information from his home in Princeton, N.J., T 609 924-1773.

Members of Harley Owners Group can make arrangements to rent a Harley in Europe through H.O.G. in Milwaukee.

Bikes can also be rented from a Honda dealer in Switzerland: Grisoni; CH-7302 Landquart; T 81 322-7288; F 81 322-6615. Landquart is in Graubunden, east of Zurich.

Ad-Mo-Tours; Box 1803, Wrightwood, CA 92397; T 800 944 2356; F 760 249 1105; www.admo-tours.com; e-mail: office@admo-tours.com. Admo cooperates with many rental sites throughout Europe.

Any rental should be ready to ride; serviced, good tires, insured.

Buy One There

Some factors beyond the control of individuals, and even dealers and manufacturers, bear on the choice, and they vary from year to year and season to season.

The rate of exchange is crucial, along with the rules and cost of shipping. In some years American currencies are high and that makes everything in Europe, including motorcycles, seem like a bargain. In such circumstances, shipping a bike from America won't make much sense since they're cheaper in Europe than America and almost all bikes are available for sale. Then the opposite happens. American currency sinks in relative value and everything is cheaper in America. It then may make sense to ship your bike from America.

Then there's the matter of U.S. specifications. Only the manufacturer can certify to them, and it's practically impossible to get a non-U.S.-spec bike into the U.S. Of course, if the goal is to leave the bike in Europe, then U.S. specs are not so important, unless U.S. registration is desired.

BMW no longer has a program for European delivery of U.S. specification bikes.

Dealers all over Europe are selling new and used bikes. Magazines and papers are full of ads, just like in America. Investing some time and patience can result in a good deal. Europeans do have strict vehicle inspection, called TUV in German, that limits modifications and maintains safety and pollution controls. They also have a significant value-added tax. A dealer selling to a non-resident alien should be able to take care of everything including insurance, and possibly, the refund of the value-added tax upon proof of export.

Ship a Bike From Home

Shipping from America can be a good deal, but it's an ever-changing game. What worked well one time may not the next. Shipping by sea, short of taking a bike as baggage, takes time and planning. Usually the bike must be crated or containerized, and then it must be forklift handled to the dock, and the process reversed at the other end. Docks are often inconveniently located. Rats can eat the plastic! Freighters may not be on an exact schedule, so time at both ends is required.

So air freight is almost always the choice. On some airlines, bikes must be crated to be flown. It is fun to get off the airplane in Europe, go around to the freight terminal, go through customs, and ride away from the airport. Agents for carriers are hungry for business, and are willing to talk both price and crating. Sometimes containers can hold several bikes for the price of one. Prices are related to cubic space needed.

The airline and agent that worked wonders one time may not the next. Call a variety of airline freight agents. One of them may be a biker. If you're planning on bringing the bike back to the U.S., arrange both ways at the same time.

Michael Mandell in New York and Warren Motorcycle Transport in Florida specialize in arranging the shipping of motorcycles by air.

Mandell; T 800 245-8726; F 516 822-0172.

Warren; T 800 443-7519; F 954 726-7336.

To get your bike out of customs in Europe, you will need proof of European insurance (see "Good Stuff to Know"), and the customs agent will want to be assured that the bike is just passing through, not being imported. If the bike is legal in America, then it's legal for an American to operate it on holiday in Europe.

If the bike is ever sold to a European, then it will have to be imported with all the taxes and inspections Europeans require.

Keep a Bike in Europe

Sometimes it's harder to find a good air freight deal back from Europe to America. Many Americans are so hooked that they keep bikes in Europe from one holiday to the next. Some rent garages. Some leave them in bonded warehouses. Some leave bikes with cooperative dealers. Then the only problem is how to keep the thing registered in America, while avoiding permanently importing it to Europe.

Only locals use the tight narrow road chiseled out of the cliffs and spanning gorges on awesome bridges, all on the south side of the Rhein, between Ilanz and Bonaduz.

An Organized Tour?

Most every road is better shared. It's possible to meet new lifelong motorcycle friends on an organized tour. Other smart, creative, attractive, motorcycle crazies like you. If time is limited, the tour folk will take care of the details and leave the riding to you. They just may have some good ideas about where to go and how to get there. And they've had practice helping if something should not go as planned.

Tours are a good bet for anyone with limited time and/or Euro-riding experience. You meet the nicest people . . . .

Recently, an American couple riding a very narrow and rarely traveled Italian pass (Vivione, Trip 37) sideswiped a protruding rock. It split the transmission housing. For anyone traveling independently, that might have been the end of the trip. Their next worry would have been how to get themselves and the busted bike down out of the boondocks. Then, how to get the bike fixed. Then what to do while it's getting fixed. In this case, the couple was on a Beach trip. The Beach luggage van carries a cellphone. A phone call was made, the bike stashed beside the road, and the couple continued to the next hotel aboard other tour members' bikes. Later, after delivering all the luggage, the Beach van took off for the little pass and retrieved the bike. Next day, the couple continued their trip on a different bike.

Here are several tour operators who specialize in trips through the Alps. They'll even carry the hair dryer.

Many makes and styles of bikes are inclined to ride together in Europe. Explore the Alps with a tour group and you'll make lifelong friends. (photo by Stacy Silverwood)

Beach's Motorcycle Adventures, Ltd.
2763 West River Parkway
Grand Island, NY 14072-2053
T (716) 773-4960
F (716) 773-5227
e-mail: bmastaff@buffnet.net
web site: bma.buffnet.net

Bosenberg Motorcycle Excursions
Mainzer Strasse 54
D-6550 Bad Kreuznach
GERMANY
T (49) 671-67312
F (49) 671-67153
e-mail: bosenberg@compuserve.com
web site: www.bosenberg.com

Edelweiss Bike Travel
Steinreichweg 1
A-6414 Mieming
AUSTRIA
T (43) 526-45690
US T (800) 877-2784
F (43) 526-458533
e-mail: edelweiss@tirol.com
web site: www.netwing.at//bike_travel

European Adventures
2 The Circle, Bryn Newydd
Prestatyn, Clwyd LL19 9EU
WALES
T (44) 745 85-3455
F (44) 745 88-8919

Jed Halpern's S.A.P. Tour
(Swiss Alps and Passes Tour)
Route du Simplon 35A; CH-1907 Saxon
SWITZERLAND
T (41) 79 225-1988
F (41) 27 744-3073
e-mail: saptour@bluewin.ch
web site: ourworld.compuserve.com/homepages/goldwing_tours/

mhs Motorradtouren GmbH
Donnersbergerstrasse 32
D-80634 Munich
GERMANY
T (49) 89 168-4888
F (49) 89 166-5549
e-mail: motorradtouren.mhs@t-online.de
web site: www.motorrad.reisen.de

Muenchner Freiheit
Postfach 44 01 48
D-8000 Munich 44
GERMANY
T (49) 89 39-5768
F (49) 89 34-4832
e-mail: MuenchnerFreiheit@compuserve.com
web site: www.motorrad.bmw.de/erlebniswelt/fernreisen

Team Aventura
Karlsebene 2
D-8924 Steingaden
GERMANY
T (49) 8 862-6161
F (49) 8 862-6161

Von Thielmann Tours
P.O. Box 87764
San Diego, CA 92138
T 619 463-7788 or 619 234-1558
F 619 463-7788
e-mail: 105114.3154@compuserve.com

World Motorcycle Tours
7106 NW 108th Avenue
Tamarac, FL 33321
T (800) 443-7519 or (954) 726-0494
F (954) 726-7336
e-mail: bikeship@icanect.net

Ad-Mo-Tours
Box 1803
Wrightwood, CA 92397
T 800 944 2356
F 760 249 1105
e-mail: office@admo-tours.com
web site: www.admo-tours.com

Glossary

aiguille - French word for needle, applied especially to peaks in the Mt. Blanc massif, as Aiguille du Midi

albergo - Italian word for inn or small hotel

Allemagne - the French word for Germany

Alpenglow - the almost flourescent pink glow of snow covered peaks at sunrise and sunset.

Alpenstrasse - German, a road in the Alps, plural is Alpenstrassen

Alpinist - a mountain climber in the Alps; alpinist is a mountain climber in general

Alpinitis - a Hermannism, infected by the Alps

alt, alte - German word for old

aperto - Italian word for open

Apfel - German word for apple

aubergine - French word for eggplant

Ausfahrt - German word for freeway exit (a pedestrian exit is Ausgang)

Ausstellung - German word for exhibition

Autobahn - German word for freeway; plural is Autobahnen

autoroute - French word for freeway

autostrada - Italian word for freeway, plural is autostrade

aux - French preposition, "to the;" hotel Aux Mille Etoiles, Les Marecottes (CH)

bain - French word for bath

basilica - a special name for a large church; not a cathedral

Bayern - German word for Bavaria

Bayrisch - adj. German word for Bavarian

bei - German word, prep. for at or near; Trimbach bei Olten

Berghaus - German for house on a mountain; Berghaus Gurnigel (CH)

Bergstrasse - German for mountain road; Bergstrasse Ferrenau (A)

Berner - German word for Bernese, adj. of Bern (CH)

Bernese - adj. & n. pertaining to Bern

besonder - German word for special

bis - German word, prep., until

bleu - French word for blue

bolognese - Italian adjective for the town Bologna, often applied to a meat sauce on pasta

bourg - French word for village

Brot - German word for bread

Brucke - German word for bridge

Bundesstrasse - German for federal road, *i.e.*, not a freeway

cambio - Italian word for change, exchange

campanile - bell tower

cannelloni - a kind of pasta

cappuccino - Italian coffee with steamed milk

carne - Italian word for meat, flesh

centro - Italian word for center, downtown

certosa - Italian word for charterhouse; Hotel Certosa (I) near Merano, called Karthaus in German

chiuso - Italian word for closed, shut, locked

cognoscente - a connoisseur, one in the know

col - French word for pass, as a mountain pass

corso - Italian word for course, large street; *in corso* is Italian for in progress

creme de la creme - the very choicest

Cyrillic - Slavic alphabet, Russian

Danemark - German word for Denmark; Coupe Danemark, hot fudge sundae

del - Italian "of the" masculine before a consonant

della - Italian "of the" feminine before consonant, singular

demi - French word for half

der - German word for article "the," masculine

des - French prep., "of the"

Deutsch - German word for German; adj., requires declension; Deutsche Alpenstrasse

Deutschland - (D) German word for Germany

deviazione - Italian word for detour

di - Italian word, prep. "of," "by," "with"

d' - French prep., "of," before a vowel

Dolomiten - German word for Dolomites

Dolomiti - Italian word for Dolomites

Dorf - German word for village

drei - German word for three

Edelweiss - German name for Alpine flower

einfach - German word for simple

Eisenbahn - German word for railroad; name of a restaurant known as motor-cycle meeting place (CH)

Eisenwaren - German word for hardware

Eis - German word for ice, also ice cream

entrecot - French for sirloin steak

etoile - French word for star, pl. etoiles

Euro - prefix for European

Fahrrad - German word for bicycle

ferme - French word for closed

formaggio - Italian word for cheese; often Parmesan

forno - Italian word for furnace, oven; al forno means baked

franc - French and Swiss unit of money

frei - German word for free, vacant; Zimmer Frei, room for rent

Furstentum - German word for principality; Furstentum Liechtenstein (FL)

Furst - German word for prince

Gasthaus - German word for inn

Gasthof - German word for inn

gelateria - Italian word for ice cream parlor

gelato - Italian word for ice cream

gemutlich - German word for comfortable

Gemutlichkeit - German word for coziness

Germania - Italian name for Germany

glace - French word for ice, ice cream

grosse - German adj., big

Hauser - German word for houses, plural of Haus

haut, haute - French adjective for high

Heidi - German woman's name; fictional Alpine story for children

heiss - German word for hot

Hochalpenstrasse - German for high Alpine road

Hochberghaus - German for high mountain house

hoch - German word for high

Hof - German word for court, court yard, yard, as in Gasthof

Hohe - German word for height

Hohenstrasse - German for high road

Hutte - German word for hut, a mountain refuge

insalata - Italian word for salad

Italia - (I) Italian word for Italy

Joch - German word for yoke, often applied to a pass

joli - French word for pretty

Kaiser Schmarrn - sweet Austrian dessert

Kalte - German word for cold (coldness)

Kaserne - German word for barracks

Kirche - German word for church

Konige - German word for kings

Konigschloss - German word for royal castle, palace

Kurort - German word for health resort, also see Aflenz Kurort

lac - French word for lake

lago - Italian word for lake

lavoro - Italian word for work, labor

le, les - French word for "the," singular and plural

linguini - pasta

magno - Italian word for great; see Campo Carlo Magno

malhereusement - French word for unhappily

marmottes - mountain animal; Les Marmottes, a restaurant in La Thuile (I)

massif - a principle mountain

militaire - French word for military; see Route Militaire

mille - French word for thousand, see Les Mille Etoiles

Mitte - German word for middle, center, Stadtmitte means downtown

Montessori - Italian educator

Motorrad - German word for motorcycle; German motorcycle bi-monthly; plural is Motorrader

Moto Sport Schweiz - Swiss motorcycle weekly

Munchs - German motorcycle brand

Nasse - German word for wet

nazionale - Italian word for national

neu - German word for new

Novembre - Italian for November

ober - German word for upper

Osterreich - German name for Austria

ost - German word for east

ouvert - French word for open

parco - Italian word for park

parmesan - Italian variety of cheese

passo - Italian word for pass

Perrier - bottled water from France

Pinzgau - region (A) S of Salzburg

pomodoro - Italian word for tomato

ponte - Italian word for bridge

pre - prefix denoting priority

Prix - French word for prize

Puch - Austrian motorcycle

Rader - plural of Rad, German word for wheel

rifugio - Italian mountain refuge

ristorante - Italian word for restaurant

Rivella - a bottled soft drink in Switzerland

Romansch - the language of Graubunden (CH)

sacrario - Italian word for sanctuary, cemetery

Sattel - German word for saddle or pass

Schlucht - German word for gorge

Schweinshax'n - typical Austrian and Bavarian cut of pork

Schweiz - German word for Switzerland

See - German word for lake

Semmelknodel - an Austrian and Bavarian dumpling

Sinalco - soft drink in Switzerland

Sonne - German word for sun

Spezi - soft drink in Austria and Bavaria

Spitze - German word for top, tip, point; Edelweiss Spitze

Stadt - German word for city

Stau See - German word for reservoir created by a dam

Strasse - German word for road or street

sud - German word for south

Suisse - French name for Switzerland

Svizzera - Italian name for Switzerland

Tal - German word for valley

telepherique - French word for cable car

terme - Italian word for hot spring

Tiroler - German for pertaining to Tirol

Toffel Strudel - an Austrian dessert

Toffler - Swiss German for motorcyclist

Toff - Swiss German word for motorcycle

Tofftreffpunkt - Swiss German for a motorcycle meeting place

Tor - German word for gate

toutes - French word for all; toutes directions means all directions

trattoria - an Italian word for restaurant

tre - Italian word for three

Uberwachung - German word for oversee, supervise; Besonder Uberwachung means special supervision

Umleitung - German word for detour

und - German word for and

val - Italian, short for valle (valley)

valle - Italian for valley

Verkehrsburo - German for travel bureau

Versicherung - German word for insurance

viale - Italian word for avenue

vietato - Italian word for forbidden

vorder - German word for front

vous - French word for you

vue - French word for view

Wald - German word for forest

WC - common sign for toilet (Water Closet)

wechseln - German word for change, exchange

weiss - German word for white

Wienerschnitzel - cutlet (meat) Viennese style

Wurst - German word for sausage

Zimmer - German word for room; Zimmer Frei means room for rent

Index

About the Author

John Hermann bought his first bike in 1960. Since then he's ridden about 850,000 miles.

A couple of car trips in Europe persuaded him that the Alps were for biking. So, in 1970, he took off on a solo trip via a European-delivered BMW, only to discover that a bike trip through the Alps requires more planning, understanding, and skills than he'd anticipated.

So, in 1975, he tried it with Beach's Motorcycle Adventures. Even though he rode his BMW90S from early to late every day of the Beach trip, he couldn't get to all the roads begging to be explored. He had such a good time that he left the bike in Europe and went back for more riding that same year.

That's been his pattern ever since; one or two trips to the Alps every year, exploring every nook and cranny of the Alps as well as other parts of Europe that might possibly have a twisty road. His is a never ending search for twisty roads, breathtaking views, local customs and food, fun hotels, almost always riding with motorcycle friends from America and Europe.

Home is a couple of blocks from the Pacific in Coronado, California, with nearby mountains and canyons for year-round riding. Coronado's sort of an island just 18 miles from Mexico and just a bridge away from San Diego.

Hermann is member number 13 of BMWMOA and BMWRA. In 2001, he was designated a "Friend of the Marque" by BMW. When he's not riding, he surfs, snorkels, appraises real estate, enjoys the piano, and for 18 years he sang with the San Diego Opera (always commuting to rehearsals and performances by bike). He's been

The special license is a gift from the BMW owners of San Diego. The lower emblem is the outline of Corsica, bearing the Corsican black head.

351

a trustee of his church and of Meals on Wheels of Greater San Diego. Twice he's participated in the riding school at the Nurburgring in Germany. In California, he has been to riding schools at Willow Springs and Laguna Seca.

One of his greatest pleasures in recent years has been this book. "How lucky can you get," he asks, "getting to check all those wonderful roads with good friends, and then getting to write about them for more good friends?"